The Cambridge Introduction to
Russian Poetry

The Cambridge Introduction to Russian Poetry presents the major themes, forms, genres, and styles of Russian poetry. Using examples from Russia's greatest poets, Michael Wachtel draws on three centuries of verse, from the beginnings of secular literature in the eighteenth century up to the present day. The first half of the book is devoted to concepts such as versification, poetic language, and tradition; the second half is organized along genre lines and examines the ode, the elegy, ballads, love poetry, nature poetry, and patriotic verse. All poetry appears in the original followed by literal translations. This book is designed to give readers with even a minimal knowledge of the Russian language an appreciation of the brilliance of Russian poetry. It will be an invaluable tool for students and teachers alike.

MICHAEL WACHTEL is Professor in the Department of Slavic Languages and Literatures at Princeton University. He is the author of *Russian Symbolism and Literary Tradition: Goethe, Novalis, and the Poetics of Vyacheslav Ivanov* (1994) and *The Development of Russian Verse: Meter and its Meanings* (Cambridge, 1998).

The Cambridge Introduction to
Russian Poetry

MICHAEL WACHTEL

CAMBRIDGE
UNIVERSITY PRESS

CAMBRIDGE UNIVERSITY PRESS
Cambridge, New York, Melbourne, Madrid, Cape Town, Singapore,
São Paulo, Delhi, Dubai, Tokyo

Cambridge University Press
The Edinburgh Building, Cambridge CB2 8RU, UK

Published in the United States of America by Cambridge University Press, New York

www.cambridge.org
Information on this title: www.cambridge.org/9780521004930

First published 2004

A catalogue record for this publication is available from the British Library

Library of Congress Cataloguing in Publication data
Wachtel, Michael.
The Cambridge Introduction to Russian Poetry / Michael Wachtel.
       p.   cm.
Includes bibliographical references and index.
ISBN 0 521 80881 2 (cloth) – ISBN 0 521 00493 4 (pbk.)
1. Russian poetry – History and criticism   I. Title
PG3041.W328 2004   891.7Г009 – dc22   2003065619

ISBN 978-0-521-80881-1 Hardback
ISBN 978-0-521-00493-0 Paperback

Transferred to digital printing 2010

For Nathaniel and Benjamin Erasmus,
whose joy in language reminds me daily why poetry exists

Contents

Part II Interpretation

Preface

The achievements of Dostoevsky and Tolstoy notwithstanding, Russian literature is a tradition of poetry, not prose, and Russian readers have always recognized it as such. This poetry has been poorly served in translation and remains one of the great rewards for foreigners willing to invest the effort in learning the language.

This book is not a history of Russian poetry, but rather a guide to reading, interpreting, and appreciating it. The only prerequisite – beyond a healthy intellectual curiosity – is a knowledge of the Russian language. How much knowledge? The more, the better, of course, but even students who have only completed their first year of study should be able to understand the general principles and much of the textual analysis. The first part of the book introduces fundamental concepts of poetic literacy, the things that any educated reader (or poet) must know. In the second part, these concepts are applied to the interpretation of specific poems, always set in the context of other poems that share their formal qualities, themes, or genres. Students without much prior exposure to poetry are urged to read the first section in its entirety before beginning the second. Within the second section, however, the chapters need not be read consecutively. From a linguistic standpoint, Chapters Five, Six and Seven are probably the most accessible (though it must be admitted that each concludes with a highly challenging poem). More experienced readers should be able to orient themselves easily and move immediately to the chapters that most interest them.

Throughout, I have included poems from a variety of styles and periods, in most cases favoring recognized classics over lesser-known works. It seemed appropriate that an introductory book should discuss some of the poems that Russians themselves consider an essential part of their cultural identity. However, broad coverage was not my primary concern. I hope that those who first encounter Russian poetry in this book will be inspired to explore further. (The bilingual anthologies listed in Section I of "Suggested further reading" offer a convenient starting point.)

Acknowledgments

The idea for this book came from Linda Bree, humanities editor at Cambridge University Press, and I am grateful for her initial suggestion, her subsequent encouragement, and her patience throughout.

I am immensely indebted to Caryl Emerson, Mikhail Gasparov, John Malmstad, Barry Scherr, and Charles E. Townsend, all of whom scrutinized early versions of the manuscript and gave numerous precise recommendations for its improvement. I also sincerely thank my students at Princeton University – both graduate and undergraduate – who will recognize many of the poems (and some of their own insights) in the pages that follow.

It may seem paradoxical that I have chosen to dedicate this book to my children, who contributed primarily by delaying its composition. The real hero, as always, is my wife, Anna, whose generosity and good humor warrant much more than a dedication.

Farrar, Straus & Giroux Inc. and the Brodsky Estate have graciously allowed me to cite Joseph Brodsky's poem ". . . i pri slove 'griadushchee'" in its entirety in Russian and to use my own literal translation of it. Brodsky's English rendering of the poem, highly interesting but too free for my purposes, can be found in Joseph Brodsky, *Collected Poems in English* (New York: Farrar, Straus & Giroux Inc., 2000), p. 114.

Note on translations and transliterations

To make the book maximally accessible, I have provided my own literal translations of all Russian passages. Throughout, Russian poetry and poem titles are given in cyrillic. Because Russian stress can be a source of perplexity for students – and because rhythm is such an essential part of poetry – I mark the stress in all Russian words (and even in proper names, when they first appear in the "Introduction"). Where transliteration is necessary – usually for individual words or phrases already cited in cyrillic – I use the system that seems to me the most straightforward (essentially that found in Victor Terras [ed.], *A Handbook of Russian Literature*, New Haven: Yale University Press, 1985, p. xix). In the bibliography, I use the less readable but more precise Library of Congress system.

If a poem has no title, I refer to it by its first line (or by the first words of that line). For poems with titles, the English translation (as against the Russian) will have all significant words capitalized (e.g., "Wave and Thought"). If a Russian poem lacks a title and is named by its first line, the English translation gives only the first word capitalized (e.g., "I loved you"). In most of the translations, in order to save space, the graphic form of the original has been altered, with the line breaks rendered by a single slash (/) and stanza breaks by a double slash (//). Occasionally the Russian syntax makes it impossible to retain the line breaks in English translation, in which case only stanza breaks are indicated.

Introduction

Поэ́т – издалека́ заво́дит ре́чь.
Поэ́та – далеко́ заво́дит ре́чь.

Цветаева, «Поэ́ты»

The poet brings language from afar.
Language brings the poet far.

Tsvetaeva, "Poets"

When poets read their works aloud, we may not understand every word, but we immediately recognize that their intonation differs from that of everyday speech. This "unnatural" declamation often causes confusion among those who first encounter it. "Why don't they just read it *normally?*" one is tempted to ask. The reason is simple: poets *want* to set their speech off from everyday language. Individual poets vary widely in the degree of "unnaturalness" they introduce to their readings, but in virtually all cases their goal is the same: to destabilize the familiar world of their listeners, to make them hear anew.

All of us, poets or not, alter our tone of voice and choice of words in accordance with specific circumstances. We speak differently with our parents than with our peers, we address the auto mechanic differently than the policeman, we speak differently when giving a toast than we do when calling for an ambulance. In many life situations, what might be called the prosaic attitude toward language dominates. Our object is to relay information as quickly and unambiguously as possible. At other times, getting the point across is not enough; it is essential to do so convincingly and fervently. We select our words carefully and consciously organize them. In this case, we are not necessarily creating poetry, but it is fair to say that we are moving in the direction of poetry. It is no coincidence that most of the rhetorical terms now associated with poetry originated in the law courts of antiquity. The court is a place where eloquence matters, and the lawyers of ancient Greece and Rome were trained in the art of persuasion.

A precise example may make it easier to distinguish between the poetic and the prosaic poles. Readers who opened *The New York Times* on July 11, 2000 were greeted by the following article on the upper left-hand corner of the first page.

Thirty-five years after the dismantling of legalized segregation,
a majority of Americans maintain that race relations in the
United States are generally good,
but blacks and whites continue to
have starkly divergent percep-
tions of many racial issues and
they remain largely isolated from
each other in their everyday lives,
according to a nationwide poll by
The New York Times.

Despite a superficial visual resemblance to verse, it is highly unlikely that any of the countless readers confused this passage with poetry. No sane person would stop to ponder why each line of this passage ends at the precise point where it does. No one would ask questions like "Is the word 'dismantling' broken into 'dis' and 'mantling' to emphasize the concept of 'break'?" or: "Does the second line end on the word 'segregation' because this emphasizes a concept pivotal to the history of race relations in America?" We do not ask such questions because, as experienced newspaper readers, we know that the layout of individual lines is determined by printing necessity and does not reflect the individual author's intent. Likewise, no reader would notice (let alone puzzle over) the unusual frequency with which the letters "m" and "a" appear in adjacent positions in the first lines: *m*antling, *m*ajority, *A*mericans, *m*aintain. We assume that the reporter's primary goal is to convey basic factual information. If certain combinations of letters recur, we attribute this to coincidence, not to a conscious attempt to achieve some sort of aural patterning. News writing is focused almost entirely on the message, and whatever might distract from its direct and unambiguous presentation is considered inappropriate.

In poetry, on the other hand, the presentation becomes part of the message. Every aspect of the word (sound, spelling, placement on the page) is potentially meaningful. If the newspaper writer aims for immediate and unambiguous communication, the poet seeks to communicate in such a way that the audience will want to read (or hear) *again*, so that the individual word becomes maximally expressive and the audience maximally alert to that expression. For this reason, repeated encounters with the same poem will deepen – and at times even contradict – the first impression, while rereading a news item produces only tedium. This opposition between the newspaper (with its immediate cognitive gratification) and poetry (with its subtle interplay of sight and sound) is at the basis of Marina Tsvetaeva's poem «Читáтели газéт» ("Readers of Newspapers"), of which the opening lines follow:

Ползёт подзёмный змёй,	The underground snake crawls,
Ползёт, везёт людёй.	[It] crawls [and] carries people.
И ка́ждый – со своёй	And each of them is with his
Газётой (со своёй	Newspaper (with his
Экзёмой!) Жва́чный тик,	Eczema!) A chewing reflex,
Газётный костоёд.	A newspaper bone-eater.
Жева́тели мастик,	Chewers of mastics,
Чита́тели газёт.	Readers of newspapers.

Tsvetaeva's short lines mimic the effect of a newspaper column. However, even a novice reader of poetry will recognize that the length of these lines is not determined by coincidence or printers' conventions, but by the poet's careful planning. If read aloud (and poetry should *always* be read aloud, if only to oneself), it becomes evident that the end of each line is marked by rhyme. This gives prominence to the final word of each line, which causes the experienced reader to make a slight pause. Ordinarily, the end of a line of poetry coincides with a logical break, usually reflected in the punctuation (a comma or period). Tsvetaeva's opening lines satisfy this expectation, but already in lines three and four, the reader is torn between pausing at the end of the line to emphasize the rhyme and rushing onwards to reach the thought's logical completion: «И ка́ждый – со своёй / Газётой (со своёй / Экзёмой!)» – "And each of them is with his / Newspaper (with his / Eczema!)" In this case, exact repetition at the end of the line helps us to recognize the symmetry of what follows. Both lines conclude with the same truncated prepositional phrase, leaving the object of the preposition to the *beginning* of the next line. These grammatically parallel words ("Gazetoi" and "Ekzemoi" are both feminine nouns in the instrumental case) are placed in graphically parallel positions. In everyday language, they would rarely be used in the same sentence, but Tsvetaeva wants us to see (and hear!) their similarities. In Russian, both words consist of three syllables, with a stress on the second. Moreover, they have a high percentage of repeated sounds: "Ga*z*étoi" and "Ek*z*émoi" (according to rules of Russian pronunciation, "k" before "z" is pronounced as "g"). Why does Tsvetaeva do this? Presumably, she wants us to equate newspaper reading with disease (a theme she develops in the lines that immediately follow). She establishes this point indirectly, through rhyme and parallelism. By placing dissimilar concepts in the identical position in the line, she emphasizes their similarity in sound and suggests that they are related by sense. Our English translation can preserve the word order but not the essential sound play.

Indeed, English translation proves wholly inadequate as early as the poem's first line. Rather than stating the setting directly, Tsvetaeva introduces the image of a «подзёмный змёй» ("underground snake"). Some ingenuity is required to recognize this as a roundabout way of describing a subway. What has Tsvetaeva gained by this indirect locution (a metaphor, to use a term we shall define later)? For one thing, she introduces a certain foreboding, not simply because the subterranean realm ("podzemnyi") is traditionally associated with unclean things, death, and hell (all of which will be directly relevant to this poem), but also because the snake ("zmei") recalls the biblical tale of the fall from Eden (which Tsvetaeva will allude to a few lines later when she compares a newspaper to a fig leaf, punning on Russian «лист» as "leaf of paper" and "leaf of a tree"). No less important is the acoustic quality of these words. "Podzemnyi" not only shares its "po . . . ze" with the previous word ("*polzet*"), but it also contains in anagrammatic form every single letter found in the subsequent word ("zmei"). Thus, the striking opening image is supported – perhaps even motivated – by the sound.

Like so much of Tsvetaeva's verse, this poem brims with linguistic inventiveness. These few comments cannot begin to do it justice, but they allow us to make some general observations on poetry. Tsvetaeva's theme in "Readers of Newspapers" is, on the surface, absolutely prosaic. (She is writing about tabloids, the lowest form of journalism.) It is not the subject that makes her work poetic, but rather her approach to that subject. By taking advantage of the very sound of words, she introduces a coherence to language that one would never find – or even seek – in a newspaper. The more one ponders her specific images, the deeper their meaning becomes. For example, the comparison of a subway to a snake could upon first glance be understood simply in terms of their crawling motion. However, additional reflection (prompted by the knowledge of the entire poem) allows one to see this as part of a carefully structured system of biblical references, which in this poem range from Genesis to Revelation. For Tsvetaeva, the newspaper is not simply the nemesis of poetry. It is poetry's demonic double, whose surface resemblance masks infernal designs. Such a view appears to have been shared by other modern Russian poets: Vladislav Khodasevich's «Газётчик» ("The Newspaper Vendor") is based on a similar assumption.

Whereas a newspaper concerns itself with current events, a poem tends to focus on the general or even archetypal. However, the two forms differ less in what they say than in how they say it. The effect of poetry depends on the combination of a number of elements (concision, imagery, grammatical parallelism, sound organization). It is this constant and complex interplay that distinguishes poetry not simply from newspapers, but from virtually all prose. While a novel or short story will undoubtedly reveal more careful organization than a newspaper article, it will never achieve the concentration and variety of patterning found in poetry.

The present book is conceived of as an introduction to Russian poetry, not a literary history. However, the task of introduction will be simplified if the reader has at least a rough knowledge of who the leading poets were, when they lived, and what "school" or "movement" they represented. The following thumbnail sketch is intended to situate *only* those poets cited in this book.

Compared to other national traditions, Russian poetry has a brief history. In the centuries when England enjoyed the creativity of Chaucer and Shakespeare, when Germany and France celebrated a flowering of medieval and baroque poetry, Russia's muse was silent, at least as far as literáte secular culture was concerned. Epochal events like the Renaissance and Reformation left no trace on the Russian cultural consciousness. Even had a talent of Shakespearean proportions arisen, three conditions would have conspired against it: the lack of a literary language, the lack of a literate public, and the overt hostility of church and state toward any form of artistic expression not intimately linked to the liturgy. Among the people at large, various forms of folklore existed, but these were independent oral traditions.

Peter the First (the Great), who ruled from 1689 to 1725, altered every aspect of Russian life, including commerce, social interaction, the military, education, and the arts. While there had been isolated attempts at Westernization under his immediate predecessors, no one could match Peter in terms of energy and urgency. However, not all reforms could be implemented as quickly as lopping the beard off a boyar. With typical impatience, Peter built a theater on Red Square, succeeding in shocking centuries-old religious sensibilities, but not in creating serious art. After all, the physical edifice alone could not compensate for the absence of a theatrical tradition.

Peter's reign was essentially a gestation period for Russian secular culture, which only came into its own after his death. A handful of ambitious and talented individuals from the new educated class took it upon themselves to create Russian poetry. Most of these pioneers spent time abroad, so their innovations tended to be adaptations of models they encountered in Europe's most advanced countries. However, historical and social circumstances specific to Russia also left their mark. Most obviously, Russian poets were completely dependent on the patronage system. Without support from the ruling institutions, nothing could be earned or published. These institutions included the court and the Academy of Sciences (which was itself controlled by the tsar). With the rare exception of men whose livelihood was not dependent on their verse (e.g., Antiokh Kantemir [Антио́х Кантеми́р], a professional diplomat whose work was not published in his lifetime), poets were members of the Academy of Sciences and therefore essentially court employees. Their work consisted largely in writing odes to commemorate specific occasions and praise the wisdom of the sovereign and the valor of the military. The primary means of dissemination of verse was recitation, which meant that poets gave considerable thought to performance (public reading). Though continuous squabbling complicated their task, Mikhailo Lomonosov [Михáйло Ломонóсов] and Vasily Trediakovsky [Васи́лий Тредиакóвский] achieved remarkable success in domesticating poetry in Russia. In the course of a few decades, a genuine poetic tradition was established, with erudite talents contributing both verse and treatises on verse composition. If Lomonosov and Trediakovsky codified the poetic language, more unorthodox talents toward the end of the century experimented with it. These included Aleksandr Radishchev [Алексáндр Ради́щев] and, in particular, Gavrila Derzhavin [Гаври́ла Держáвин], the most inventive and aesthetically significant poet of the century.

In the early decades of the nineteenth century, Russian poetry changed direction. Poets emerged from the ranks of the aristocracy. Most served the country in some capacity, but not as poets. State-sponsored poetry ceased to exist, and the salon replaced the court as the primary venue. Instead of an audience of rulers and high-ranking nobles, poets wrote for their peers and, especially, for their friends. Accordingly, the themes of poetry now concentrated on the personal (friendship, longing, love) rather than the civic. Even the language of poetry changed. Influenced by the French-flavored Russian of Nikolai Karamzin [Николáй Карамзи́н], poetry sounded much closer to the spoken idiom than it had in the previous century.

The first few decades of the nineteenth century are traditionally considered Russia's "Golden Age." Ushered in by the Italophile Konstantin Batiushkov [Константи́н Бáтюшков] and the Germanophile Vasily Zhukovsky [Васи́лий Жукóвский], it reached its apogee in Aleksandr Pushkin [Алексáндр Пýшкин], who seamlessly adapted the innovations of his predecessors and added his own. Pushkin brought his "Midas touch" to everything he wrote, from epigrammatic insult to religious verse, from love poem to fairy tale, from comedy to tragedy. His works, characterized by a surface clarity that often masks their profundity, set the standard for contemporaries and successors. Most of the other major poets of the time were Pushkin's friends. Nikolai Iazykov [Николáй Язы́ков], who made a name for himself singing the carefree joys of student life, later devoted his poetry to nationalistic themes and conservative causes. Evgenii Baratynsky [Евгéний Бараты́нский], the only contemporary poet who could rival Pushkin, began as a follower of Batiushkov, but developed a distinctly brooding tone and a complicated syntax and language unique in his day. Petr Viazemsky [Пётр Вя́земский], who outlived all of his friends and grew increasingly stodgy and conservative, was in his youth a free-thinker and poet of great wit and irreverence.

After Pushkin's death, Russian poetry enjoyed a final brief outburst of creativity in Mikhail Lermontov [Михаил Лёрмонтов], a Romantic in the Byronic mode, whose powerful, uncompromising, and always dissatisfied persona dominated his verse. After Lermontov's death, Russian poetry went into relative decline. It was not so much that great poets ceased to exist as that the sudden emergence of prose made poets less numerous and poetic interaction less animated. The greatest flowering of Russian poetry has always occurred in eras when numerous excellent poets are at work together, spurring each other on. In the decades following Pushkin's death, the handful of outstanding poets worked more or less independently. Fedor Tiutchev [Фёдор Тютчев], whose early poems were published in a journal that Pushkin himself edited, was a diplomat. He wrote poetry primarily for himself, took little interest in whether it was actually published, and at one point inadvertently destroyed a stack of his own manuscripts, in one stroke depriving posterity of some of the century's potentially finest verse. If Lermontov represented the Romantic cult of the poetic personality, Tiutchev followed the more speculative side of Romanticism. Afanasy Fet [Афанасий Фет], whose "art for art's sake" credo alienated him from the socially engaged critics of his time, withdrew to his estate, refraining for decades from publishing his introspective and innovative verse. Only Nikolai Nekrasov's [Николай Некрасов] poetry really fit in with the spirit of the times; in his work, the plight of the masses gets expression, often in satiric or folkloric style.

The last years of the nineteenth century marked a rebirth of interest in poetry and the dawn of Russia's "Silver Age" (as the period from the 1890s to the early 1920s has come to be known). The term is somewhat misleading, since in quantity of excellent poets and quality of work the "Silver Age" is not inferior to the "Golden Age." The first phase of the "Silver Age" saw the ascent of Russian Symbolism. After Valery Briusov's [Валерий Брюсов] adaptations of European Decadence, Symbolism soon took a strong religious turn in the works of Zinaida Gippius [Зинаида Гиппиус]. Building on Vladimir Soloviev's [Владимир Соловьёв] philosophy and mystical poetry, the influential triumvirate of Aleksandr Blok [Александр Блок], Andrei Bely [Андрей Белый], and Vyacheslav Ivanov [Вячеслав Иванов] sought to redefine the goals of art. Consciously fusing myth and religion with aesthetics, they saw poetry as a means of transcending the physical world and achieving knowledge of a mysterious other world. Blok began as a love poet, but later turned his attention to urban and civic themes. Bely, an inveterate experimenter, explored almost every aspect of verse language in works that ranged from the confessional to Nekrasov-like folk stylizations. For Ivanov, whose fascination with antiquity affected both the texture of his verse and its themes, poetics meant mythopoetics, with personal and contemporary themes always submerged in the timeless and selfless world of myth. The Symbolists' contributions went beyond the writing of verse, for they were untiring educators and proselytizers. Through translations, public lectures, and personal example, they raised public consciousness about art. Though not a Symbolist, Mikhail Kuzmin [Михаил Кузмин] had similarly wide-ranging talents and interests: his poetry ranges from the precise miniature to the mystical and hermetic.

The Symbolists continued to write for decades, but the movement as such more or less collapsed in 1910. At this point, many new schools appeared, the two most significant being Acmeism and Futurism. Acmeism was a neo-classical form of modernism, which purported to reject the excessive mysticism of Symbolism and replace it with a new ideal of clarity. In many respects, however, the Acmeists were a logical extension of the Symbolists, with their emphasis on poetic craft and cultural continuity. Acmeism left its mark on Russian poetry less as a unified movement than through the achievements of its two greatest poets: Anna Akhmatova [Áнна Ахмáтова] and Osip Mandel'shtam [Óсип Мандельштáм]. Perhaps even less unified than Acmeism, Futurism sought to provoke and outrage. If the Symbolists and Acmeists revered the past, the Futurists – at least the Cubo-Futurists, who represented the most extreme of several Futurist camps – claimed to reject it entirely. In its place, they proposed either a neo-primitivism (which sought its linguistic ideal in a historically nonexistent form of early Slavdom) or a cult of the new technology (machines, speed). The former was represented by the eccentric Aleksei Kruchenykh [Алексей Кручёных] and visionary Velimir Khlebnikov [Велимир Хлéбников], the latter by Vladimir Mayakovsky [Владимир Маякóвский]. Arguing that radical poetics went hand in hand with radical politics, Mayakovsky greeted the Revolution with open arms and became one of the most visible apologists for the Soviet regime. His influence, which waned toward the end of his life and for a few years after his suicide in 1930, ultimately proved decisive through the entire Soviet period.

Two of Russia's most outstanding poets emerged from the ferment of the pre-revolutionary years without belonging to any "school." Boris Pasternak [Борис Пастернáк] began his career close to one of the more docile Futurist factions, but soon became a poet without an "ism." Marina Tsvetaeva's [Маринá Цветáева] poetry reflects the influence of Cubo-Futurism, but she herself never joined this or any other movement. Both Pasternak and Tsvetaeva synthesized the most compelling aspects of many rival groups, creating exuberant yet profound poetry with linguistic brilliance and extraordinary emotional range. Their works are among the most challenging, but also the most rewarding in the entire Russian tradition.

The Russian revolution was a watershed event not only in terms of politics, but also in the cultural sphere. If Russian visual artists and musicians could easily continue their careers in emigration, poets found themselves choosing between highly undesirable alternatives. Many emigrated, only to live unhappy and often creatively unproductive lives in countries that could not appreciate them. In Paris, the capital of the Russian emigration, Vladislav Khodasevich [Владислáв Ходасéвич] and Georgy Ivanov [Геóргий Ивáнов] provided bleak but powerful poetic voices. Others remained in a Russia they distrusted, often with tragic professional and personal consequences. Akhmatova endured years of persecution, while Mandel'shtam was arrested twice and perished on his way to a Stalinist labor camp. Tsvetaeva combined the worst of both fates, spending bitter years as an émigré, only to return to Russia, where, obscure and destitute, she committed suicide.

The Soviet regime valued culture insofar as it could inspire loyalty to the party. A new patronage system arose, with the party leaders standing in for the tsars and the ever more powerful Writers' Union playing the role that the Academy of Sciences had played in the eighteenth century. However, the stakes were even higher, since a poem that misinterpreted the often inscrutable party line could result in a stiff prison sentence or worse. As in the eighteenth century, panegyric genres were favored. With the exception of Mayakovsky's work, little of the reams of officially published poetry is worthy of serious attention. On the other hand, a rich tradition of unofficial poetry emerged in the relative freedom after Stalin's death. In the 1960s, Evgeny Evtushenko [Евгéний Евтушéнко] tried to resurrect the tribune that Mayakovsky had established, filling stadiums with crowds who came to hear his daring, if somewhat compromised (both poetically and politically) verse. More influential, perhaps, was the quiet revolution of the bards, genuine non-conformists who sang their verse, accompanying their unschooled voices on the traditional Russian seven-string guitar. Of these, Bulat Okudzhava's [Булáт Окуджáва] plaintive lyrics were among the most celebrated. Though never officially produced, cassette recordings of the bards' work spread throughout the country, making it known far and wide. Various non-conformist poetry movements also took shape in the 1960s and 1970s, ranging from avant-garde experimenters like Nina Iskrenko [Нúна Искрéнко], who embraced a diverse panoply of styles ("polystylistics"), to conceptualist poets like Dimitri Prigov [Дмúтрий Прúгов] and Timur Kibirov [Тимýр Кибúров], who questioned the validity of all previous discourse (especially the official Soviet language). Finally, some poets built on the legacy of the officially repudiated "Silver Age," celebrating the richness and variety of pre-revolutionary poetry. Though a member of the Writers' Union, Viktor Sosnora [Ви́ктор Сосно́ра] wrote on unorthodox themes in unorthodox style, revitalizing Futurist experiments with language. A complete outsider to the system, Joseph Brodsky [Ио́сиф Бро́дский] created a richly allusive poetics, combining high and low genres and styles. After his forced emigration, he tried tirelessly to inculcate his reverence of tradition to American audiences through interviews, readings, and translations, as well as in the capacity of university professor, American poet laureate, and Nobel prize winner.

By the time of Brodsky's death in 1996, Russian culture had experienced perhaps the most decisive paradigm shift in its entire history. For an outsider, it is difficult to appreciate the extent to which the demise of the USSR altered the landscape of Russian poetry. On the one hand, poets experienced an unprecedented sense of freedom. For the first time in Russian history, censorship was abolished. For the first time in living memory, poets could write without giving a thought to political expediency, without depending on the state as the sole sponsor and publisher of literature. On the other hand, a rich culture of secrecy was demolished in a single stroke. Through threats, admonishments, punishments, and rewards, the Soviet Union had granted the poet an exalted place in society. Evtushenko, who fully appreciated this status, had been right on the mark when he entitled one of his books *A Poet in Russia Is More Than a Poet* (1973). The "system" created no shortage of sycophants, but it also gave birth to non-conformist poets as well as a colorful vocabulary to describe their subversive activities: «спи́ски» (copies of unofficial verse which circulated among the conspiratorial cognoscenti), «самизда́т» (the system of unofficial publication [typewriter and carbon paper being the primary means of reproduction]), «эзо́пов язы́к» (Aesopian language, needed to express the truth in a fashion sufficiently obscure to sneak it past the censor), «писа́ть в стол» ("to write for the desk drawer," the term for work so critical that it could only be put in a folder to await publication in some distant era). The dissident poet was an extremely appealing figure, and the attendant mythology helped make him (or her) a cultural hero unimaginable in the West.

In a society that controlled all sources of information, people looked to literature as a secret source of wisdom and a moral compass. With the fall of the Soviet Union, the familiar and accepted roles of poet as martyr or poet as prophet lost their relevance. If the non-conformist Soviet poet had to outwit the increasingly clumsy totalitarian system, the post-Soviet poet has to contend with new adversaries, more mundane, but no less powerful. As entertainment, poetry now competes with Harlequin romances, television sit-coms, and Hollywood-style films. As social commentary, it has lost considerable ground to the news media. While many bemoan this turn of events, Westerners recognize it as the inevitable fate of the modern poet. At the present time, poetry in Russia is probably no more prominent a cultural force than it is in English-speaking countries, yet the relatively small readership remains as devoted and educated as anywhere in the world. And Russian poets have proved resilient, responding to new challenges with wit and imagination.

Part I

Concepts

Chapter 1

Versification: how to do things with words

Какáя глубинá!
Какáя смéлость и какáя стрóйность!

Пушкин, «Мóцарт и Сальéри»

What profundity!
What daring and what just proportion!

Pushkin, "Mozart and Salieri"

All forms of communication – both artistic and quotidian – are based on rules. These rules may be arbitrary, but we depend on them nonetheless. There is no particular reason why a red light should mean "stop" and a green light "go," but drivers or pedestrians who disregard this binary opposition will not survive long. Likewise, it is hard to explain logically why English speakers call that tall plant with branches and leaves a "tree," while Russians call it a "derevo," but the fact is that English-speakers and Russian-speakers have agreed, consciously or not, to respect these designations.

When we speak English, we rarely appreciate its complexity. We do not struggle to make the subject agree with the verb, but this is not because English lacks rules (or that one need not know them), but precisely because we know them so well that they have become automatic. Studying a foreign language teaches us, among other things, the ubiquity and necessity of grammar.

Like any other language, poetry has its own grammar: versification. Of course, obeying this set of rules does not guarantee brilliant verse, just as following the rules of English grammar will not necessarily produce scintillating conversation. But it is only within an agreed-upon system that brilliance can stand out.

Contemporary linguists assure us that no sentiment is unique to a given language, that all ideas are translatable. In practical terms, this is surely a good thing: it would be dangerous, for example, if a peace treaty were unable to be ratified because it could not be comprehensibly rendered in the language of one of the warring parties. However, poetic meaning moves uncomfortably across linguistic borders. Because poetry is created not simply through dictionary definition, but by using grammatical, rhythmical, and aural means to temper – and at times to tamper with – dictionary definition, a translation may say more or less than the original, yet never offer a precise equivalent.

Poetry is a universal phenomenon, but versification differs from tradition to tradition. The principles of modern Russian verse were mainly derived from Western European models, but certain qualities of the Russian language itself forced poets to make adaptations. Readers familiar with English versification, for example, will find many familiar concepts in this chapter. However, the same terminology will at times be applied in a manner inconsistent with common English usage.

It is surprising how often one encounters objections to the study of versification on the grounds that it runs counter to the creative spirit. One such argument goes something like this: only bad poets follow the rules, while great poets flout them. There is, of course, no denying that the rules of poetry – as opposed to those of chemistry or biology – are not *a priori* part of our universe. Over time, they can and do change. However, poetic innovation need not be construed as a rejection of versification *per se*. In any epoch, poets have a very precise understanding of the rules of verse. Depending on their own needs and proclivities, they will accept some of them, while rejecting (or revising) others. Insofar as the innovations are successful, they themselves become part of an ever-evolving grammar of poetry. In studying versification, then, we must be mindful that we are examining a dynamic system, a set of rules that each poet to a certain extent redefines. However, it is easy to overestimate the importance of rule-breaking. In all historical periods, a powerful current of continuity is essential, if only to provide the background against which innovation can be recognized. To be comprehensible, a great poet, like a great orator, must rely on a grammar that is widely understood.

A second argument against versification runs along the following lines: poetry is the result of inspiration, not calculation. Once again, there is no need to refute this claim altogether; it simply needs to be placed in a broader context. The creative process appears to differ widely depending on the individual. Some great poets work methodically and edit painstakingly while others do indeed produce at extraordinary speed with little revision. Such outbursts of creativity – one thinks, for example, of Pushkin's «Бóлдинская óсень» (the fall of 1830, which he spent at his Boldino estate, writing one masterpiece after another) – reveal powers of concentration verging on the miraculous, yet they do not refute the presence or relevance of rules. Clearly, inspired poets (or composers, or painters) have internalized the rules to the extent that they no longer have to ponder them while creating. Inspiration is by no means a rejection of rules, but testimony to their having been thoroughly mastered and instantaneously applied.

Meter

The most obvious way to set poetry off from prose is through meter. When, in the eighteenth century, Russians consciously decided to create a secular literary culture, they had several possible sources to choose from. Though Russia had a rich and varied oral tradition of folk song and heroic poetry, this could not serve as a point of departure. The new literature had to be urbane and "European," maximally distinguished from the uneducated entertainment of the common folk. Russian poets therefore ignored native traditions (which they would rediscover when Romanticism took hold almost a century later) and looked abroad.

One possibility was syllabic poetry, which had firmly taken root in Poland. Kantemir, the greatest Russian exponent of this type of verse, begins his first satire as follows:

> Умé недозрéлый, плóд недóлгой наýки!
> Покóйся, не понуждáй к перý мои рýки:
> Не писáв летя́щи дни вéка проводи́ти
> Мóжно, и слáву достáть, хоть творцóм не слы́ти.

(Oh, my immature mind, fruit of brief study! / Remain calm, do not force my hands to the pen: / It is possible to spend the fleeting days of life not writing, / To achieve glory, yet not to be known as a writer.)

Ignoring the now archaic forms (truncated non-predicative adjectives [летя́щи дни], unfamiliar infinitive endings [проводи́ти]) and grammatical constructions (the opening vocative case [Умé], the imperfective gerund [писáв]) and focusing only on the formal elements, we can see three organizational principles at work. The first is the syllable count (hence the term "syllabic" verse): each line contains precisely the same number of syllables (thirteen). The second organizational feature is rhyme, found in pairs at the end of the line. This passage is typical of Russian syllabic poetry in that only "feminine" rhymes are used. Such rhymes are based on a two-syllable pattern of stressed/unstressed (e.g., наýки/рýки [from the Kantemir excerpt] or уви́дел/оби́дел). Masculine rhymes, in which stress falls on the final syllable (e.g., дóм/однóм, любóвь/крóвь) were avoided by Russian syllabic poets, who in this regard clung tenaciously to their Polish models. (Since the Polish language has fixed stress on the penultimate syllable [except, of course, in monosyllabic words], masculine rhymes are rarely found.) In addition to syllable count and rhyme, each line has a word break (called a "caesura") between syllables 7 and 8. This mandatory pause between words is common in long lines of verse, and it often – though by no means necessarily – corresponds to a pause in syntax or logic. Just as rhyme marks the end of each line, so the caesura marks the middle. Taken together, these three principles (syllable count, rhyme, caesura) served to set the poetic utterance starkly apart from everyday language.

There is no *inherent* reason why syllabic verse did not become the dominant verse type in Russia. In the hands of able practitioners, it was extremely effective. (Those patient enough to familiarize themselves with the linguistic archaisms will find that Kantemir's satires remain amusing even today.) However, the historical fact is that, within in a matter of decades, syllabic verse ceased to exist in Russia.

The demise of Russian syllabic verse was the result of the triumph of syllabo-tonics. Like syllabic verse, syllabo-tonic poetry was already widely used in other countries before it appeared in Russia. Lomonosov, who pioneered it, was well acquainted with German models. The essential feature of syllabo-tonic poetry is the regular alternation of stressed (accented) and unstressed (unaccented) syllables. There are five patterns ("feet") on which syllabo-tonic poetry can be based. In the following examples, a stressed syllable (a "strong position") is indicated by "‒́", an unstressed syllable (a "weak position") by "∪":

iambic: ∪‒́
trochaic: ‒́ ∪
dactylic: ‒́ ∪ ∪
amphibrachic: ∪‒́ ∪
anapestic: ∪ ∪‒́

Lines of syllabo-tonic poetry are created by connecting a number of these feet in a row. Iambic and trochaic meters, based on feet of two syllables, are called binary, while dactylic, amphibrachic, and anapestic meters (i.e., those built on feet of three syllables) are called ternary. Rather than giving examples of meters based on each of the five possible feet (all of which we will encounter in this book), we will now focus only on iambic tetrameter, the most common meter in the history of Russian poetry. According to the scheme introduced above, one would expect a four-foot iambic line to look like this:

∪‒́ ∪‒́ ∪‒́ ∪‒́

The following excerpt, from Lomonosov's «Вече́рнее размышле́ние о Бо́жием вели́честве при слу́чае вели́кого се́верного сия́ния» ("Evening Meditation on God's Greatness on the Occasion of the Great Northern Lights"), follows this pattern exactly. Every line contains four stresses (on syllables 2,4,6,8), the last of which forms a masculine rhyme (in the pattern a–b–a–b).

Лицé своé скрывáет дéнь,
Поля́ покры́ла мрáчна нóчь,
Взошлá на гóры чóрна тéнь,
Лучи́ от нáс склони́лись прóчь.

(Day hides its face, / Dark night has covered the fields, /A black shadow has risen onto the mountains, / The rays of light have turned away from us.)

In actuality, one very rarely encounters passages that fit the iambic pattern so perfectly. The Russian language itself resists. In contrast to English (or German, the language that directly influenced Lomonosov's practice), Russian lacks secondary stress. This means that no matter how long a word is, it will contain only one stress. Accordingly, once Lomonosov decided that every second syllable needed to be accented, he had no choice but to reject any word of more than three syllables. And even three-syllable words had to be limited to those in which the stress fell on the second syllable (скрывáет, покры́ла, склони́лись). Lomonosov himself soon recognized that iambs of this type severely restricted his creativity. He began to allow "pyrrhics" (feet with no stresses) to substitute for iambs. As a result, iambics came to be defined less by the strong syllables than by the weak ones. It was not essential that all even-numbered syllables be stressed, but rather that all odd-numbered syllables remain *unstressed*.

As an innovator, Lomonsov initially opposed pyrrhic feet because they obscured the basic rhythmic pulse so essential to syllabo-tonic verse (and so unfamiliar to the Russian ear). However, once Russians became accustomed to the alternation of unstressed/stressed syllables, omitted stresses seemed quite natural. Standard Russian iambic tetrameter would sound noticeably different from Lomonosov's earliest experiments.

Духóвной жáждою томи́м,
В пусты́не мрáчной я́ влачи́лся,
И шестикры́лый серафи́м
На перепýтье мнé яви́лся.

(Tormented by spiritual thirst, / I dragged myself along in a dark desert, / And a six-winged seraph / Appeared to me at a crossroads.)

This passage comes from Pushkin's «Прорóк» ("The Prophet"). Every line is written in iambic tetrameter, yet only one of them has four stresses. Instead of the constant alternation of unstressed/stressed in the Lomonosov excerpt, we find rich rhythmic variation, no two lines having the identical stress pattern. It now becomes important to distinguish between *meter* (the generalized scheme) and *rhythm* (the actual realization of that scheme in a given line). In the Pushkin excerpt, meter and rhythm coincide only in the second line. Unlike the early Lomonosov, Pushkin can use four-syllable words (шестикры́лый, перепýтье) as well as all three-syllable words, regardless of whether they are stressed on the first (жа́ждою), second (духо́вной), or third (серафи́м) syllables. Once pyrrhic feet are allowed, any Russian word can fit into an iambic pattern. Only in the final foot of the line are pyrrhic feet unacceptable (a rule that, with very rare exceptions, remains constant throughout the history of Russian syllabo-tonic poetry).

Another change from the Lomonosov example is the presence of an unstressed ninth syllable in Pushkin's second and fourth lines. This is by no means Pushkin's innovation; in fact, Lomonosov himself championed it. In any case, the essential point is that this additional syllable does not alter the meter, but only the rhyme. The rules of versification demand that the last strong position in every line be stressed (i.e., the eighth syllable in iambic tetrameter), but they do not restrict the number of unstressed syllables that follow. The additional syllable in two of Pushkin's lines results in a more varied rhyme scheme. Masculine rhymes alternate with feminine rhymes according to the pattern of a–B–a–B (masculine rhymes are conventionally designated by small letters, feminine rhymes by capital letters).

Russian poems sometimes have two unstressed syllables after the rhyming syllable, e.g., Aleksandr Blok's famous «Незнако́мка» ("The Stranger"):

> По вечера́м над рестора́нами
> Горя́чий во́здух ди́к и глу́х,
> И пра́вит о́криками пья́ными
> Весе́нний и тлетво́рный ду́х.

(In the evenings above the restaurants / The hot air is wild and thick, / And a malevolent spring spirit / Directs the drunken screams.)

This poem, like those of Lomonosov and Pushkin, is written in iambic tetrameter. The second and fourth lines contain masculine rhymes and therefore have 8 syllables. The first and third lines, however, have 10 syllables, but these are *not* pentameter lines. To have an iambic pentameter line, the tenth syllable (final potential stressed syllable) would necessarily be stressed. In the present case, the eighth is stressed, but not the tenth, which signals the presence of a so-called dactylic rhyme (i.e., the stressed syllable of the rhyme is the third to last).

Already in Lomonosov's day, pyrrhic feet became a permanent fixture of Russian syllabo-tonic poetry. The use of pyrrhics means that stress is not completely predictable. We know where it may *not* fall, but not where it *will* fall. The question thus arises: how does one distinguish the words that receive stress from the ones that do not? In general, poetic usage reflects ordinary vernacular usage, where lexical parts of speech (nouns, verbs, adjectives, adverbs) receive stress, but grammatical elements (prepositions, conjunctions) do not. Pronouns complicate the picture slightly. The rule of thumb for poetic scansion is that a pronoun (or possessive pronoun) is stressed only if it falls on a metrically strong syllable. In the Pushkin line «На перепу́тье мне́ яви́лся» ("Appeared to me at a crossroads"), "mne," receives stress because it falls on an even-numbered syllable (even-numbered syllables being strong in iambic meters). Had Pushkin written, «И в то́м саду́ мне вдру́г яви́лся» ("And suddenly appeared to me in that garden"), it would still be a metrically irreproachable iambic line, but the word "mne" would necessarily remain unstressed.

The following Blok poem demonstrates two additional freedoms that distinguish the Russian iambic line.

> Но́чь, у́лица, фона́рь, апте́ка,
> Бессмы́сленный и ту́склый све́т.
> Живи́ ещё хоть че́тверть ве́ка –
> Всё бу́дет та́к. Исхо́да не́т.
>
> Умрёшь – начнёшь опя́ть снача́ла,
> И повтори́тся всё, как вста́рь:
> Но́чь, ледяна́я ря́бь кана́ла,
> Апте́ка, у́лица, фона́рь.

(Night, a street, a streetlight, a pharmacy, / Senseless and dull light. / Even if you live another quarter century – / Everything will be this way. There is no way out. // If you die, you'll begin again from the start, / And everything will repeat as it did long ago: / Night, the icy ripple of a canal, / A pharmacy, a street, a streetlight.)

Blok's meter is iambic tetrameter (with rhyme scheme A-b-A-b), but he uses great rhythmic variation. In some lines (4,5) all stresses are realized. In line 6, the first potential stress is unrealized. In line 2, the second potential stress is unrealized. In line 8, the third potential stress is unrealized.

All of these possibilities are typically found in iambic tetrameter. However, the first and seventh lines seem to contradict the rules for iambs, since both begin with a stressed syllable. Both are, in fact, acceptable variants in Russian iambic verse. The first line begins with a spondee, i.e., a foot with two consecutive stresses. (One might conceive of a spondee as the opposite of a pyrrhic.) While spondees can in principle occur anywhere in a line, they are most frequently found in the first foot of an iamb. The seventh line has a stress on the first and fourth syllables. This variant (which, following the terminology of Vladimir Nabokov, we will call a "tilt"), is possible in Russian iambic lines only when the first syllable is a monosyllabic word.

Both the spondaic opening and the tilt are relatively rare. As readers (or listeners), we should learn to recognize them because they have interpretive significance. In the Blok poem, it is not surprising that these striking rhythmical variations occur in lines that are closely related semantically. In the first line, the spondee creates a ponderous effect, as the poet lists a series of visual impressions. In the seventh, the identical first word suggests that we are dealing with a recapitulation of the opening statement. The rhythmic tilt produces a sudden shift, which is ultimately shown to be yet another version of the senseless repetition that is the poem's theme (a bleak Symbolist revisitation of Nietzsche's concept of "eternal recurrence").

It may be helpful to give a few more examples of spondees and tilts to show how poets take advantage of rhythm to emphasize thematic concerns. The following lines come from Pushkin's famous description of the 1709 battle of Poltava (from the long poem of that name), which marked the turning point in Peter the Great's decade-long war with Sweden:

> Швед, русский – колет, рубит, режет,
> Бой барабанный, клики, скрежет,
> Гром пушек, топот, ржанье, стон,
> И смерть и ад со всех сторон.

(Swede, Russian – stabs, hacks, slices, / A drumbeat, cries, grinding, / The thunder of canons, stamping, neighing, moaning, / And death and hell from all sides.)

In this iambic tetrameter passage, Pushkin uses numerous poetic means to portray the fierce combat between the Swedes and the Russians. One way he does this is through a partial breakdown in grammar, where lists of words (e.g., nouns in nominative case, third-person singular verbs) replace ordinary sentences. Rhythmic virtuosity underscores this chaotic impression. Pushkin not only combines two spondaic openings with a tilt, but he fully realizes the stresses, in the spondaic lines achieving the rare effect of *five* stresses in a four-foot line. Of course, the function of these rhythmic variations is quite different here than in the Blok poem. The spondee «Ночь, улица» ("Night, a street"), thanks to the words' meanings and the larger semantic context, makes a ponderous impression, while «Швед, русский» ("Swede, Russian"), because of the very different semantic coloring of the passage, mimics rhythmically the impetuous clash of antagonists in battle. In short, a spondee (like a tilt) does not have a fixed meaning. It simply serves as a signal, a means of poetic emphasis. It is up to the interpreter to determine why the poet chooses to highlight these particular words.

One final example of an expressive use of rhythm in iambic tetrameter can be seen in the laconic first poem of Osip Mandel'shtam's first book, *Камень* (*Stone*), cited here in its entirety:

> Звук осторожный и глухой
> Плода, сорвавшегося с древа,
> Среди немолчного напева
> Глубокой тишины лесной . . .

(A cautious and mute sound / Of a fruit, which has fallen from a tree, / Amid the unceasing melody / Of deep forest silence . . .)

The theme of Mandel'shtam's poem, the interplay of sound and silence, is reinforced and even developed on the level of form. A tilt opens the poem, varying the iambic tetrameter before it has even been established. The first stress falls on the very first word ("zvuk" – "sound"), thereby giving prominence to that single sound that interrupts, as it were, a larger, incessant melody. Together with the striking adjective "cautious" (an odd description of a sound, but an ordinary description of a person), it invites us to understand this sound as an autobiographical statement, a personification of the poet himself. (The fact that mention of the fruit itself is delayed until the second line encourages the initial uncertainty as to whether the sound is human or natural. This is the syntactic effect of enjambment, which we have already seen in Tsvetaeva and which we shall discuss in due course.) Mandel'shtam introduces himself with extreme rhythmic subtlety, beginning his "first" poem with an unexpected stress on a semantically loaded concept.

This brief examination of iambic tetrameter should suffice to demonstrate that syllabo-tonic poetry, while rhythmically predictable to a great extent, still leaves room for variation, and that poets take advantage of these rhythmic freedoms to draw our attention to certain words. The popularity of syllabo-tonic poetry indicates its vitality: it has been the versification of choice for Russian poets from the eighteenth century to the present.

On the other hand, syllabo-tonics do not hold a monopoly on Russian poetry. Accentual poetry, another system of versification, appeared sporadically in the early nineteenth century, and was used with some frequency by the beginning of the twentieth century. While it never replaced syllabo-tonics (in the way syllabo-tonics had made syllabic verse obsolete), it did offer a viable alternative, so that most twentieth-century poets have used both.

Strict accentual poetry is defined by a constant number of *realized* stresses in each line, with variable intervals between them. If the intervals are only one or two syllables, the form is called a «дóльник» (there is no agreed upon English equivalent, so we will simply transliterate it as "dol'nik"), essentially a compromise between syllabo-tonic verse and purely accentual verse. The following excerpt, from the beginning of an untitled Blok poem, demonstrates how regular a "dol'nik" can be:

Крыльцó Её, словно пáперть.
Вхожý – и стихáет грозá.
На столé – узóрная скáтерть.
Притаи́лись в углý образá.

На лицé Её – нéжный румя́нец,
Тишина́ озарённых тенéй.
В душé – кружа́щийся та́нец
Мои́х улетéвших днéй.

(Her porch is like that of a church. / I enter and the storm quiets down. / On the table is a patterned tablecloth. / The icons have hidden themselves in the corner. // On Her face there is a tender blush, / The silence of illuminated shadows. / In [her] soul is a twirling dance / Of my days that have flown away.)

Line 2 can be scanned as amphibrachic trimeter (stresses on syllables 2,5,8) and lines 4 and 6 as anapestic trimeter (stresses on syllables 3,6, and 9). By omitting the stress on the pronoun, one could also read line 5 as anapestic trimeter. However, none of the other lines fits this or any other syllabo-tonic pattern, because the unstressed intervals vary between one and two syllables; line 3 would scan unambiguously as: $\cup\ \cup\acute{-}\cup\acute{-}\cup\ \cup\acute{-}\cup$, line 7 as $\cup\acute{-}\cup\acute{-}\cup\ \cup\acute{-}\cup$, line 8 as $\cup\acute{-}\cup\ \cup\acute{-}\cup\acute{-}$. (Line 1 could be read just as line 7, though there is some uncertainty here because of the pronoun. In any case, it cannot be scanned as a syllabo-tonic line.) In short, when there is no longer complete predictability of where the unstressed syllables occur, we have crossed over from syllabo-tonic to accentual verse. "Dol'nik" is the transitional form, and one often finds individual lines in it that scan as syllabo-tonics. A further element of "dol'nik" verse (and accentual verse in general) that resembles much Russian syllabo-tonic poetry is its consistent rhyme scheme, which lends a high degree of predictability to the end of each line. The excerpt above uses the common A-b-A-b pattern.

The opening of Mayakovsky's «О́блако в штана́х» ("A Cloud in Trousers") demonstrates a less predictable type of accentual verse. Here the unstressed intervals vary widely, leaving the reader (or listener) little sense of where the next stress will appear:

Вашу мы́сль,
мечта́ющую на размягчённом мозгу́,
как вы́жиревший лакéй на засалённой кушéтке,
буду дразни́ть об окрова́вленный сéрдца лоску́т;
до́сыта изъиздева́юсь, наха́льный и éдкий.

(Your thought, / which dreams away on a softened brain, / like a servant run to fat on a greasy cot, / I will tease against the bloodied rag of my heart, / I, nasty and caustic, will sate myself in mockery.)

For purposes of scansion, it should be noted that the first two lines of verse shown above are actually one line. Mayakovsky's liberties in graphic layout need not detain us here; suffice it to say that the a-B-a-B rhyme scheme (мозгу́/лоску́т, кушётке/е́дкий) indicates the actual structure of the passage more accurately than the graphic presentation (which is used to highlight the peculiar syntax and thus underscore the theme). To understand the accentual principles at work here, it will be useful to break down each line:

line 1 (= graphic lines 1 and 2): 15 syllables, stress on 3,5,12,15
line 2 (= graphic line 3): 15 syllables, stress on 2,7,11,14
line 3 (= graphic line 4): 14 syllables, stress on 4,8,11,14
line 4 (= graphic line 5): 14 syllables, stress on 1,7,10,13

Each line has four stresses, but beyond the rhymes at the end of the line, the placement of the stresses do not form a pattern. It might be tempting to see this rhythmic confusion as a reflection of the poem's theme (the poet's mockery of his audience), but that is unlikely. Mayakovsky uses accentual meters frequently, and his themes vary widely. Moreover, accentual meters can be found in any number of more tradition-conscious poets (Joseph Brodsky, for example), where they are applied to an even wider range of genre and subject matter.

Not all examples of accentual verse will retain even a consistent number of stresses per line. However, all will rhyme according to a predictable (i.e., recurring) scheme. If even this minimal requirement of accentual verse is removed, the result is free verse, exemplified in the following passage from Nina Iskrenko's «Друга́я же́нщина» ("Another Woman"):

> Когда́ мне невмо́чь
> пересилить беду́
> когда́ у меня́ бессо́нница
> и це́лый ба́к гря́зного белья́
> когда́ я
> пу́таю дете́й
> с диноза́врами
> а благоприя́тное расположе́ние свети́л на не́бе
> принима́ю за просту́ю любе́зность
> когда́ без
> че́тверти во́семь мне уже́ пора́
> и без че́тверти де́вять мне уже́ пора́
> и без че́тверти оди́ннадцать мне
> уже́ пора́
> и по ра́дио
> говоря́т вся́кие нехоро́шие ве́щи
> когда телефо́н наконе́ц отключа́ется
> потому́ что бо́льше уже́ не мо́жет
> а мы́сленно предста́вленный кусо́к ма́сла

не ма́жется на воображ́аемый хлéб
и вдобáвок в темноте́ среди нóчи я натыкáюсь на
велосипéд в коридóре

(When I am powerless / to overcome misfortune / when I have insomnia / and a whole container of dirty laundry / when I / confuse my children / with dinosaurs / and I take as a simply courtesy / the favorable position of stars in the sky / when at / quarter of eight it's time for me [to go] / when at quarter of nine it's time for me [to go] / when at quarter to eleven / it's time / for me [to go] / and on the radio / they are saying all sorts of bad things / when the telephone cuts off / because it can't bear it any more / and the piece of butter pictured in my mind / won't spread on the imagined bread / and in addition in the darkness in the middle of night I smack myself against / a bicycle in the corridor)

A Russian of Iskrenko's generation would immediately recognize the first two lines as a citation from «Полнóчный троллéйбус» ("Midnight Trolley"), a famous song of the bard Bulat Okudzhava. It is significant that Iskrenko's polemic response to Okudzhava is not simply semantic (a feminist revision of a masculine pose), but is also reflected in verse form. Okudzhava's poem is written in amphibrachs, which Iskrenko initially retains by beginning her poem with a direct quotation (strictly speaking, she already breaks the amphibrachs by splitting a single line of Okudzhava's poem into two lines of her own). But as soon as the citation ends, all semblance of syllabotonics disappears. By line 3, there is no discernable pattern of stressed and unstressed syllables. Intervals between stressed syllables range from as few as zero ("bák griáznogo" in line 4) to six ("mázhetsia na voobrazháemyi" in the third line from the end). The passage cannot qualify as accentual verse not only because the number of stresses in each line varies widely and unpredictably, but because there is no rhyme. (In the Mayakovsky excerpt, the rhyme scheme encouraged us to combine the initial short line with the second line, but since Iskrenko dispenses with rhyme altogether, there is little reason to combine the short lines. Even were we to do so, no consistent rhythmic pattern would emerge.)

The absence of all of these organizing features indicates that we have entered the realm of free verse. Until quite recently, free verse has played a marginal role in Russian poetry, and we will therefore not consider it in this book. However, it should be emphasized that free verse does not reject poetic structure *per se*, but only the traditional organizing principles of rhythm and rhyme. In the Iskrenko excerpt, one immediately notes the insistent repetitions of whole words ("kogda" at the start of many lines, "pora" at the end), which create certain patterns and even expectations. Iskrenko also plays on sounds (e.g., "*b*edu, *b*essonnitsa, *b*el'ia" at the ends of lines 2–4, "*po*ra" and "*po* *r*adio" in lines 14–15) and carefully considers the structure of individual lines, taking advantage of the natural pauses at the end of each line to create anticipation (e.g., "kogda bez / chetverti," where the reader expects an object after "bez" [e.g., "nadezhdy" – "hope"], rather than a time expression). In short, free verse is still a form of poetry, but it removes the traditional constraints and replaces them with new ones.

Free verse (i.e., without rhyme and meter) should not be confused with blank verse (i.e., without rhyme, but *with* meter). Blank verse was already used by Russian poets in the eighteenth century in imitations of antiquity (since rhyme did not exist in ancient Greek or Latin poetry) and, beginning in the nineteenth century, in drama (following Shakespeare's example), lyric meditations, and some imitations of folklore. The term blank verse is sometimes restricted to mean only unrhymed iambic pentameter, its most common incarnation:

> Ещё одно, последнее сказанье –
> И летопись окончена моя,
> Исполнен долг, завещанный от Бога
> Мне, грешному. Недаром многих лет
> Свидетелем Господь меня поставил
> И книжному искусству вразумил.
>
>   (from Pushkin's drama «Борис Годунов» ["Boris Godunov"])

(Just one last tale – / And my manuscript is finished, / My duty is fulfilled, [which was] bequeathed by God / To me, the sinner. Not in vain for many years / Did the Lord place me as a witness / And teach me the art of books.)

> Вот холм лесистый, над которым часто
> Я сиживал недвижим – и глядел
> На озеро, воспоминая с грустью
> Иные берега, иные волны.
>
>   (from Pushkin's poem « . . . Вновь я посетил» [". . . Again I visited"])

(There is the wooded hill, above which frequently / I would sit motionless – and look / At the lake, remembering with sadness / Other shores, other waves.)

Why do these two passages sound so different, despite their being written in the same meter? In the absence of rhyme, the caesura plays an especially prominent role. In the first example, a caesura comes after the second foot, lending a measured, formal quality to the utterance. The second example, much more conversational in style, dispenses with caesura. (The fact that two of the four lines have a word break after the second foot is immaterial; a caesura must fall in the identical position in *every* line.) Pushkin's early work in blank verse always contains the caesura; he clearly felt the need for an ordering principle that could offset the absence of rhyme. Only when he became accustomed to the form was he willing to relinquish the caesura.

Rhyme

Blank verse (and free verse) notwithstanding, rhyme has been a crucial element in Russian versification from the eighteenth century to the present day. We have already introduced the three main types of rhyme: masculine (stress on the final syllable, e.g., са́д/лимона́д, до́м/одно́м), feminine (stress on the penultimate syllable, e.g., са́да/лимона́да, во́ля/до́ля), and dactylic (stress on the third syllable from the end, e.g., мгнове́нного/пле́нного, еди́нственный/таи́нственный). This last type, acknowledged but rarely used in the eighteenth century, became popular in the Romantic period in imitations of folklore. (Russian folk poetry was generally unrhymed, but had frequent dactylic line endings.)

Two details should be mentioned lest they cause confusion. Russian rhyme demands an adjacent stressed vowel and consonant. For this reason, it would be incorrect to label кни́га/фи́рма a rhyme (though the words *are* linked by sound, as we shall see in the next chapter). On the other hand, водо́й/густо́й form a completely acceptable rhyme, because the «й» is a consonant (linguists call this a "glide" and refer to it as "j" or "jot"). It is essential to remember that sound is more important than spelling in determining rhyme. Russian has only five basic vowel sounds, but they are written ten ways (а/я, о/ё, и/ы, э/е, у/ю). For this reason, pure rhymes may be spelled with different forms of the same "vowel pair," e.g., лёг/но́г, бью́т/принесу́т, люби́л/бы́л (even though English speakers are apt to perceive «и» and «ы» as different vowel sounds). Likewise, paired consonants (д/т, з/с, б/п, в/ф, г/к, ж/ш) can be rhymed with each other as long as they are both devoiced, e.g., шумя́т/са́д, потеря́в/гра́ф, челове́к/сне́г. In feminine rhymes, poets often allow some freedom in the exactitude of the syllable that follows the rhyme. Even Pushkin, who was unusually strict in his usage, allowed feminine rhymes like дубро́вах/суро́вых and хо́чешь/проро́чишь (in this last case, the words are phonetically identical – only the spelling differs).

Since its introduction to Russian poetry, rhyme has undergone radical change. Most twentieth-century poets would reject the rhyming practice of their eighteenth-century counterparts in favor of rhymes that those earlier poets would themselves have rejected. The following examples (all taken from Lomonosov's version of the first psalm, which he translated at some point between 1743 and 1751) are typical of his time: хо́дит/приво́дит, ступа́ть/заседа́ть, поспе́шны/гре́шны, дела́х/пра́х. Such rhymes are called "exact" (or "pure"). They not only contain the identical stressed vowel/consonant combination, but they coincide completely in all letters that follow the rhyming syllable. Another essential feature of these rhymes is that they are grammatical: verbs rhyme with verbs, nouns rhyme with nouns. With one exception, they simply match morphological endings, a task which – truth be told – does not require great ingenuity. (A first-year student of Russian could easily come up with any number of rhymes for, say, чита́ешь: понима́ешь, зна́ешь, извиня́ешь, etc.)

A comparison of these rhymes to those of Mayakovsky (see the excerpt cited above) or Joseph Brodsky shows clearly the enormous changes that occurred. The following pairs, from Brodsky's cycle «Ча́сть ре́чи» ("A Part of Speech"), typify the rhyming practice found in much twentieth-century Russian poetry: нева́жно/не ва́ш но, го́ру с/го́лос, с мы́са/смы́сла, едва́ ли/подва́ле, ба́не/зуба́ми. While Brodsky by no means dispenses with grammatical rhyme, he limits it severely. Rhymes based on morphological endings, so frequent in Lomonosov, almost never appear in Brodsky. Instead, one finds frequent use of approximate rhymes (which still have the minimal requirement of adjacent stressed vowel and consonant, but play very freely with the sequence of vowels and consonants that follow). This does not mean that Brodsky's rhyme is necessarily *better* than Lomonosov's, but merely that its type and function has changed. When the first Russian poets introduced rhyme in the eighteenth century, they were seeking nothing more than a euphony that would highlight the end of the line. Rhyme itself was a novelty, and exact rhyme was prized for its very obviousness. Freer rhyming practice became possible only after exact rhyme had been established and accepted. Once the reader/listener anticipated it, the need – and freedom – to experiment arose.

It would be incorrect to suggest that the path from Lomonosov to Mayakovsky and Brodsky was a gradual move from strict rhyme to approximate rhyme (or from uninteresting to interesting ones). Derzhavin's rhymes were far more approximate than Pushkin's. The main test of good rhyme is not simply whether it succeeds in linking two lines aurally, but whether it creates a meaningful connection between them. Pushkin placed severe constraints on himself in terms of exact rhyme, yet he demonstrated great ingenuity within these constraints.

Не да́й мне Бо́г сойти́ с ума́;	God forbid that I go mad;
Нет, ле́гче по́сох и сума́.	No, better the staff and the bag.
А что́ же де́лает супру́га	But what does a wife do
Одна́, в отсу́тствие супру́га?	Alone, in the absence of her husband?

These two excerpts are based on homonymic rhyme, identity of sound. Both use grammatical rhyme (in the sense that nouns rhyme with nouns), yet both contain an element of surprise. The first, the opening of an untitled poem of the utmost gravity, sets madness (in the fixed expression «сойти́ с ума́») against homelessness («сума́» being the traditional attribute of the wanderer), which is clearly deemed preferable. The second, from the comic «Гра́ф Ну́лин» ("Count Null") functions by showing how absolute identity (of sound and spelling) is illusory: the two "identical" words are in fact opposed ("wife" in nominative singular, "husband" in the genitive singular). This rhyme introduces the work's basic constellation of characters and theme: solitary wife and absent husband.

Stanza

Poets often choose to organize their poems into what might be called verse paragraphs. When each paragraph contains the same number of lines and an identical rhyme scheme (or with minor variation thereof), it is called a stanza. The most common stanza consists of four lines (the "quatrain"), but virtually any number of lines is possible. A stanza ordinarily stands as a complete unit, both syntactically and logically. It generally ends with a full stop (period, exclamation point, or question mark), a signal that the thought has been completed. (Some poets – Tsvetaeva and Brodsky, for instance – often disregard this convention, but they do so not out of ignorance, but as a conscious violation of a self-imposed boundary.) Sometimes stanzas build logically on one another, like chapters in a story or links of a chain. At other times, they may be used to highlight a series of parallels or even digressions, in which case certain stanzas could be removed without anyone necessarily noticing their absence. Whatever the function, the stanza serves as another means of organizing verse language. If rhyme is primarily aural, the stanza is largely visual. A listener may hear the recurring rhyme scheme and sense the stanzaic breaks, but there can be no certainty that the poet has actually written them as stanzas until one sees that they are set off graphically (marked by a skipped line between stanzas).

Tiutchev's «День и ночь» ("Day and Night"), quoted in its entirety below, can illustrate the function of a stanza.

> На ми́р таи́нственный духо́в,
> Над этой бе́здной безымя́нной,
> Покро́в набро́шен златотка́нный
> Высо́кой во́лею бого́в.
> Де́нь – сей блиста́тельный покро́в
> Де́нь, земноро́дных оживле́нье,
> Души́ боля́щей исцеле́нье,
> Дру́г челове́ков и бого́в!

Но ме́ркнет де́нь – наста́ла но́чь;
Пришла́ – и с ми́ра рокова́ого
Тка́нь благода́тную покро́ва,
Сорва́в, отбра́сывает про́чь . . .
И бе́здна на́м обнажена́
С свои́ми стра́хами и мгла́ми,
И нет прегра́д меж е́й и на́ми –
Вот отчего́ нам но́чь страшна́.

(Onto the mysterious world of spirits, / Above this nameless abyss, / A veil woven of gold is thrown / By the lofty will of the gods. / Day is this shining veil / Day, the animation of the earthborn, / The healing of the ailing soul, / The friend of men and gods! // But day darkens – night has fallen. / It has come – and from the fateful world / Having torn off the beneficent cloth of the veil, / It casts it away . . . / And the abyss is exposed to us / With its fears and mists / And there are no barriers between us and it – / This is why we fear the night.)

The poem consists of two eight-line stanzas. As we should expect, the meter (iambic tetrameter) remains constant throughout. There is a slight variation in the rhyme scheme. Each stanza consists of two four-line units (marked by punctuation and syntax), in which the masculine rhymes surround the feminine rhymes. The difference is that the first stanza employs the same masculine rhyme in lines 1,4,5,8, while the second stanza uses two different masculine rhymes.

The title simply introduces day and night, but the poem itself contrasts them, devoting the first stanza to day and the second to night. The fact that the second stanza begins with the word «Но» ("But") marks this contrast explicitly. Other shifts contribute to this opposition: the first stanza is written exclusively as third-person narration, while the second switches midway, unexpectedly introducing the first person plural. The first stanza is essentially a song of praise, while the second becomes an admission of fear. These juxtapositions are enhanced by an opposition dormant in the Russian language: "den'" is masculine, while "noch'" is feminine. Grammatical gender, ordinarily a fact of Russian language without special significance (i.e., there is nothing inherently feminine about a "tetrad'" or masculine about "bloknot," though both refer to notebooks), becomes in this poem another means of creating contrast. All Slavic, Germanic, and Romance languages have masculine day and feminine night, yet only poets (as against ordinary native speakers) are apt to consider this opposition semantically significant. Tiutchev even uses different rhythmic and aural techniques to set apart his two crucial concepts. In the first stanza, he accentuates the word "den'" by placing it in tilts in the initial position of two consecutive lines. As if in balance, the word "noch'" appears twice in the second stanza, in the first and final lines. If "day" occurs in the central lines of the stanza, night is found at the extremes. If "day" is always found at the start of the line, "night" comes towards the end. The first time it occupies the rhyming position as the last word of the line, always a position of prominence. (In the first line of the second stanza, day yields to night in the very literal sense, with the word "den'" occurring on the second foot and "noch'" on the fourth.) The final time "night" appears is as the penultimate word of the final line, where it echoes the "noch'/proch'" rhyme of lines one and four and builds on the sounds that immediately precede it: "Vot ot*chego n*am *noch'*". Tiutchev carefully weaves both key concepts into the sound texture of the poem, but he does so *differently* in each stanza.

In short, the stanzaic structure underlines in numerous ways the poem's theme. In order to create a contrast, Tiutchev sets two stanzas against each other and activates numerous linguistic qualities that would, in ordinary speech or prose, pass unnoticed: rhythm, grammatical gender, the position of words in a line. The first stanza, apparently a celebration of day, is essentially undone by the second. Ultimately night takes priority, ripping asunder day's superficial cover and forcing us to confront the abyss that lurks beneath.

Certain stanzaic forms are invented for a specific work and rarely, if ever, used again. Pushkin devised the Onegin stanza for his novel in verse *Eugene Onegin*, and all subsequent poets who used the form consciously emulated his work in one way or another. Other fixed stanzaic forms have longer and more complicated histories. The sonnet, for example, a fourteen-line poem that originated in thirteenth-century Italy, has been accepted – and adapted – by innumerable poets. As a result, there is no single "correct" sonnet form, but a number of possible models. With few exceptions, though, a sonnet consists of two logically enclosed quatrains followed by two tercets (groups of three lines) that develop the theme raised in the quatrains.

Russian sonnet writing reached a fevered pitch in the Symbolist period, and Vyacheslav Ivanov's «Любо́вь» ("Love") displays a mastery of the form.

Мы – два́ грозо́й зажжённые ствола́,
Два пла́мени полу́ночного бо́ра;
Мы – два́ в ночи́ летя́щих метео́ра,
Одно́й судьбы́ двужа́лая стрела́.

Мы – два́ коня́, чьи де́ржит удила́
Одна́ рука́, – одна́ язви́т их шпо́ра;
Два о́ка мы еди́нственного взо́ра,
Мечты́ одно́й два тре́петных крыла́.

Мы – дву́х тене́й скорбя́щая чета́
Над мра́мором боже́ственного гро́ба,
Где дре́вняя почи́ет Красота́.

Еди́ных та́йн двугла́сные уста́,
Себе́ сами́м мы Сфи́нкс еди́ный о́ба.
Мы – две́ руки́ еди́ного креста́.

(We are two tree-trunks burned in a thunderstorm / Two flames in a midnight forest; / We are two meteors that fly at night, / A two-pointed arrow of one fate. // We are two steeds, whose bridle is held / By one hand, – one spur pricks them; / We are two eyes of a single gaze, / Two quivering wings of one dream. // We are a grieving pair of two shadows / Above the marble of a divine coffin, / Where ancient Beauty rests. // Two-voiced lips of single mysteries, / We both are a single sphinx for each other. / We are two arms of a single cross.)

Part of the sonnet's appeal lies in its difficulty. Ordinarily, rhymes come in pairs. In the sonnet, however, the first eight lines (the octet) are based on only two rhymes, a test of the poet's resourcefulness. The final six lines (the sestet) are generally composed of three different rhymes, though Ivanov here adds an additional challenge by rhyming four of the lines on "-ta." (It is conceivable that he viewed the rhymes on "-ta" and "-sta" as distinct and thus is using the canonical three-rhyme sestet.) Ivanov writes "Love" in iambic pentameter, the standard meter of Russian sonnets, placing an additional constraint on himself by including a caesura after the second foot.

The sonnet brings with it structural as well as strictly formal expectations. It introduces an idea in the initial quatrain, varies, develops or otherwise complicates it in the second, and synthesizes the two quatrains in the concluding sestet. The ninth line is a particularly important landmark, often (though not in this particular sonnet) beginning with a contrastive word, e.g., «Но» ("But"). Each of these three sections is set off graphically (the skipped line) as well as by syntax and punctuation. The graphic break after line 11 is the only one that need not correspond to a logical break, though Ivanov does make a full stop in this poem. While the sonnet can in principle treat any subject, certain themes recur with particular frequency. The love sonnet goes back to the very origins of the form (Petrarch's sonnets to Laura), and Ivanov builds on this tradition.

On first glance, it may seem that Ivanov's poem has little development, that it simply presents a set of variations on the theme of love as a unifying force that combines two discreet things into one. This theme has its source in eastern (Arabic) verse; in Russian poetry one finds direct echoes of it in Pushkin and Fet (in works that Ivanov would certainly have known). Through careful patterning, Ivanov makes this inherited theme very much his own. The opening quatrain relies entirely on inanimate images, drawn with one exception (line 4) from nature. These images are elemental and powerful, yet, it would seem, of brief duration (in this regard the "arrow" of the fourth line is fully in keeping with the spirit of the other imagery).

The second quatrain shifts to the animate world, with the emphasis again on motion, speed, and – implicitly – impermanence. The ninth line, while structurally parallel to many of the preceding statements, marks a decisive break. The ubiquitous motion of the octet yields to an image of stasis, as a couple grieves at the grave of an ancient divinity. This image of antiquity is then developed in the reference to the sphinx (ancient mythology) and its riddle. In the final line, Ivanov moves to an explicitly Christian image, with its implication of resurrection. The quatrains thus combine the spheres of the natural, the animal, and the human world, while the tercets supply a mythological foundation, merging Greek and Christian traditions. Ivanov thereby traces the development of love from passion to Passion, from an impulsive spark of flame to a permanence beyond death. All of this is done by careful adherence to the norms of the sonnet, which has itself been through the ages a favored medium for love poetry.

Chapter 2

Poetic language

Пошло слово любовь, ты права.
Я придумаю кличку иную.
Для тебя я весь мир, все слова,
Если хочешь, переименую.

Пастернак, «Без названия»

You are right, the word 'love' is banal.
I will think up another term.
For you, if you like,
I'll rename the whole world, all the words.

Pasternak, "Without a Name"

In poetry, as in any other kind of speech, our specific words reveal an enormous amount about us. All languages are rich enough to offer multiple ways of expressing the same sentiment. The poet, it has been claimed, chooses "the best words in the best order." But what are the "best words"? Since there is no litmus test to determine whether a given word is worthy or unworthy, poets must determine for themselves what vocabulary is appropriate for what work. The results vary widely, depending on the era, the genre, and the personal taste of the individual.

Lexicon

With the advent of secular poetry in Russia, the need for a distinct poetic language became imperative. One of Lomonosov's seminal ideas was to apply the classical notion of three styles (high, middle, low) to the Russian literary language. Since Lomonosov felt that poetic language should be maximally differentiated from spoken language, he gave pride of place to the high style, which was based on words borrowed from Church Slavonic (the Russian recension of Old Church Slavonic, a written language devised in the ninth century in order to translate liturgical texts from Greek). By Lomonosov's day, Church Slavonic was already distant from the Russian vernacular, but nonetheless comprehensible to the educated public, who encountered it in church and scripture. Distant yet understandable, with powerful religious/historical associations, this language served Lomonosov's purposes well. After all, serious poetry was meant to commemorate elevated subjects, and Russian poets thus had at their disposal a ready-made vocabulary for panegyric genres.

Reading Lomonosov today, we are struck by the archaic quality of his diction. It is worth remembering that, even in his own time, this language would not have sounded "natural." The opening lines of his ode on the occasion of Catherine's ascension to the throne (1762) display a number of his lexical preferences:

Внемлите все преде́лы све́та	Hearken, all ends of the earth
и ве́дайте, что мо́жет Бо́г!	And know what God can do!
Воскре́сла на́м Елисаве́та:	Our Elizabeth has risen:
лику́ет це́рковь и черто́г.	Church and court rejoice.

This passage (and the rest of this lengthy work, for that matter) flaunts the high stylistic register. In addition to direct borrowings from religious discourse ("Bog" [God], "voskresla" [is risen]), Lomonosov creates a distinctively poetic diction by using "vnemlite" in place of the colloquial "slushaite" (hear), "vedaite" instead of "znaite" (know), "likuet" rather than "raduetsia" (rejoice).

Lomonosov's powerful example set the tone for subsequent eighteenth-century poets. Toward the end of the century, Derzhavin began to move away from Lomonosov's injunctions, but one can still detect their influence. In one of the great works of his last years, the 1807 verse epistle «Евге́нию. Жи́знь зва́нская» ("To Eugene: Life at Zvanka"), Derzhavin devotes numerous stanzas to the joys of simple country life (a theme alien to Lomonosov's poetic world):

Пасту́шьего вблизи́ внима́ю ро́га зо́в,
Вдали́ тетереве́й глухо́е токова́нье,
Бара́шков в во́здухе, в куста́х сви́ст соловьёв,
Рёв кра́в, гро́м жо́лн и ко́ней ржа́нье.

(I hearken to the summons of the shepherd's horn nearby, / To the muted mating call of the black grouses in the distance, / To the whistle of the nightingales in the bushes, [like] lambs in the air / To the bellowing of cows, the thunder of woodpeckers and the neighing of horses.)

Derzhavin uses a simple lexicon to depict the bucolic life on his estate. For a poet of this time, he is remarkably specific, not only in explicitly naming animals and birds, but even adding local color through the word "zholná" (a distinct type of woodpecker; the general Russian word is "diátel"). Yet the entire passage is governed by the distinctly literary verb "vnimaiu" ("hearken to"). Moreover, Derzhavin produces a jarring effect when he rejects "koróv" – the standard genitive plural of "cows" – in favor of the Church Slavonic "krav." These two words are identical in meaning, but worlds apart in terms of stylistic resonance. (For a more familiar example, compare "górod" and "grad." Both mean "city," but the former is standard Russian, while the latter is an archaism found only in special contexts, e.g., Leningrad.) The distinction has played a crucial role in the history of the Russian language and in the poetic tradition. "Koróv" (like "górod") is typical of modern Russian, with its predilection for "polnoglásie" (the "full vowel" variant, technically termed "pleophony"). "Krav" (like "grad") is a Church Slavonicism, an archaic, high-style form, which Derzhavin – unlike Lomonosov – places in a mundane context. Derzhavin presumably chose this variant not because of its high stylistic register, but because it fit in with the thick consonantal texture of the line (which describes – and even mimics – animal noises). In any case, Derzhavin's conscious decision to avoid "polnoglasie" demonstrates his allegiance to Lomonosov's basic principles (for more on these, see the discussion of the ode in Chapter Four).

Karamzin broke decisively with Lomonosov in theory and practice. His heirs, the nineteenth-century elegists, created a new poetic ideal, the "language of polite society." The church-slavonicisms that so dominated the eighteenth century were now felt to be bombastic and appeared only in works that required a religious or elevated tone (e.g., Pushkin's «Пророк» ["The Prophet"], cited in Chapter One and discussed later in this chapter). Instead, a French-influenced poetic idiom took shape. It would be a mistake to confuse this new lexicon with the vernacular, for it relied heavily on Gallicisms (direct translations from the French which sounded artificial in everyday Russian), periphrastic expressions, and mythological allusions. Nonetheless, this poetic language was much closer to the spoken language, albeit one spoken only by a highly literate segment of the populace.

Batiushkov's poetry epitomized the new style, as this excerpt from «Выздоровлéние» ("Convalescence") demonstrates:

> Как лáндыш под серпóм убийственным жнецá
>   Склоняет гóлову и вя́нет,
> Так я в болéзни ждáл безврéменно концá
>   И дýмал: Пáрки чáс настáнет.
> Уж óчи покрывáл Эрéба мрáк густóй,
>   Уж сéрдце мéдленнее билóсь:
> Я вя́нул, исчезáл, и жи́зни молодóй,
>   Казáлось, сóлнце закати́лось.

(Just as a lily of the valley under the murderous sickle of the reaper / Bends its head and fades, / So I in my illness awaited a premature end / And I thought: Fate's hour is coming. / Erebus' thick darkness had already closed my eyes, / My heart was already beating slower: / I was fading, disappearing, and it seemed that the sun / Of my young life had set.)

One is struck by the mythological references and the rather complicated means by which a single idea (illness) is expressed. The passage begins with a comparison of the ailing speaker to a lily of the valley – presumably growing amid the grain – about to be cut down by the harvester's sickle. (Pushkin would later note the inaccuracy of this comparison in the margins of his own Batiushkov edition – a lily grows in the meadow, hence it would be cut by scythe. Such precision was clearly unimportant to Batiushkov.) Batiuskov's specific word choices are striking: he assiduously avoids the key word "smert'" ("death"), choosing instead euphemisms (forms of the verb "to fade") and imagery (closing eyes, setting sun). He also incorporates two references to Greek mythology.

One of Pushkin's major contributions to Russian poetry was to revise Batiushkov's language by stripping away the periphrastic qualities and introducing words and phrases that were genuinely colloquial.

> Порá, мой дрýг, порá! покóя сéрдце прóсит –
> Летя́т за дня́ми дни́, и кáждый чáс унóсит
> Части́чку бытия́, а мы́ с тобóй вдвоём
> Предполагáем жи́ть . . . И гля́дь – как рáз – умрём.

(It's time, my friend, it's time! The heart asks for peace – / Days fly after days, and each hour takes away / A small part of existence, but you and I together / Propose to live . . . And before you look, we'll up and die.)

Pushkin's theme – the brevity of life – could hardly be more traditional, yet it is expressed with remarkable directness. Rather than resorting to convoluted synonyms and paraphrases for death, Pushkin uses the standard Russian verb "umeret'." The mythological allusions are absent, as is the comparison to a flower. In general, Pushkin's vocabulary is strikingly simple, at times even conversational. Idiomatic expressions like "gliad'" and "kak raz" might have been used in earlier poetry, but only in "low" genres such as comedy or fable. Such words would have been unthinkable in a Batiushkov elegy, not to mention a Lomonosov ode. Yet they do not strike us here as jarring colloquialisms, but rather meld harmoniously into the pared-down style of the whole.

After Pushkin, Russian poetic diction moved in several directions. In Nekrasov's work, the lexicon expanded to include something approximating the spoken language of the common man. In Tiutchev, the rhetorical traditions of the eighteenth century were to some extent revitalized. Compare, for example, the opening of Nekrasov's «О погóде» ("About the weather") with the opening of Tiutchev's roughly contemporaneous «Двá гóлоса» ("Two Voices"):

Сла́ва Бо́гу, стреля́ть переста́ли!
Ни мину́ты мы ны́нче не спа́ли,
И едва́ ли кто в го́роде спа́л:
Но́чью пу́шечный гро́м грохота́л,
Не до сна́!

(Thank God they've stopped shooting! / We didn't sleep a minute today, / And surely no one in the city slept: / Cannon thunder rumbled at night, / We weren't up to sleeping!)

Мужа́йтесь, о дру́ги, бори́тесь приле́жно,
Хоть бо́й и нера́вен, борьба́ безнаде́жна!
Над ва́ми свети́ла молча́т в вышине́,
Под ва́ми моги́лы – молча́т и оне́.

(Take courage, o friends, fight diligently, / Though the battle be unequal, the struggle hopeless! / Above you the stars are silent in the heights, / Beneath you are the tombs, and they too are silent.)

Nekrasov's subject matter is itself taken from daily life. The "shooting" he describes is not part of an epic battle, but refers to the cannon shots traditionally used to warn Petersburg's inhabitants of an impending flood. Tiutchev's poem is set in mythic time, the speaker an unidentified bard of antiquity, who urges warriors on to glorious deeds in battle. Nekrasov's speaker is clearly just an average Petersburg citizen, and his lexical choices reflect this. (Note how he speaks in the first person plural, rather than the more individualized singular.) The poem begins with an unabashed colloquialism ("Slava Bogu" [Thank God]) and includes any number of low stylistic forms ("nynche" [today]) and idioms ("ne do sna" [up to sleeping]). The Tiutchev example relies on a completely different register, with archaic forms ("drugi" instead "druz'ia" [friends], the archaic feminine plural «оне́» instead of «они́» [they]), and markedly literary diction (e.g., "svetila" rather than "zvezdy" [stars]).

In the twentieth century, such variety becomes even greater. Vladimir Mayakovsky brought the language of the streets to Russian poetry, while Vyacheslav Ivanov used a language replete with archaisms. Compare the diction of Mayakovsky's «На́те!» ("Take this!") to Ivanov's «В Колизе́е» ("In the Coliseum"):

Через ча́с отсю́да в чи́стый переу́лок
вы́течет по челове́ку ваш обрю́згший жи́р,
а я ва́м откры́л столько стихо́в шкату́лок,
я́ – бесце́нных сло́в мо́т и транжи́р.

(In an hour into the clean lane / your flaccid fat will pour out person by person, / while I revealed so many precious boxes of verses to you, / I, the prodigal and spendthrift of priceless words.)

Дéнь влажнокýдрый досия́л,
Меж тýч огóнь вечéрний сéя.
Вкруг помрачáлся, вкруг зия́л
Недви́жный хáос Колизéя.

Гляде́ли из стихи́йной тьмы́
Судéб безврéменные óчи . . .
Дéнь бýрь истóмных к пра́гу нóчи,
Дéнь áлчный провожда́ли мы́.

(Day with its moist curls shone its last, / Sowing evening fire among the dark clouds / The unmoving chaos of the Coliseum / Darkened all around, yawned all around. // From the elemental darkness, / Untimely orbs of fate glanced . . . / We accompanied the thirsting day, / The day of exhausting storms to the threshold of night.)

It is no coincidence that Mayakovsky's poem has a modern urban setting, while Ivanov's is set in the Roman Coliseum, with its direct link to history and mystery. The vocabulary of each poem makes this eminently clear: Mayakovsky revels in the colloquial (e.g., his title) and sub-literary, while Ivanov relies on archaisms ("alchnyi" [thirsting], "prag" instead of the standard modern form "poróg" [border] – note the rejection of "polnoglasie") and a neologism that imitates ancient Greek epithets ("vlazhnokudryi" [literally: "moist-curled"]). Ivanov also makes use of tilts and spondees in this iambic tetrameter poem to lend weight to the word "day." He borrows this technique from Tiutchev, one of his beloved precursors, who used similar rhythmical techniques to accentuate that very same word in "Day and Night" (see Chapter One).

Sound

Poets determine their choice of words based on considerations both stylistic and aural. It is not sufficient to select a series of words from a specific lexical sphere; a poet always thinks in terms of the interaction of those words, of the aural effect they create. Different poetic movements have distinctly different preferences as far as the sound of verse is concerned. Radishchev, an unusually inventive eighteenth-century writer, has often been taken to task for the rough quality of his verse, but this was precisely his goal. In one chapter of his prose work *A Journey from Petersburg to Moscow* (1790), a poet (a thinly veiled version of Radishchev himself), reads aloud portions of his ode «Вóльность» ("Freedom"). His comments on the line «Во свéт рабствá тьмý претвори́» ("Transform the darkness of slavery into light") show a subtle awareness of the importance of sound texture in poetry. "[This line] has been criticized [. . .] It is heavy and difficult to pronounce because of the frequent repetition of the letter 't' and the concatenation of frequent consonants: 'bstva t'mu pretv' – there are only three vowels for ten consonants, and in Russian one can write as sweetly as in Italian . . . I agree . . . though some have considered this verse successful, finding in its unevenness a graphic expression of the difficulty of the deed itself." Radischev thus justifies the harshness of his verse on poetic grounds: the sound texture should reflect the difficulty of the subject matter.

This unashamedly cacophonous style was rejected by the succeeding generation. The comparison of Russian and Italian recurs with a very different evaluation two decades later in one of Batiushkov's letters: "[O]ur language in and of itself is rather bad and coarse – it smells of Tartar. What is an «ы»? What is a «щ», what are «ш», «ший», «щий», «при», «тры»? Oh, barbarians! [. . .] Excuse me for my anger at the Russian people and their language. I was just reading Ariosto, breathing the pure air of Florence [. . .]"

While Batiushkov could hardly avoid using the sounds that he so disdainfully enumerates, he could at least shun the cumbersome consonant clusters so fundamental to Radishchev's poetic voice. Famed for his mellifluous verse, Batiushkov sought to recreate the melodies of his revered Italian poets. One of his techniques was hiatus, the use of consecutive vowel sounds. (Lomonosov had inveighed against hiatus in his theoretical writings on Russian poetry, presumably because it encouraged the reader to elide syllables and thus obscure the rhythmic pulse):

> От во́лн *Уле́и и* Байка́ла,
> От Во́лги, До́*на и* Днепра́,
> От гра́да на́шего Петра́,
> С верши́н Кавка́з*а и У*ра́ла!

(From the waves of Oulu and Baikal, / From the Volga, the Don, and the Dnepr, / From the city of our Peter, / From the peaks of the Caucasus and the Urals!)

In this passage from his patriotic «Перехо́д через Ре́йн» ("Passage over the Rhine"), Batiushkov uses several of those "barbaric" sounds (e.g., "na*sh*ego Pe*tr*a / S ver*sh*in"), but the overall effect is by no means jarring. On the contrary: he combines the distinctly Russian names of rivers, lakes, and mountains in the most harmonious fashion. The "barbarisms" are overwhelmed by the hiatus (indicated by italics) and the numerous phonetic echoes (e.g., "*Ot vol*n . . . *Ot vol*gi," "*Don*a i *Dn*epra"). The Oulu, a river in northern Finland (then part of the Russian empire), was surely chosen by Batiushkov as much for its vowel-rich name as for its geopolitical significance.

In the history of Russian poetry, the same stylistic battle would be fought repeatedly. Among the twentieth-century poets, Mandel'shtam, with his personal cult of Batiushkov, might be said to represent the principle of euphony. It is characteristic that Mandel'shtam would write phrases like «рыда́нья *Аони́д*» and «пе́нья *Аони́д*» (the Aonides were the muses), which combine his reverence for antiquity with the consecutive vowel sounds made famous by Batiushkov. In fact, Mandel'shtam originally planned to exploit this hiatus in the very title of his second book by calling it *Аони́ды.*

The Cubo-Futurists, Mandel'shtam's contemporaries, exhibit an altogether different attitude to sound organization. Aleksei Kruchenykh and Velimir Khlebnikov, in their manifesto «Сло́во как таково́е» ("The Word as Such"), cite two famous lines of nineteenth-century poetry (from Lermontov's «А́нгел» ["The Angel"], which we will discuss in Chapter Five), as an example of the old, which they contrast unfavorably to their own approach.

"Writers before us had a completely different sound instrumentation, e.g.,

> По не́бу полу́ночи а́нгел лете́л
> И ти́хую пе́сню он пе́л . . .
> (An angel flew along the midnight sky / And he sang a quiet song . . .)

Here the "пе", "пе" gives a bloodless coloration . . . Like paintings done with pudding and milk, we are also not satisfied with verses built on

> па-па-па
> пи-пи-пи
> ти-ти-ти

A healthy person will only ruin his stomach on such food.

We have given an example of another sound and word combination:

> дыр бул щыл
> убешщур
> скум
> вы со бу
> р л эз

(Incidentally, in these five lines there is more truly Russian [*bol'she russkogo natsional'nogo*] than in all of Pushkin's poetry.)"

These five lines constitute an entire poem by Kruchenykh, perhaps the most celebrated example of "zaum'" ("trans-rational poetry" or, more poetically, "beyonsense"). In "zaum'," new words, unburdened by fixed meanings, were called into being by expressive combinations of sounds. Kruchenykh opens his "manifesto" poem by giving special prominence to those very phonemes that Batiushkov had decried as barbaric: the vowel «ы» and the consonant «щ». Precisely these sounds, so alien to the "civilized" languages of Europe, represent for the radical Futurists the uniquely

Russian spirit. It is somewhat difficult to explain Kruchenykh's neologism «щыл», since only substandard (Polish influenced?) Russian would allow for the "hard" variant of the Russian letter «щ». As a "slap in the face" of Russian spelling rules, however, it aptly reflects the Cubo-Futurist ethos.

Of course, no poet can entirely avoid using certain sounds. (It is true that Derzhavin wrote «Соловей во сне» ["A Nightingale in a Dream"] without the letter "r," which he considered harsh and thus unsuited to the tranquil atmosphere he sought to evoke. However, this poem is exceptional and quite short.) Batiushkov, as we have seen, could not completely renounce the "barbarisms," just as the Futurists (with the exception of the most radical "zaumniki") could not do without the "bloodless," Europeanized "pa," "pi," and "ti." The real issue is not whether certain sounds occur, but how prominently they occur.

It will be useful to compare the following two passages (both written in 1914), each of which exhibits careful sound patterning. The first comes from Mandel'shtam's «Я не слыхал рассказов Оссиана» ("I never heard Ossian's tales"):

> И не одно́ сокро́вище, быть мо́жет,
> Мину́я вну́ков, к пра́внукам уйдёт,
> И сно́ва ска́льд чужу́ю пе́сню сло́жит
> И как свою́ её произнесёт.

(And more than one treasure, perhaps, / Skipping the grandsons, will go to the great-grandsons, / And again the bard will set down another's song / And pronounce it as his own.)

The second is from Mayakovsky's «Война́ объя́влена» ("War Is Declared"):

> Бро́нзовые генера́лы на гранёном цо́коле
> моли́ли: «Раску́йте, и мы́ пое́дем!»
> Проща́ющейся ко́нницы поцелу́и цо́кали,
> и пехо́те хоте́лось к уби́йце – побе́де.

(The bronze generals on the faceted pedestal / begged: "Unfetter us, and we will ride!" / The kisses of parting cavalry clattered, / and the infantry wanted [to get] to the murderer, – to victory.)

In Russian, stressed vowels contribute much more to the sound texture of verse than unstressed ones, since the latter (with the exception of «у» and «и») are reduced and thus less prominent. It is appropriate to speak of assonance (the technical term for a repeated vowel sound) on "o" in the first line of the Mandel'shtam excerpt because it is found in all three stressed vowels. The fact that "o" also appears in several *unstressed* positions in no way enhances this effect. It looks the same, but sounds different. One can nonetheless speak of assonance on "u" in the second line, largely because the unstressed (yet also unreduced) "u" in the final two words amplifies the emphatic repetition of the first two stressed syllables. In this instance, the sound fabric is particularly rich, since repeated consonant sounds (a technique known as either consonance or alliteration) accompany the assonance: «Мин*у́*я в*н*у́ков, к пра́в*н*укам уйдёт». The sound texture of Mayakovsky's verses is no less rich, but the alliterations in this passage occur on the harsher, less mellifluous, sounds of the Russian language. The final two lines are particularly illustrative in this respect: «Проща́ющейся ко́нницы поцелу́и *ц*о́кали / и пехо́те хоте́лось.»

The interpreter of poetry must exercise extreme restraint in ascribing precise meaning to specific sounds. On the basis of the previous two examples, it might appear that Mandel'shtam uses the gentle "nu" repetition because he writes about the smooth transmission of cultural tradition, while Mayakovsky uses "harsh" sounds to depict war. Yet there is nothing inherently martial about Mayakovsky's sounds, just as there is nothing inherently tranquil about Mandel'shtam's. One could imagine phrases like «*Х*оть *х*о́чет *х*оро́шее» ("Though he wants good") or «Зан*у́*ду *н*у́жно ун*и́*зить» ("It's necessary to humiliate the bore"), where these same sounds would have quite different associations. Recurring sounds draw attention to themselves and, in poetry, take on the semantic coloration of what they depict. Mayakovsky's poem describes a war, and once we recognize this, we hear the specific sounds as military. Likewise, Mandel'shtam's poem celebrates cultural continuity and, *in that context*, we associate the insistent "nu" repetitions with this theme. The sounds of poetry cannot determine meaning, but only support it.

Even if specific sounds are not endowed with *a priori* meaning, their significance should not be underestimated. One need only observe a young child repeating what appear to be nonsense syllables to see that pure sound is in itself a distinctly human pleasure, and that poets are in some sense attempting to recreate that initial joy of naming. Yet sound repetition is not simply the province of children and poets. Upon reflection, one finds that many of our most routine and seemingly "unpoetic" expressions (e.g., "sp*ee*d *d*emon" or "n*u*mb*er* cr*u*n*cher*") owe their longevity – and perhaps their very existence – to consonance and assonance. Such expressions "sound right" because they are easily pronounced and easily remembered.

Tropes and syntax

Our discussion of poetic language has so far been limited to lexicon (stylistic register) and sound. However, poetry is made not only of individual words and sounds, but of entire sentiments. In everyday speech, we may speak directly or indirectly. For example, on an average day, if asked to respond to the question, "How are you?" most people say "Fine." Less direct answers would also be possible, all of which depend on figures of speech, e.g., "Not bad," (meiosis [i.e., understatement]), "Disastrous" (hyperbole [i.e., exaggeration]). Even the answer "Fine" may be used ironically, in which case it, too, is an indirect answer.

In short, indirectness seems to be a fundamental property of language itself, and it should come as no surprise that poets take advantage of it. Such indirect statements are known as tropes (from the Greek "tropos" or "turn") or figures of speech (from the Latin "figura" or "shape"). In this section, we will consider some of the most important of them. Those that occur with less frequency will be introduced in the course of poetic analyses in the second part of the book.

Tropes and figures (the terms are essentially synonymous) introduce new and unexpected shifts to a poem. In many cases, they are used for purposes of comparison. Metaphor posits an identity between two things. For example, Boris Pasternak entitled a volume of poetry «Сестра́ моя – жи́знь» ("My Sister – Life"). In this case, the metaphor seems to be supported by grammatical gender: both "sestra" and "zhizn'" are feminine. A wholly different image is created by Petr Viazemsky, who begins one of his last poems with the metaphor: «Жи́знь наша в ста́рости – изно́шенный хала́т» ("Our life in old age is a worn-out dressing gown"). Pasternak's metaphor posits a kinship between the poet and life. Viazemsky's reflects a distance; life is associated with lethargy and thus sapped of its vitality.

At times, a poet seeks to create a relationship of similarity rather than identity. In English, this is known as a simile (a comparison using "like" or "as"); in Russian it is simply called a comparison («сравне́ние»). When discussing simile, it is useful to distinguish the "tenor" (the thing actually being described) from the "vehicle" (what that thing is compared to). For example, in Pushkin's lines «Безу́мных ле́т уга́сшее весе́лье / Мне тяжело́, как сму́тное похме́лье» ("The faded joy of wild years / Weighs on me like an unsettling hangover"), "joy" is the tenor and "hangover" is the vehicle. A simile recognizes the distinctiveness of the objects under comparison, an awareness of an inexact fit. In this way, it accentuates difference as well as likeness. Mayakovsky, who often pushes comparisons to the breaking point, favors similes, e.g., «Как тракти́р мне стра́шен ваш стра́шный су́д» ("Your last judgment is as terrifying as a tavern to me"). Alliteration gives additional support to this simile (*traktir/strashen/strashnyi*). The Russian instrumental case can also be used as a type of simile (this appears with special frequency in modernist verse): «Я во́лком бы вы́грыз бюрократи́зм» ("I would gnaw through red tape like a wolf"), to cite Mayakovsky once again.

Simile and metaphor are based on principles of similarity, while metonymy depends on contiguity, drawing things together because of their proximity. One of the reasons why Pasternak's poetry is so rich in striking juxtapositions is his reliance on metonymy. The poem «Сложа вёсла» ("With Oars At Rest"), in which the poet and his beloved are together in a rowboat, begins with the line «Лодка колотится в сонной груди́» ("The boat pounds in the sleeping breast"). The word "lodka" ("boat") takes the place of the more logical "serdtse" ("heart"). The boat does not "symbolize" the heart; rather, it is connected by location (the poet is sitting inside the boat). In making this metonymic substitution, Pasternak was surely guided by sound as well as sense: "*lódka kolótitsia.*" Synecdoche (the substitution of a part for the whole) is a special type of metonymy. For example, when Mayakovsky describes the revolutionary masses storming the Winter Palace, he names them only by their clothing (presumably their most visible attribute, but also an indication of their social position): «А в двери́ – бушла́ты, шине́ли, тулу́пы» ("And through the doors [come] sailors' coats, soldiers' coats, and peasant coats").

One of the more striking tropes is oxymoron (contradiction), which is generally used to express not a lack of logic, but a sense of awe or a particularly intense impression. Oxymoron is often found in mystical and religious writings, but it extends to any experience that defies ordinary rational understanding. One of Mandel'shtam's late poems from his exile contains the line: «В роско́шной бе́дности, в могу́чей нищете́» ("In luxuriant poverty, in powerful destitution"). Here the poet forces us to reconsider the usual associations of familiar concepts, to consider a state of physical poverty that – paradoxically – can be spiritually rich and even empowering.

Apostrophe (direct address) is a particularly important trope for poetry. In everyday life, we tend to limit our use of apostrophe to people or animals in our immediate vicinity. Poets are much more liberal. Not only do they address people who are distant or even deceased, they frequently address inanimate objects. Turning to speak to someone or something establishes a more immediate relationship, and apostrophe often marks a poem's emotional climax. Tiutchev's «Фонта́н» ("The Fountain") opens with a turn to the listener/reader: «Смотри́, как о́блаком живы́м / Фонта́н сия́ющий клуби́тся; / Как пламене́ет, как дроби́тся / Его́ на со́лнце вла́жный дым.» ("Look how like a living cloud, / The shining fountain swirls; / How its moist smoke / Burns and breaks in the sun.") Though we readers cannot possibly see the specific fountain in question, the direct address invites us – even *causes* us – to become spectators. The second (and final) stanza begins with yet another apostrophe: «О сме́ртной мы́сли водоме́т, /

О водомёт неистощи́мый! / Како́й зако́н непостижи́мый / Тебя́ стреми́т, тебя́ мятёт?» ("O, font of mortal thought, / O, inexhaustible font! / What incomprehensible law / Spurs you on, disturbs you?") Leaving his readers behind, the poet turns to the fountain itself, which now is not merely a physical object, but a metaphor for human thought. In this second apostrophe, Tiutchev shifts lexical registers, rejecting the standard Russian "fontan" (with its latinate origin) of the title and first stanza in favor of the archaic Slavic synonym "vodomet." The sudden shift of addressees, combined with this elevated diction, heightens the emotional tone of the poem. From the first to the second stanza Tiutchev moves from the physical to the metaphysical, from detached observation (statements) to impassioned participation (questions and exclamations). The use of two different apostrophes is thus essential to the structure of the poem as a whole.

Some figures of speech are syntactic rather than semantic. In other words, they are achieved through manipulation of word order. Repetition at the beginning of a line is called anaphora. A classic example comes from Pushkin's «Проро́к» ("The Prophet"):

> Мои́х уше́й косну́лся о́н, –
> И и́х напо́лнил шу́м и зво́н:
> И вня́л я не́ба содрога́нье,
> И го́рний а́нгелов полёт,
> И га́д морски́х подво́дный хо́д,
> И до́льней ло́зы прозяба́нье.

(He touched my ears, – / And noise and sound filled them: / And I perceived the shudder of heaven, / And the lofty flight of angels, / And the underwater motion of sea beasts, / And the growth of vines in the valley.)

In this case, the anaphora is also an instance of polysyndeton, the repetition of a conjunction ("and"). This technique is often found in the Bible, which is one reason Pushkin chooses it for this particular poem. Anaphora serves as an ordering principle at the beginning of the line, much as rhyme usually orders the end of the line.

Two common – and related – syntactic figures are parallelism and chiasmus. The former uses the same parts of speech in the same order (e.g., «Мча́тся ту́чи, вью́тся ту́чи» ["Dark clouds rush, dark clouds twirl"]), the second uses the same parts of speech in reverse order (e.g., «Му́тно не́бо, но́чь мутна́» ["Turbid is the sky, the night is turbid"]) or even a series of nouns with reversed case order. For example, Derzhavin begins his poem «На сме́рть кня́зя Меще́рского» ("On the Death of Prince Meshchersky") with two exclamations: «Глаго́л време́н! мета́лла зво́н!» (Literally: "Word of time! Of metal the sound!") This example of chiasmus is based solely on nouns: the "crossing" occurs between the nominative and genitive cases. (It might be noted that Derzhavin's line contains two additional tropes: metaphor [the striking of a clock is being described] and personification [time "speaks"].)

In English, rules of word order ensure that parallelism occurs much more frequently than chiasmus. In Russian, however, the elaborate case system allows for extraordinarily free word order, making the language just as amenable to chiasmus as to parallelism. To see how Russian poets take full advantage of syntax (and not merely syntactic figures), one need only look at the first line of one of Baratynsky's elegies: «Рассéивает грýсть пирóв весёлый шýм.» Russian grammar allows for four translations of this sentence:

1) "The happy sound of feasts disperses sadness."
2) "Sadness disperses the happy sound of feasts."
3) "The happy sound disperses the sadness of feasts."
4) "The sadness of feasts disperses a happy sound."

The first of these renderings is the most logical, with the list becoming increasingly counter-intuitive. However, there is reason to think that Baratynsky recognized and wished to suggest all of these meanings. In the remainder of the poem, the speaker describes his melancholy amidst a crowd of revelers. In this context, the first translation reflects the speaker's hope that his sadness will disappear among his carefree companions, while the second adumbrates his ultimate realization that external happiness cannot alter his internal sadness. The third and the fourth variants seem less plausible, but the oxymoronic phrase "sadness of feasts" has definite relevance to the paradoxical situation in which the speaker finds himself. In short, syntactic and grammatical ambiguities can suggest alternate interpretations or reinforce thematic paradoxes.

Enjambment is a syntactic technique unique to poetry. Since the cadence of a verse line is strongly marked (either rhythmically or by rhyme), it implies an endpoint. This tends to be indicated by a period or comma, but even when punctuation is lacking, a sentence segment usually concludes. For example, one of Pushkin's great love poems begins:

> Для берегóв отчúзны дáльной
> Ты покидáла крáй чужóй;
> В чáс незабвéнный, в чáс печáльный
> Я дóлго плáкал пред тобóй.

(For the shores of a distant homeland / You left a foreign realm; / At an unforgettable hour, at a sad hour / I cried at length before you.)

Pushkin places punctuation marks only after lines two and four, yet lines one and three, which contain complete prepositional phrases, also conclude at logical pauses. The punctuation notwithstanding, there is no enjambment in this passage.

Comparing these lines to a passage from Tsvetaeva's «Поэты» ("Poets"), we can see the decisive break characteristic of true enjambment:

> Кто в ка́менном гробу́ Басти́лий
> Как де́рево в свое́й красе́.
> Тот, чьи следы́ – всегда́ просты́ли,
> Тот по́езд, на кото́рый всё
> Опа́здывают . . .

([He], who in the stone grave of Bastilles / Is like a tree in its beauty. / He, whose footprints – have always gone cold, / He is a train, for which everyone / Is late . . .)

The excerpt begins with each line breaking at a logical pause, but in the fourth line, Tsvetaeva ends on the subject ("vse") and forces the finite verb to fall onto the next line. With this verb, the whole sentence comes to an abrupt end. In short, one would ordinarily expect the words "vse opazdyvaiut" ("everyone is late") to come in the same line. By splitting them over two lines, Tsvetaeva uses the verse form to reflect the meaning. The line describes a late arrival, so the key word also arrives "late."

The "meaning" of enjambment is not always as transparent as in the above example. At times it merely pushes the reader forward, adding an excited quality to the utterance. In any case, enjambment always sets syntax against semantics, adding special emphasis whenever it occurs.

If enjambment is unique to verse, most poetic techniques can also be found in prose and even in everyday conversation. What sets verse language apart is the extent to which poets consciously organize diction, tropes, and grammar to develop and accentuate their statements. Not every linguistic element is necessarily a poetic element, but every linguistic element has the *potential* to become one. Seemingly inexpressive grammatical categories, when carefully structured, take on a host of subtle and powerful meanings, all of which contribute to a poem's message. The multiplicity and concentration of complementary systems (syntactic, lexical, aural, semantic) distinguishes poetry from other forms of verbal art.

Chapter 3

Tradition and the individual talent

Всё бы́ло встáрь, всё повтори́тся снóва,
И слáдок нáм лишь узнавáнья ми́г.

Мандельштам, «Tristia»

Everything was before, everything will repeat again,
And for us only the moment of recognition is sweet.

Mandel'shtam, "Tristia"

In any sphere of creativity, an unspoken directive to "make it new" coexists with an equally strong tacit imperative to retain qualities of the old. Pure repetition is tedious; pure innovation is incoherent. To see how traditions evolve, one need look no further than the local movie theater. Seventy years ago, audiences flocked to "King Kong," quaking in their seats as the eponymous beast screamed, raged, and took on New York City. Today's viewers may admire this same film as a historical document, but few will react with the gasps and screams that the film originally aroused. In particular, the special effects, so daring in their day, now contribute more to mirth than to fear. Producers of the latest monster films rely on myriad technical advances to shock a generation inured to cinematic horror, yet they generally preserve the basic plot outline of a wild creature's encounter with civilization. Many retain the love subplot and even specific details, like the monster's appearance at or on top of famous buildings or a "bad guy" becoming one of its victims. Such repetitions reflect less a lack of creativity than a genuine insight: what worked well once can work well again. Consciously or not, the audience itself wants to be terrified only within familiar parameters. The quality of the newer films depends less on invention than on the clever manipulation of "traditional" elements. If the director can rework them and still shock us, we are dealing with a first-rate monster flick. If the old formulas are trotted out in completely predictable ways, we head for the popcorn.

There are, of course, significant differences between Hollywood entertainment and poetic tradition, but they share the impulse to revisit successful works of an earlier era. In all national literatures, continuity plays a decisive role. In Russia, as if literature could compensate for the brutal twists and turns of history, continuity is regarded as an especially great virtue. Lermontov began his career by lifting whole passages from Pushkin in works whose very titles he took verbatim from his beloved precursor. Mandel'shtam, whose verses celebrating repetition form the epigraph to this chapter, saw the past as the wellspring for all great poetry. The Symbolist Fedor Sologub so valued the work of his predecessors that he advocated a theory of creativity verging on plagiarism.

"Intertextuality" is the general term for the numerous possible means by which one work of literature alludes to and engages others. The more one has read (and remembered), the more one is likely to appreciate the often subtle interplay among poems. On the other hand, those with little prior experience will justifiably ask whether it is possible to understand a work without charting its relationship to various "subtexts." In the case of monster movies, which attract a young audience, most of today's viewers have surely not seen the original "King Kong." This lack of context hardly means that they cannot enjoy the new movie. Some may actually like it precisely because they do not recognize its derivativeness. Others may have a vague sense of the tradition, even if they miss the specific conscious references. But those who have seen "King Kong" will certainly have a richer understanding of the strengths, weaknesses, and even intentions of the new film.

Likewise, though neophyte readers of Russian poetry cannot possibly know the rich resonances of certain words or phrases, they should be aware of this dimension of poetic communication. Toward the beginning of a 1979 poem entitled "Дóн Жуáн" ("Don Juan"), Viktor Sosnora writes the laconic line «Стóл яств» ("A table of victuals"). At face value this can be understood as a realistic detail from one of the innumerable feast scenes associated with Don Juan's legendary escapades. However, a knowledgeable Russian reader immediately hears in these words a specific poetic reference. Exactly two hundred years earlier, Derzhavin had written «На смéрть кня́зя Мещéрского» ("On the Death of Prince Meshchersky"), a lament on life's brevity. That work contained a famous line about the rapidity with which celebration turns into mourning: «Где стóл был яств, там грóб стоúт» ("Where there was a table of victuals, there is now a coffin"). By citing this line in abbreviated form, Sosnora cleverly foretells, as it were, Don Juan's own final "act," in which a feast leads swiftly to his death.

To a greater or lesser extent, all new works engage their predecessors, and it would be senseless to pretend otherwise. Textual echoes add depth and breadth, making a poem profoundly dialogical, yet they rarely *determine* its meaning. Moreover, they can be daunting to a reader not intimately familiar with the tradition. In this book, such discussions will be kept to a minimum. With a few unavoidable exceptions (e.g., Mandel'shtam), we will limit questions of intertextuality to forms that are either marked explicitly by the poet or can be logically intuited by the resourceful reader.

Citation

When a politician wishes to win over his audience, he often draws on the words of an illustrious predecessor. "As Abraham Lincoln said," intones the speaker, and the effect is already there, almost regardless of what follows. In short, the politician refers to a recognized authority in order to align his own message with one that is hallowed by tradition. Other methods of allusion are possible. The politician may omit Lincoln's name but say, "Four score and seven years ago," obviously assuming that his audience will recognize the reference. He could even alter those words to "Two score and seven years ago" and still be confident that the source (and its aura of authority) would resonate.

To a far greater extent and in much richer variety than politicians, poets refer to other poets. Some may know the tradition better than others, some may know it earlier than others, but all serious poets must at some point or another acquaint themselves with the accomplishments of their predecessors. Such an acquaintance entails a challenge. How can the new poet match up to what has already been said? It has been argued that whole national literatures are formed through this "anxiety of influence." Yet the existence of a rich tradition is not simply constricting, but also enlightening and enriching. Russian poets have generally delighted in the poetry of others, regarding it as a precious resource that can be creatively exploited in numerous ways.

An early poem of Aleksandr Blok offers a relatively straightforward example of this process:

> И тя́жкий со́н жите́йского созна́нья
> Ты отряхнёшь, тоску́я и любя́.
>
> Вл. Соловьев

> Предчу́вствую Тебя́. Года́ прохо́дят ми́мо –
> Все в о́блике одно́м предчу́вствую Тебя́.
>
> Весь горизо́нт в огне́ – и я́сен нестерпи́мо,
> И мо́лча жду́, – *тоску́я и любя́.*
>
> Весь горизо́нт в огне́, и бли́зко появле́нье,
> Но стра́шно мне: изме́нишь о́блик Ты,
>
> И де́рзкое возбу́дишь подозре́нье,
> Смени́в в конце́ привы́чные черты́.
>
> О, как паду́ – и го́рестно, и ни́зко,
> Не одоле́в смерте́льныя мечты́!
>
> Как я́сен горизо́нт! И лучеза́рность бли́зко.
> Но стра́шно мне: изме́нишь о́блик Ты.

([Epigraph: "And you will shake off the burdensome dream of earthly consciousness, / Yearning and loving." Vladimir Soloviev] I anticipate You. Years pass by – /

I anticipate You always with the same visage. // The entire horizon is aflame – and unbearably clear, / And I silently wait, – *Yearning and loving.* // The entire horizon is aflame, and [Your] appearance is near, / But I am afraid that You will change [Your] visage, // And arouse an impertinent suspicion, / Having replaced in the end [Your] ordinary features. // O, how I will fall – grieving and low, / Having not overcome [my] mortal dream! // How clear is the horizon! And radiance is near. / But I am afraid that You will change [Your] visage.)

Blok's poem comes from a book of poems called «Стихи́ о Прекра́сной Да́ме» ("Verses about the Beautiful Lady"). Many of these laconic and enigmatic works describe a meeting (or, more precisely, an anticipated meeting) between the male speaker and a female figure who is at once a source of joy and fear. This specific poem characteristically combines the language of love poetry (e.g., "podozrenie" [suspicion], "cherty" [features]) with that of religious poetry ("luchezarnost'" [radiance], "oblik" [visage]). The emphasis is on expectation and anxiety, with the speaker balancing the certainty of the woman's imminent appearance against the uncertainty of the form this will take. One is struck by the poem's insistent repetitions; whole phrases are reiterated numerous times, giving the impression that the entire scene has itself been rehearsed over and over. Blok's image of the "eternal feminine" had numerous sources, but one of the most direct was the mystical poetry of Vladimir Soloviev, who had died in 1900, the year before «Предчу́вствую Тебя́» was written. In this poem, Blok explicitly establishes his lineage with Soloviev. Not only does he italicize the words he borrows, he even cites the exact source in an epigraph.

The Soloviev poem, written in 1892, is indeed close in spirit to Blok's verses. It, too, focuses on an imminent meeting between the speaker and an unnamed female figure. (The fact that the speaker is male and his addressee female is not stated explicitly, but – as in the Blok poem – is obvious from the lengthy tradition of love lyrics that these poems draw on.)

Заче́м слова́? В безбре́жности лазу́рной
Эфи́рных во́лн созву́чные струи́
Несу́т к тебе́ жела́ний пла́мень бу́рный
И та́йный вздо́х неме́ющей любви́.

И, трепеща́ у ми́лого поро́га,
Забы́тых грёз к тебе́ стреми́тся ро́й.
Недалека́ возду́шная доро́га,
Оди́н лишь ми́г – и я́ перед тобо́й.

И в э́тот ми́г незри́мого свида́нья
Незде́шний све́т вновь озари́т тебя́,
И тя́жкий со́н житейского созна́нья
Ты отряхнёшь, тоску́я и любя́.

(What good are words? In the azure boundlessness / The harmonious streams of ethereal waves / Carry to you the powerful flame of desires / And the secret sigh of mute love. // And, shaking at the dear threshold, / A swarm of forgotten dreams rushes to you. / The aerial path is not far, / Only an instant – and I am before you. // And in that instant of invisible meeting / The unearthly light will again illuminate you, / And you will shake off the burdensome dream of earthly consciousness, / Yearning and loving.)

In Soloviev, we find the same conflation of love poetry (e.g., "u milogo poroga" [at the dear threshold]) and religious verse (e.g., "nezdeshnii svet" [unearthly light]), the same motif of anticipation. Nonetheless, there are significant differences between these poems. Most striking is that Soloviev's speaker displays no doubts whatsoever. He has experienced this meeting before (note the "vnov'" [again] in the final stanza) and is certain that it will recur ("odin lish' mig" [only an instant]). The oxymoronic "mig nezrimogo svidaniia" ("instant of invisible meeting") points not at the impossibility of this meeting, but rather at its mystical, quasi-religious nature. (English translation cannot preserve the essential opposition: both "nezrimogo" and "svidaniia" are based on verbs meaning "to see" [cf. the archaic "zret'" versus standard "videt'"].) Blok's speaker has not experienced this meeting, but has long anticipated it. Though he senses it ever more strongly, he is clearly troubled by fears. Interestingly, the phrase "toskuia i liubia" ("yearning and loving") refers in Blok to the speaker himself, while in Soloviev it is attributed to the mysterious feminine figure.

What, then, is the function of the epigraph? In taking just two lines from Soloviev's poem, Blok minimizes the differences between his poem and that of his predecessor. One of the striking elements of Blok's poem is that the word "Ty" is capitalized, making it unambiguously a divine figure. In the Soloviev poem, the "ty" is most likely also a divinity, but it is not written with a capital letter. By selecting a passage for his epigraph in which the word "ty" only appears at the beginning of a line, Blok erases this difference. The same phenomenon can be observed on the level of stanza. Blok's poem is written in two-line stanzas, while Soloviev's is in quatrains. Yet by citing only two lines from Soloviev, Blok eliminates the distinction. Even the metrical differences are diminished. Soloviev's poem is in iambic pentameter, while Blok's vacillates between iambic pentameter and hexameter. When only two lines are cited, however, the metrical incongruities disappear. In short, Blok uses the epigraph in this case not merely to express his admiration for his precursor, but to align himself with him all the more emphatically.

Epigraphs are perhaps the most explicit means through which a poet indicates an awareness of his place in a tradition. They invite the reader to view the new poem against the background of an earlier one. In less direct ways, however, such a dialogue is almost always in progress. Anna

Akhmatova's «Реквием» ("Requiem"), a cycle of poems about the Stalinist repressions, contains a poem entitled «Посвящение» ("Dedication"), which begins as follows:

> Перед этим горем гнутся горы,
> Не течёт великая река,
> Но крепки тюремные затворы,
> А за ними «каторжные норы»
> И смертельная тоска.

(Before this grief mountains bend, / The great river ceases to flow, / But the prison bolts are strong, / And behind them are the "convicts' burrows" / And deadly anguish.)

The phrase "katorzhnye nory" ("convicts' burrows") is in quotation marks because it is indeed a quotation. The source is Pushkin's «Во глубине сибирских руд» ("In the depths of Siberian mines"), a political poem addressed to the exiled Decembrists. The third stanza of that poem reads:

> Любовь и дружество до вас
> Дойдут сквозь мрачные затворы,
> Как в ваши каторжные норы
> Доходит мой свободный глас.

(Love and friendship / Will reach you through the dark bolts, / Just as into your convicts' burrows / My free voice reaches.)

Akhmatova, it will be noticed, not only repeats these two words, but also borrows the underlying rhyme "zatvory/nory." Such repetition serves to point out a parallel that is both historical and literary. On the one hand, Akhmatova suggests that the senseless brutality of Stalinism has a direct precedent in Tsar Nikolai's cruel reprisals against the Decembrists. On the other hand, Akhmatova likens her own role to Pushkin's: in both cases the poets are left to support and console their unjustly imprisoned friends. Pushkin's poem ends with the hope that an age of freedom will ultimately prevail. Akhmatova, not quite so optimistic, nonetheless tries in "Requiem" to posit some future peace that might offset the present sufferings. The poet's role, she emphasizes, is both to bear witness and give hope. In short, Akhmatova cites Pushkin not only to lay claim to his authority as poet, but also to continue the tradition of poet as social critic and spokesman for the politically repressed.

Citation can also be used parodically, to undermine earlier convictions. The contemporary poet Dimitri Prigov has developed a genre he calls «Банальное рассуждение» ("The Banal Disquisition") in which well-known proverbs and familiar quotations are subjected to close scrutiny from a practical vantage point. His "Второе банальное рассуждение на тему: быть знаменитым некрасиво" ("Second Banal Disquisition on the Subject of 'To Be Famous Isn't Nice' ") begins:

> Когда ты скажем знаменит –
> Быть знаменитым некрасиво
> Но ежели ты незнаменит
> То знаменитым быть не только
> Желательно, но и красиво

(When you are, let's say, famous – / To be famous isn't nice / But if you're not famous / Then to be famous is not only / Desirable, but even beautiful)

Prigov's verses are fundamentally reactive. To understand them it is essential to know their context – a poem of Boris Pasternak.

> Быть знаменитым некрасиво.
> Не это подымает ввысь.
> Не надо заводить архива,
> Над рукописями трясись.
>
> Цель творчества – самоотдача,
> А не шумиха, не успех.
> Позорно, ничего не знача,
> Быть притчей на устах у всех.

(To be famous isn't nice. / This is not what elevates [one]. / One need not set up an archive, / Tremble over manuscripts. // The aim of creativity is self-abnegation, / Not to create a stir or a public success. / It is shameful, when one is meaningless, / To be on everyone's tongue.)

As this excerpt makes clear, Pasternak's poem is aimed at writers who seek glory without having anything to say. The real poet, he argues, is concerned less with his reputation than with his art. Poetry, according to his conception, is essentially selfless and thus directly opposed to fame.

Prigov takes this lofty sentiment not as a profound truth, but as a display of disingenuousness. Pasternak's verses were written when the poet was not simply established, but almost legendary. It is easy, Prigov reasons, for the famous to deplore fame, but the obscure poet does not have this luxury. Playing on Pasternak's choice of the word "nekrasivo" ("not nice" in the given context, but literally "not beautiful"), he rejects Pasternak's judgment, viewing fame as something beautiful ("krasivo"). Prigov criticizes Pasternak not simply on the basic level of statement, but also in terms of diction and form. He introduces jarring colloquialisms such as "skazhem" ("let's say") and "ezheli" (rather than the more standard "esli" [if]). Like most parodists, he borrows the meter of his target text (in this case, iambic tetrameter), yet he introduces a "mistake" in line three. When Prigov rhymes Pasternak's key word "znamenit" with its negation ("neznamenit"), he adds an extra syllable that throws off the scansion, thus undermining in a single stroke Pasternak's content *and* form. (The line scans correctly only if the reader swallows the middle syllable of the word "ezheli," something an uneducated or inebriated speaker might do. If this is Prigov's intention, then he diminishes Pasternak's sentiment not by a rhythmic break, but by including a colloquial word with a substandard pronunciation.)

Prigov's allusion is motivated differently than Blok's and Akhmatova's, but all three examples demonstrate the interconnectedness of poetic tradition. Blok seeks to create a seamless link to his predecessor. Akhmatova draws similarities and parallels while recognizing the distinctiveness of two historical epochs. Prigov emphasizes the falseness in a statement that has become such a classic that few stop to think about it. What is important in all three cases is that the poets themselves clearly direct their audience to a specific prior text. Such poetry is profoundly dialogical, and it demands to be read in conjunction with an earlier text. This fascination with others' words and worldviews is an essential part of Russian poetry.

Topos

At times, politicians rely on a different technique to win over their audiences. Rather than citing a specific authority, they include a general "feel-good" reference to their country's glory. "And in this great country of ours" they intone and, again, what follows is almost immaterial. The phrase "our great country" gives the audience a feeling of patriotic well-being and lends the speaker the status of benevolent preserver of traditional values. In such instances, we are dealing with a commonplace, a constantly repeated cliché which is reiterated precisely because novelty is, in this context, undesirable.

This technique is also used in literature, where it is called a "topos" (from the Greek word for "place"). Topoi cross generations and national boundaries with extraordinary fluidity, making it difficult to find their precise source. If we read a detective novel and our suspicion falls on the butler, chances are that our author is not referring to a specific work in which "the butler did it," but to a topos common to a multitude of works. Literary topoi associated with certain physical places may vary. For example, in some works a cemetery will supply the setting for an illiterate shepherd's plaint. In others, it will be the place where villains congregate, perform sacrilegious deeds, and get their comeuppance in supernatural adventures.

A literary topos need not be an actual location. When an epic poet breaks off his narration and turns to the muses to seek inspiration, he is invoking a topos (the modesty topos, where the poet bewails his inadequacy to the difficult task ahead). When Mandel'shtam compares a landscape to Homer's poetry (in the poem «Есть и́волги в леса́х» – "There are orioles in the woods"), he is developing the medieval topos of nature as a book. Topoi may be understood simply as frequently recurring motifs – the shoot-out in a Western, the pie in the face of slapstick comedy. Their value is two-fold. On the one hand, their very predictability offers a convenient means of orienting the reader. Familiarity inevitably creates an expectation. (When the lightning crashes suddenly during a horror movie, we know that something terrible is about to happen.) On the other hand, it allows the poet to vary the expected element and break the norms. (The lightning might strike, but the inevitable terror scene not materialize.) In either case, the reference is not to one specific usage (as in a citation), but to an entire tradition of usage.

Let us look at one such topos. In poetry of various types, the moon is a frequent visitor. Most commonly, it is associated with mystical apparitions and poetic inspiration. Russian has two words for "moon": the folklorically-tinged «ме́сяц» (Slavic in origin) and the more standard, latinate «луна́». (The novelist Ivan Goncharov describes the nostalgic atmosphere of Oblomov's youth using this very opposition: «В э́том краю́ никто́ и не зна́л, что́ за луна́ така́я, – всё называ́ли её ме́сяцем.» ["In this land no one even knew what the *luna* was – everyone called it *mesiats*"]. Conveniently, this choice of words allows the poet to designate the moon as either masculine or feminine. Still more conveniently for syllabo-tonic poetry, one of the words is stressed on the first syllable and the other on the second. In short, depending on the poet's needs, "mesiats" and "luna" can be opposed or synonymous.

Lermontov's «Каза́чья колыбе́льная пе́сня» ("Cossack Lullaby"), a poem in a stylized folk idiom, includes in its opening lines an image of the moon:

> Спи, младе́нец мо́й прекра́сный,
> Ба́юшки-баю́.
> Ти́хо смо́трит ме́сяц я́сный
> В колыбе́ль твою́.

(Sleep, my beautiful baby, / Lullaby. / The bright moon looks quietly / Into your cradle.)

A lullaby is a night poem, and it is hardly surprising that the moon is mentioned. In this case, Lermontov chooses "mesiats" for its folk coloration. Despite the presence of a trope (personification), this is not a startling image, nor is it intended to be.

Both "mesiats" and "luna" are found in Pushkin's poem «Бе́сы» ("The Demons"), written from the perspective of a traveler who gets lost in a snowstorm and suddenly finds himself surrounded by demons. Circularity (of motion and time) is a central theme, and Pushkin suggests this formally by repeating a passage in the first, fourth, and seventh (final) stanzas: «Мча́тся ту́чи, вью́тся ту́чи; / Невиди́мкою луна́ / Освеща́ет сне́г лету́чий» ("Dark clouds rush, dark clouds twirl; / The invisible moon / Illuminates the flying snow"). In this "realistic" depiction, Pushkin writes about a "luna." However, in the penultimate stanza, innumerable demons appear «в му́тной ме́сяца игре́» ("in the turbid play of the moon"). At the moment when reality gives way to the supernatural, Pushkin switches to the more folkloric "mesiats."

At other times, poets vary the expected image of the moon. Iazykov, in the spirited style characteristic of his student days, writes in the poem «К хала́ту» ("To His Dressing Gown"):

> Ночно́го не́ба президе́нт,
> Луна́ сия́ет золота́я;
> Усну́ла су́етность мирска́я –
> Не дре́млет мы́слящий студе́нт.

(The president of the night sky, / The golden moon shines; / Worldly vanity has fallen asleep – / [But] the thinking student does not doze.)

Iazykov aligns the student-philosopher with the moon, a comparison suggesting that the night is the time of profound thoughts. However, to understand this passage, it is essential to know that in the student slang of Iazykov's day, "president" was the word used to designate the leader of a drinking society. Hence the "traditional" image of the night sky is undercut by the amusing association of dissolute student life.

Blok's «Незнако́мка» ("The Stranger") offers another image of the dissolute moon.

> Над о́зером скрипя́т уклю́чины,
> И раздаётся же́нский ви́зг,
> А в не́бе, ко всему́ приу́ченный,
> Бессмы́сленно криви́тся ди́ск.

(Oarlocks screech above the lake, / And a woman's squeal resounds, / But in the sky, inured to everything, / The disc grimaces senselessly.)

Blok uses neither "luna" nor "mesiats," but opts for the geometric designation "disc," thus removing any hint of the romantic or supernatural. The accompanying verb "krivit'sia" has a double meaning: literally, it means to be crooked (it presumably depicts a crescent moon), but it also has the secondary meaning of "to grimace." Blok is creating a scene of spiritual destitution, and he achieves this effect through the inclusion of a moon too jaded to care about the squalor it observes.

Mayakovsky, in «Юбиле́йное» ("A Jubilee Poem"), in which he quite literally addresses Pushkin, calls up the traditional motif of the moon to ingratiate himself with his predecessor. But he gives the topos a characteristic twist:

> В не́бе во́н
> лу́на́
> така́я молода́я,
> что её
> без спу́тников
> и выпуска́ть риско́ванно.

(Up there in the sky / the moon / is so young // that even to let her out / without companions / is risky.)

Mayakovsky takes advantage of the feminine gender of "luna" and puns on several words: "molodaia" (the standard word for a "new" moon, but also, of course, the ordinary word for "young") and "sputnikov" (a term used for heavenly bodies but also for companions generally). The word order delays the humorous effect of this passage until the very end of the sentence (the last "step" of Mayakovsky's idiosyncratic "stepladder" layout). Rather than offering a hackneyed paean to nature, Mayakovsky makes nature reflect a scene from human life, personifying the moon as an inexperienced girl who should not be allowed out without chaperones.

«Тво́рчество» ("Creation"), an early programmatic poem of the arch-symbolist Briusov, contains a truly unprecedented depiction of the moon.

> Всхо́дит ме́сяц обнажённый
> При лазо́ревой луне́ . . .

(The naked moon [mesiats] rises by the azure light of the moon [luna])

This image provoked great mirth in Vladimir Soloviev, who found it "not only indecent, but also impossible, since 'mesiats' and 'luna' are simply two names for the same object." Yet Briusov defended his choice, arguing that the poem itself was about the creative act, and that the true poet need not restrict himself to the material of mundane reality. His poem is full of oxymoron, synaesthesia, and other techniques that combine to evoke an atmosphere maximally distant from the quotidian world. In that context, the "mesiats" can be taken to be the signal of poetic creation, which has an ontological status every bit as valid as the "luna" (the "standard" feature of a nocturnal scene).

Genre

We have already had occasion to speak about genre without particularly emphasizing the concept as such. Genre is simply a way of classifying forms of artistic endeavor (e.g., the novel, the drama, the poem) into smaller groups (e.g., the detective story, the tragedy, the elegy). Such classifications, it should be emphasized, originate in the producers of art, not in the consumers. Classical composers do not by chance write for two violins, a viola, and a cello. Rather, they choose this combination of instruments with the full awareness that this is the standard string quartet. Since Haydn more or less canonized it, this instrumentation gave subsequent composers very precise ideas about what sort of music they should write. Granted, Mozart and Beethoven had stricter conceptions of string-quartet form than composers of the twentieth century. But even in the twenty-first century composers approach a string quartet differently than they would a piece for four random instruments. Likewise, no modern artist sits down and innocently draws a bowl of fruit. This image is inevitably linked to the traditional still life, and any artist in our day has in mind the models of earlier centuries. An essential element of genre (which partially explains its significance) is that it determines both the approach of the creator as well as the expectations of the audience. That is to say: if an autodidact who has miraculously avoided all contact with the history of art happens to sketch a bowl of fruit, viewers will still perceive this work as part of the lengthy tradition of still life.

How did poetic genres originate? Most likely, they arose in response to basic emotional needs. The earliest poets were using language to celebrate, grieve, pray, convince, or simply to ponder, and they created the corresponding genres. In some sense, these same fundamental purposes have guided all subsequent poets, and this probably explains the tenacity with which genres outlive specific writers, historical epochs, and even national traditions. However, the longevity of genre is more than just a tribute to the power of the emotions that first coalesced to form them. For once a genre is established, subsequent poets consciously assimilate and creatively adapt it.

If new automobile makers do not reinvent the wheel, so new poets need not reinvent genres. There have been times when poets argue that the old forms must be totally discarded. Mayakovsky, as a self-proclaimed revolutionary, attempted to create new poetic genres like the march and even the order (prikáz). However, these remained isolated experiments; most of Mayakovsky's work can be traced to previously existing generic models. Revolutionary or not, individual epochs and literary schools will favor some genres and reject others. For example, the ode had its heyday in Russia in the eighteenth century, then went into spectacular decline for much of the nineteenth, only to be revived (in spirit, if not in form) by Mayakovsky in the twentieth.

The names of many poetic genres (e.g., epic, ode, elegy, ballad) are widely used and familiar even to people only vaguely aware of literary tradition. However, the precise definition of these terms is elusive – and not only to neophytes. To begin with, it is not always evident what genre a given work represents. Even if the poet writes "ode" on the top of the page, there is no certainty that this poet has the identical conception of "ode" as previous poets. If a poem does not bear any genre designation, the complications only become greater. It may have several elements commonly associated with a genre, but lack others that are no less important.

These questions must be confronted with every individual work, and they can rarely be fully resolved. Absolute consistency of usage would simplify this problem, but one cannot demand that poets strictly adhere to previously established norms. It is only logical that the creative tendencies that influence poetic form in general also apply to genre. That is to say: genre is *inherently* unstable. The conflicting imperatives of the new and the old ensure that, to some extent, each new work recreates the genre for itself. Moreover, a genre is rarely defined by a single feature, but by a combination of features. For interpretive purposes, it is sometimes less significant to categorize a poem definitively than it is to recognize qualities characteristic of certain genres and to see how they are employed or modified by individual poets.

The value of such an approach should become evident in the second part of this book. Without attempting to sketch the entire history of any individual genre, we will simply choose a group of poems that are linked by common concerns (be they formal, thematic, or both). These poems are generally connected not in the sense of citation (where one explicitly responds to another), but in the sense of topoi, in that they present variations on a theme, implicitly invoking an unnamed – and perhaps unknown – model. By looking at a series of poems, one appreciates not merely the internal coherence and concentration that go into an individual work, but also the way each poem addresses and intersects with the tradition.

Russians distinguish between «стихотворе́ние» and «поэ́ма», both of which are often rendered in English as "poem." The former is a relatively short, usually lyric poem with a minimum of plot, while the latter is a lengthier work – often tens or even hundreds of pages long – with strong narrative tendencies, e.g., Pushkin's «Ме́дный вса́дник» ("Bronze Horseman"). The ballad, the subject of Chapter Five, while generally considered a form of «стихотворение», can be seen as a sort of transitional genre. Though both types of poems are essential to the Russian literary tradition, the second part of the book will treat only «стихотворения», simply because the inclusion of «поэмы» would entail reading passages out of context, a complication inappropriate for an introductory book. It should be kept in mind, however, that virtually all of the concepts and genres discussed in shorter poems are directly applicable to longer ones.

Part II

Interpretation

Chapter 4

From the ode to the elegy (and beyond)

Из па́мяти изгры́зли го́ды,
За что́ и кто́ в Хоти́не па́л,
Но пе́рвый зву́к Хоти́нской о́ды
Нам пе́рвым кри́ком жи́зни ста́л.

Владислав Ходасевич, «Не я́мбом ли четырехсто́пным»

The years have gnawed away from memory,
Who fell at Khotin and for what,
But the first sound of the Khotin ode
Became our the first cry of life.

Vladislav Khodasevich, "Not in iambic tetrameter"

From the vantage point of the twenty-first century, the Russian eighteenth-century ode seems a forbidding and inaccessible genre. The poems are without exception long, the language archaic, the subjects political, the tone jingoistic and/or sycophantic. However, when placed in its literary, historical, and sociological context, this poetry can become fascinating and even aesthetically interesting. What the eighteenth-century odists were doing in the cultural sphere was no less ambitious than what Peter the Great had done in the political arena a few decades earlier. This was an attempt to bring a backward, isolated country into the modern age, to take what the West had to offer and adapt it to specifically Russian needs.

Before the eighteenth century, Russia had no viable secular literature. If such a tradition was to take root, it could only do so with the support of the ruling institutions. The Church, skeptical of the value of literacy beyond religious texts, was unsympathetic. So the would-be poet needed to enlist the support of the sovereign. The most logical way to do this was to write verse that would instill patriotic feelings and – not coincidentally – reverence for the monarch.

The solemn ode, a poem of praise devoted to an event or personage of great distinction, was the eighteenth-century genre of choice. Everything about the ode was expected to be grandiose – the form, the lexicon, the style and, of course, the subject. It is indicative of the genre that the title of Lomonosov's seminal "Khotin Ode" contains almost twenty words: «Óда блажéнныя пáмяти государы́не императри́це Áнне Иоáнновне на побéду над ту́рками и татáрами и на взя́тие Хоти́на 1739 гóда» – "Ode to Her Majesty Empress Anna Ioannovna of Blessed Memory on the Victory over the Turks and Tatars and the Taking of Khotin in the Year 1739." (Actually, this was the title when Lomonosov first published this poem in 1751; the earliest version – lost to posterity – would presumably not have included the phrase "of blessed memory," since Anna was still alive.)

Historically speaking, the battle of Khotin proved insignificant, yet Lomonosov's ode on the subject set the standard for Russian poetry for decades – and in some respects, for centuries.

Востóрг внезáпный у́м плени́л,
Ведёт на вéрх горы́ высóкой,
Где вéтр в лесáх шумéть забы́л;
В доли́не тишинá глубóкой.
Внимáя нéчто, клю́ч молчи́т,
Котóрой завсегдá журчи́т
И с шу́мом вни́з с холмóв стреми́тся.
Лаврóвы вью́тся тáм венцы́,
Там слу́х спеши́т во всé концы́;
Далéче ды́м в поля́х кури́тся.

Не Пи́нд ли под ногáми зрю́?
Я слы́шу чи́стых сéстр музы́ку!
Пермéсским жáром я́ горю́,
Теку́ поспéшно к óных ли́ку.
Врачéбной дáли мнé воды́:
Испéй и всé забу́дь труды́;
Умóй росóй Кастáльской óчи,
Чрез стéпь и гóры взóр простри́
И ду́х свой к тéм странáм впери́,
Где всхóдит дéнь по тёмной нóчи.

(A sudden rapture captivated my mind / It leads to the top of a tall mountain, / Where the wind has forgotten to make noise in the forests; / In the deep vale there is silence. / Perceiving something, the spring is silent, / Which always gurgles / And rushes noisily downwards from the hills. / There laurel crowns are wound, / There one hastens to hear all around; / In the distance smoke rises in the fields. // Do I not behold Pindus beneath me? / I hear the music of the pure sisters! / I burn with the fire of Permessus / I go hurriedly to their assembly. / They have given me healing water: / Drink it and forget all difficulties; / Wash your eyes in the Castalian dew, / Stretch your gaze through steppe and mountains / And press your soul toward those countries, / Where the day [first] rises after the dark night.)

Lomonosov's complete ode consists of twenty eight ten-line stanzas, of which the first two are cited above. His stanzaic form, adapted from Western European models, soon became canonical for Russian odes. The meter (Lomonosov's major innovation, borrowed from German verse) is iambic tetrameter. The distinctive rhyme scheme consists of a quatrain (a-B-a-B), followed by a couplet (c-c), followed by a quatrain with a different rhyme scheme from the initial one (D-e-e-D). This rhyme scheme, based on French odes, had already been used in Russia by Trediakovsky (see Chapter Eight), but never with the alternating masculine/feminine rhymes, the standard pattern after Lomonosov. (Other poets, and Lomonosov himself, would from time to time vary the stanzaic form, but the general outline – ten lines of alternating rhymes composed of two quatrains and a couplet – remained fixed.) As is typical of early Lomonosov, pyrrhic feet are rare. It has been suggested that the relatively few lines with less than four stresses in "Khotin" (e.g., lines 4 and 6 in the above excerpt) were added when Lomonosov reworked his ode for publication.

According to the French neo-classicist Nicolas Boileau, who influenced the Russians as both a theoretician and a practicing poet, the ode was characterized by "beau désordre" ("beautiful disorder," or, in Trediakovsky's excellent rendering, «красный беспорядок»). The inspired poet, in keeping with the powerful emotions he sought to portray, was supposed to introduce a certain degree of confusion – albeit structured and even elegant confusion – to his verse. The confusion in Lomonosov's stanzas is immediately palpable. Though the title informs us that the poem will be devoted to a specific battle, neither Russia nor her foes are mentioned in the first two stanzas. Rather than military preparations, we encounter the poet himself, not the biographical Lomonosov, to be sure, but a sort of archetypal visionary poet. The first word ("vostorg" – "rapture") sets the tone, with the poet being led up high, presumably to observe from this elevated vantage point the epic battle that will transpire. (Mountains are the traditional locus of the sublime, that state of amazed joy tinged with fear so appropriate for battle scenes.) The second stanza, beginning with a rhetorical question (a frequent trope in this ode and in odes in general), introduces a series of explicit references to ancient Greece (e.g., the "chistykh sestr" are the muses, Pindus a mountain range, Permessus a river), through which the modern Russian odist transparently affiliates himself with his ancient counterparts.

Only in the third stanza does the poet abruptly turn to the true subject of his ode:

Корабль как ярых волн среди,
Которые хотят покрыти
Бежит, срывая с них верьхи,
Претит с пути себя склонити;

Седа́я пе́на вкру́г шуми́т,
В пучи́не сле́д его́ гори́т,
К росси́йской си́ле так стремя́тся,
Круго́м объе́хав, тьмы́ тата́р;
Скрыва́ет не́бо ко́нской па́р!
Что ж в то́м? стремгла́в без ду́ш валя́тся.

(Like a ship among furious waves, / Which want to cover it / Rushes on, cutting off their tips, / Not allowing itself to be turned aside; / The gray foam sounds all around, / Its track burns in the abyss, / So swarms of Tatars surge toward the Russian force / Riding all around it / The horses' steam covers the sky! / And what of it? The soulless ones crash down headlong.)

This stanza introduces the antagonists, but indirectly, through the use of an extended simile (also known as "epic simile" because of its frequent use in the epics of Homer, Vergil, and Dante). The Russians are likened to a boat, the hordes of Tatars – infidels, therefore "without souls" – to the waves that attempt to push it off course. However, Lomonosov's presentation complicates this image considerably. The basic grammatical expression "kak . . . tak" ("just as . . . so") is hardly unusual, yet by placing both the "kak" and the "tak" as the second elements of a clause (rather than the first), Lomonosov radically alters standard Russian syntax. Moreover, the lengthy vehicle of his simile (the boat) appears before the tenor (the Russian army). No reader or listener could possibly understand the comparison until the seventh line of the stanza. In fact, the obvious assumption (a false one, as it turns out) would be that the ship referred to in the first line is literal rather than figurative. This misleading signal is part of the odic strategy – the grandeur of the subject matter astonishes the poet himself, who transmits his excitement in an emotionally charged, somewhat wild language that his audience must struggle to comprehend.

When indirect expression is a goal, figurative language becomes essential. Not surprisingly, then, Lomonosov's ode serves as a virtual compendium of tropes. Describing the patriotic zeal of the Russian soldiers, he uses hyperbole: «Жела́ет вся́к проли́ть *всю* кро́вь» – "Everyone desires to shed *all* his blood" (italics added). At moments of especially high emotion, he apostrophizes them: «Но ва́м не мо́жет то́ вреди́ть, / О ро́ссы, ва́с сам ро́к покры́ть / Жела́ет для счастли́вой А́нны» ("But this cannot harm you / O Russians, fate itself wishes / To defend you for fortunate Anna"). In fact, Lomonosov apostrophizes any number of people and things: not only Russia's soldiers, but also the enemy's soldiers, Pindar (the long dead odist of antiquity), Anna (the living sovereign), Russia, Istanbul, etc. To enliven the battle scenes, he frequently uses a grammatical construction whereby a plural subject (more precisely: two singular nouns connected by the conjunction "and") takes a singular verb, e.g., «От ро́ву лес и брег дрожи́т» ("From the cry forest and shore shakes" [rather than "shake"]) or «Пусты́ня, лес и во́здух во́ет» ("Desert, forest, and air howls" [rather than "howl"]). This grammatical "error" not only gives the impression of spontaneity and high emotion; it also points to its source in Greek epic, yet another way of showing the poet's kinship with Homer and of claiming Khotin as a direct descendent of Troy. To achieve beautiful disorder, Lomonosov incorporates one of the most radical tropes, zeugma, whereby a single verb governs two or more mutually exclusive nouns. For example, when the enemy flees, Lomonosov describes them as «Забы́в и меч, и стан, и стыд» ("Having forgotten sword, camp, and shame"). One can forget a sword, and one can forget shame, but the first is a literal usage and the second a figurative one. When these two nouns are yoked to a single verb, the effect is startling. (Zeugma is often found in comic passages, though not in Lomonosov.) In this instance, Lomonosov augments the effect through alliteration, bringing together in sound the illogical combination of "*stan*" and "*styd*." Likewise, the image of peaceful Russia – which exists thanks to the valor of Russia's army – relies on zeugma: «С пшени́цей где поко́й насе́ян» ("Where peace is sown with wheat"). This line again demonstrates how readily Lomonosov departs from standard Russian syntax, since he places "gde" as the second sentence element.

Lomonosov's ode contains the requisite scenes of carnage, but it is much more than battle description. Indeed, the battle is constantly interrupted by commentary of various sorts. Peter the Great and Ivan the Terrible make a cameo appearance in stanzas 9–12 to congratulate Anna on continuing their great work in extending Russia's frontiers. The morning after the decisive battle (stanza 18), Phoebus Apollo accompanies the "golden finger of dawn" («Злато́й уже́ денни́цы перст», a transparent allusion to the "rosy-fingered dawn" of Homeric epic), admiring the devastation that the Russian troops have wrought. The final few stanzas move from the martial to the pastoral, praising the peace that the battle of Khotin has ensured. The poem concludes with the humility topos, whereby the poet asks the sovereign to excuse his inadequacy for attempting the monumental task of singing Russia's glory.

Lomonosov was particularly attentive to the sound quality of his verse. The opening quatrain of the sixth stanza demonstrates several key features:

За хо́лмы, где паля́ща хля́бь
Дым, пе́пел, пла́мень, смерть рыга́ет,
За Тигр, Стамбу́л, свои́х загра́бь,
Что ка́мни с берего́в сдира́ет [. . .]

(Beyond the hills, where the burning abyss / Belches smoke, ash, flame, death / Beyond the Tigris, which tears rocks from the shores, / O Istanbul, remove your own [troops] [. . .])

The second line contains five stresses, an unusual effect in tetrameter verse. Lomonosov "weighs" down this line, presumably to emphasize the horrors of the abyss which he enumerates. Another means of slowing the actual reading is the use of consonant clusters. Lomonosov complicates the texture by including barely pronounceable combinations like "Za Ti*gr*, *St*ambul." Tongue-twisters of this type are hardly exceptional; in the opening stanzas cited earlier, we find other examples: "vé*tr v* le*s*ákh" and "sé*str m*uzýku." Two elements contribute to the inordinately high number of realized stresses and directly affect the sound of the verse: Lomonosov's distaste for "polno-glasie" (in the clusters mentioned above he prefers "vetr" to "veter," "sestr" to "sester") and his predilection for using short adjectives non-predicatively (e.g., "paliashch*a* khliab'" instead of "paliashch*aia* khliab'"). Both of these factors increase the proportion of consonants to vowels. Even without them, however, Lomonosov is especially partial to alliteration, e.g., in the above passage: "*kh*o*l*my . . . *khl*iab'," "*p*é*p*el . . . *pl*a*m*en'," "*r*y*g*aet, Ti*g*r, za*g*rab', be*r*e*g*ov." This thick consonantal sound texture, together with the elevated diction, fractured syntax, and variety of tropes, give a highly distinctive flavor to a genre whose themes are largely predictable.

In the hands of a particularly resourceful poet, even the themes could be made interesting. Derzhavin wrote «Фели́ца» ("Felitsa") for the usual reasons: to flatter the sovereign, Catherine the Great. In this he succeeded admirably – Catherine rewarded him with a diamond-encrusted snuffbox. The poem's florid exordium (the second stanza is cited below) clearly displays an allegiance to the odic tradition:

Пода́й, Фели́ца! наставле́нье:
Как пы́шно и правди́во жи́ть,
Как укроща́ть страсте́й волне́нье
И сча́стливым на све́те бы́ть?
Меня́ твой го́лос возбужда́ет,
Меня́ твой сы́н препровожда́ет;
Но и́м после́довать я сла́б.
Мятя́сь жите́йской суето́ю,
Сего́дня вла́ствую собо́ю,
А за́втра при́хотям я ра́б.

(Give me, o Felitsa, instruction: / How can one live gloriously and truthfully, / How can one tame the excitement of the passions / And be happy on earth? / Your voice moves me, / Your son guides me; / But I am too weak to follow them. / Confused by life's vanity, / Today I am master of myself / But tomorrow I am a slave to whims.)

In terms of meter and rhyme, Derzhavin's odic stanza conforms exactly to the standard set by Lomonosov. He also retains the basic paradigm of flawless sovereign and unworthy poet. In this case, the poet presents himself as a supplicant, admitting his faults and seeking edification. Hence the poem contains a characteristically strong didactic element.

The most striking changes from Lomonosov can be found in the passages where the poet focuses not on the sovereign, but on himself:

> А я, проспа́вши до полу́дни,
> Курю́ таба́к и ко́фе пью;
> Преобраща́я в пра́здник бу́дни,
> Кружу́ в химе́рах мы́сль мою́:
> То плéн от пе́рсов похища́ю,
> То стрéлы к ту́ркам обраща́ю;
> То, возмечта́в, что я султа́н,
> Вселéнну устраша́ю взгля́дом;
> То вдру́г, прельща́яся наря́дом,
> Скачу́ к портно́му по кафта́н.
>
> Или в пиру́ я пребога́том,
> Где пра́здник для меня́ даю́т,
> Где блéщет сто́л сребро́м и зла́том,
> Где ты́сячи разли́чных блю́д;
> Там сла́вный о́корок вестфа́льской,
> Там звéнья ры́бы астраха́нской,
> Там пло́в и пироги́ стоя́т,
> Шампа́нским ва́фли запива́ю;
> И всё на свéте забыва́ю
> Средь ви́н, сласте́й и арома́т.

(But I, having slept until noon, / Smoke tobacco and drink coffee; / Turning working days into holidays / I let my thoughts wander in chimeras; / Now I steal captives from the Persians / Now I turn my fire on the Turks; / Now, dreaming that I am the sultan, / I frighten the universe with my glance; / Now, suddenly tempted by clothing, / I skip to the tailor for a kaftan. // Or at a splendid feast, / Where a celebration is made for me, / Where the table shines with silver and gold, / Where there are thousands of sundry dishes; / There is the famous Westphalian ham / There are chains of Astrakhan fish, / There is pilaf and pies, / I wash down Belgian waffles with champagne; / And I forget everything on earth, / Among the wines, the sweets, and the fragrances.)

The emphatic use of anaphora ("Gde ... Gde ... Gde ... Tam ... Tam ... Tam . . .") and alliterations (e.g., "*k*uriu taba*k* i *k*ofe," "*p*reobrashchaia v *p*razdnik," "*p*len ot *p*ersov *p*okhishchaiu," etc.) are perfectly in keeping with the style of the solemn ode. The tropes are also expected in odic style: hyperbole ("*tysiachi* razlichnykh bliud" [*thousands* of sundry dishes]), chiasmus ("kuriu tabak i kofe p'iu"). Yet the passage could hardly be confused with Lomonosov. To begin with, there are any number of words of distinctly non-Russian origin that would have been anathema to Lomonosov's highly prized lexical unity. Not only are they associated with mundane activities (eating, sleeping, drinking), but their very precision would have shocked those accustomed to traditional odes. For example, the general term "nariad" would be acceptable in a Lomonosov ode, but the specific "kaftan" would not. Indeed, the entire line «Скачу́ к портно́му по кафта́н» (I skip to the tailor for a kaftan) would be unthinkable. It is instructive to compare it with Lomonosov's «Теку́ поспе́шно к о́ных ли́ку» (I go hurriedly to their assembly), where the word order is scrambled and where every individual word is archaic. In passages like this, Derzhavin "domesticates" the ode. If Lomonosov sought a language maximally distanced from everyday life, Derzhavin takes significant steps in the direction of the vernacular.

In terms of genre, the truly innovative element of Derzhavin's poem was perhaps more evident to his contemporaries than to today's readers. The "I" of "Felitsa" is, despite the specificity of detail, not the poet himself. Rather, it is a composite of Catherine's courtiers, whose vices were instantly recognizable to the audience of that time. In this way, Derzhavin's ode borders on satire. This hybrid nature of the genre corresponds to any other number of hybrids, for Derzhavin routinely mixed the high and the low, the serious and the comic. In a typical display of lexical and aural repetition, Derzhavin lauds Catherine for her ability to make «Из разногла́сия согла́сье» ("agreement from disagreement," or "harmony from disharmony"). The same could be said of Derzhavin's own poetics.

The most distinctive departure from Lomonosov's norms occurred not in Derzhavin, but in the poets of the early nineteenth century. In their work, the elegy becomes the prominent genre, displacing the odic stanza and stance. The Russian elegy is defined not by obligatory formal features, but by its style. In a programmatic essay, Batiushkov introduced this new ideal (which he called «лёгкая поэ́зия» ["light poetry"]) by juxtaposing it to epic and heroic verse: "In grand genres the reader, fascinated by the description of passions, blinded by the liveliest colors of poetry, can forget its imperfections and unevenness, and he greedily hearkens to the inspired poet . . . In a light genre of verse the reader demands the utmost perfection, purity of expression, harmony of style, malleability, flow; he demands truth in feelings . . . because his attention is not diverted in any powerful way." In short, Batiushkov's vision of "grand genres" corresponds closely to the ode and its ideal of "beautiful disorder." However, what for the ode is a virtue is for light genres a vice. In the latter, everything must be carefully balanced; it cannot afford any rough edges. Batiushkhov's «Мой ге́ний» ("My Spirit") gives a good sense of the new poetic values:

О па́мять се́рдца! ты сильне́й
Рассу́дка па́мяти печа́льной,
И ча́сто сла́достью свое́й
Меня́ в стране́ пленя́ешь да́льной.
Я по́мню го́лос ми́лых сло́в,
Я по́мню о́чи голубы́е,
Я по́мню ло́коны златы́е
Небре́жно вью́щихся власо́в.
Мое́й пасту́шки несравне́нной
Я по́мню весь наря́д просто́й,
И о́браз ми́лый, незабве́нный,
Повсю́ду стра́нствует со мно́й.
Храни́тель ге́ний мо́й – любо́вью
В уте́ху да́н разлу́ке о́н:
Засну́ ль? прини́кнет к изголо́вью
И услади́т печа́льный со́н.

(O memory of the heart! you are more powerful / Than the sad memory of reason, / And often with your sweetness / You captivate me in a distant land. / I remember the voice of dear words, / I remember blue eyes, / I remember golden locks / Of carelessly curled hair. / I remember the entire simple attire / Of my incomparable shepherdess, / And her dear, unforgotten image / Travels everywhere with me. / My guardian spirit – by love / It is given in consolation for parting: / Do I fall asleep? it bends to the head of my bed / And sweetens the sad dream.)

Batiushkov's poem consists of four quatrains (not set off graphically, but marked by punctuation and rhyme) of iambic tetrameter. While iambs are not obligatory in an elegy, they do tend to predominate, just as they did in the ode. In contrast to the ode, however, the stanzaic structure, rhyme scheme, and number of feet per line vary widely from elegy to elegy. In this poem, Batiushkov uses alternating rhymes (a-B-a-B at the beginning, A-b-A-b later) except in lines 5–8, where he uses a "ring" structure (a-B-B-a). "My Spirit" shares certain figures of speech with the ode: it opens with an apostrophe and contains a lengthy anaphora. It also relies on alliteration (e.g., "*s*erdtse . . . *s*il'nei . . . ra*ss*udka") and assonance (e.g., the shift from stressed "a" to "o" in the lines: «Меня́ в стране́ пленя́ешь да́льной. / я по́мню го́лос ми́лых сло́в» and even an important wordplay in "strane/stranstvuet." Yet it lacks the ode's more radical tropes (e.g., epic simile, zeugma, grammatical "errors"). Most strikingly, Batiushkov's subject is neither a battle nor a virtuous sovereign, but the poet himself and his love for an unnamed woman (the "genii" of the title). Though physically separated, she continues to be present in spirit. The opening lines, which set the memory of the heart (feeling) against that of the mind (reason) are essential to understanding the emotional substrate of this poetry. Intimate feelings had no place in the ode, but they are the essence of the elegy. Dream, that most personal of spheres, is where Batiushkov's poem ends.

Readers familiar with English poetry often assume that all elegies are meditations on death. In the Russian tradition, such an association is not entirely wrong. After all, Zhukovsky's influential translation of Thomas Gray's "Elegy in a Country Churchyard" ushered in an entire "graveyard school" of Russian poets. Still, death was by no means a defining feature of the Russian elegy. Far more often these poems were about loss, and, more specifically, the poet's emotional response to it. In the Batiushkov example, physical loss has been transformed into spiritual gain. Batiushkov's contemporaries considered "My Spirit" an elegy, but we might just as fairly call it a love poem (which was, historically, a subgenre of elegy). Indeed, lines 5–8 include one of the most traditional features of love poetry: the blazon, a catalogue of the beloved's physical qualities (her eyes, her hair, her clothes, her face). The reference to a shepherdess should not be taken literally; it, too, points to a genre, the classical tradition of pastoral, which was populated by happy couples of shepherds and shepherdesses.

One of the essential elements of the Russian elegy is the lexicon. In a poem as short as "My Spirit," it is remarkable how many words recur: "pamiat'" (memory), "pechal'nyi" (sad), "pomniu" (I remember), "milyi" (dear), "sladkii" (sweet), implicit in the form of "sladost'" (sweetness) and "usladit" (sweetens). These words have been called "word-signals," the suggestion being that they indicate the Russian elegiac style more certainly than any specific theme or meter. In fact, virtually every adjective in this poem could classify as a "word-signal" of the elegiac school. After the unabashedly turgid language of the eighteenth-century ode, the limited vocabulary of the elegy stands out all the more starkly.

The young Pushkin was profoundly influenced by the elegiac school. «Пробуждéние» ("Awakening"), written a year after Batiushkov's poem, shares Batiushkov's theme of sleep and love. Pushkin himself categorized the poem as an elegy.

Мечты́, мечты́,	Dreams, dreams
Где вáша слáдость?	Where is your sweetness?
Где ты, где ты,	Where are you, where are you,
Ночнáя рáдость?	Night's joy?
Исчéзнул óн,	It disappeared,
Весёлый сóн,	The happy dream,
И одинóкий	And alone
Во тьмé глубóкой	In deep darkness
Я пробуждён.	I am awakened.

Кругóм постéли	Around my bed
Немáя нóчь.	There is mute night.
Вмиг охладéли,	The yearnings of love
Вмиг улетéли	Suddenly went cold,
Толпóю прóчь	Suddenly flew
Любвѝ мечтáнья.	Away in a throng.
Ещё полнá	The soul still
Душá желáнья	Is full of desire
И лóвит снá	And tries to catch
Воспоминáнья.	The recollections of sleep.
Любóвь, любóвь,	Love, love,
Внемлѝ молéнья:	Hearken to my entreaty:
Пошлѝ мне внóвь	Send me again
Свой видéнья,	Your visions,
И поутрý,	And in the morning,
Вновь упоённый,	Again enraptured,
Пускáй умрý	Let me die
Непробуждённый.	Unawakened.

Pushkin's poem is written in the unusual form of iambic dimeter, which causes the rhymes to come at an unusually rapid pace (almost every second word). The poem is astrophic, which is to say that it does not break down into a predictable pattern of quatrains or couplets. This "looser" structure may be motivated by the theme of dreams, which wander freely from one thought to the next. Like the Batiushkov elegy, this, too, is a love poem. Love is associated with sleep and memory, lost love with wakefulness. These associations explain the paradoxical final line of the poem: since waking implies the end of love, the poet asks to die "unawakened" in order to remain with his beloved.

After the hegemony of the ode, the elegy forced Russian poets to be precise, to concentrate their means of expression and thematic range. Such changes offered new directions and brought about some excellent poetry, yet the limitations of the Russian elegy were evident almost from its inception. The restrictive lexicon and the stylized protagonist were criticized by those unsympathetic to the school and, in time, even by some of its leading practitioners. While elements of elegiac diction remained dear to Pushkin throughout his life, it is remarkable how far he moved from the elegiac speaker and his repetitive vocabulary. In his novel in verse *Eugene Onegin*, Pushkin repeated the elegiac clichés in his unflattering portrait of Vladimir Lensky and, in particular, in the elegy that Lensky pens the night before his death (chapter six, stanzas 21 and 22). In an authorial intrusion in that same chapter (stanza 44), Pushkin cites – and seemingly repudiates – his own elegiac period:

Мечты́, мечты́! где ва́ша сла́дость?
Где, ве́чная к ней ри́фма, *мла́дость*?

Уже́ль и впра́вду наконе́ц

Увя́л, увя́л её вене́ц?

Уже́ль и впря́мь и в са́мом де́ле,
Без элеги́ческих зате́й,
Весна́ мои́х промча́лась дне́й
(Что я шутя́ тверди́л досе́ле?)

(Dreams, dreams! Where is your sweetness? / Where is its eternal rhyme, *youth*? / Is it possible and for real finally / That its wreath has withered, withered? / Is it indeed possible in fact / Without elegiac flourishes, / That the spring of my days has rushed by / [As I have until now repeated in jest?])

These verses transparently allude to Pushkin's own «Пробужде́ние» ("Awakening,"), written a decade earlier. Now, however, the elegiac mask has been removed. Rather than a stylized portrayal of lost youth (a favorite elegiac topos), Pushkin breaks with convention, insisting that his mourning over lost youth is no longer a pose. This unconventional approach to a conventional theme is achieved largely through lexicon. He mixes the canonic "word-signals" of the traditional elegy (e.g., "mechty" [dreams] "uvial" [withered]) with colloquialisms alien to the elegiac style ("Uzhel' i vpriam' i v samom dele" [Is it indeed possible in fact]). If the first lines of «Пробужде́ние» ("Mechty, mechty, / Gde vasha sladost'?" [Dreams, dreams, / Where is your sweetness?]) were meant to be taken at face value, their repetition here serves an entirely different function. As a citation, it sends the reader back to the earlier text and context in order to question their validity. In a typical elegy, the rhyme of "sladost'" and "mladost'" would pass by unnoticed. However, Pushkin specifically draws attention to its hackneyed quality (the italics are his), thereby undercutting the apparent logic that conjoins the two concepts.

Another way of gauging Pushkin's turn away from the elegy is to look at a later poem on a similar subject. In his «Стихи́, сочинённые но́чью во вре́мя бессо́нницы» ("Verses Composed at Night at a Time of Sleeplessness"), the mature Pushkin does not explicitly renounce his earlier elegiac self, but he nonetheless reveals an entirely new authorial stance and poetic idiom.

Мне́ не спи́тся, не́т огня́;
Всю́ду мра́к и со́н доку́чный.
Хо́д часо́в лишь однозву́чный
Раздаётся близ меня́,
Па́рки ба́бье лепета́нье,
Спя́щей но́чи трепета́нье,
Жи́зни мы́шья беготня́ . . .

Что трево́жишь ты́ меня́?
Что ты зна́чишь, ску́чный шёпот?
Укори́зна или ро́пот
Мной утра́ченного дня́?
От меня́ чего́ ты хо́чешь?
Ты́ зовёшь или проро́чишь?
Я́ поня́ть тебя́ хочу́,
Смы́сла я́ в тебе́ ищу́ . . .

(I can't sleep, there is no light; / Everywhere darkness and dreary sleep. / Only the monotonous movement of the clock / Sounds near me, / The old woman's babbling of Fate, / The trembling of sleeping night, / The mouse's bustle of life . . . / Why do you trouble me? / What do you mean, boring whisper? / Are you a reproach or a regret / Of the day wasted by me? / What do you want from me? / Do you call or prophesy? / I want to understand you, / I seek meaning in you . . .)

The poem's title is reminiscent of the eighteenth century, when "Verses composed during . . ." were common (e.g., Lomonosov's «Стихи́, сочинённые на доро́ге в Петерго́ф» – "Verses Composed on the Road to Peterhof"). However, Pushkin's poem has an urgency that separates it both from the eighteenth century and from the elegiac school of the early nineteenth. Neither the vocabulary nor the imagery is expected. The trochaic tetrameter lines themselves stand out against the background of elegiac iambs. Particularly striking stylistically is the string of metaphors in lines 5–7, which adds a new dimension to the darkness described in the opening lines. These metaphors are linked to the concrete depiction of darkness and sound that preceded them, but they show the lyric persona's tendency to *interpret* reality. The only sound in the first few lines is that of a clock, yet from this emerges the "lepetan'e" ("babbling") of Fate itself. The image "Zhizni mysh'ia begotnia" ("The mouse's bustle of life") implies that a mouse is truly present (the "realia" of the poem), but, even if this is the case, an interpretive leap is necessary to recognize the movement of life itself in this aimless scurrying. The three metaphors end in ellipsis, suggesting the sudden shift in thought that occurs immediately thereafter. A series of questions follows, addressed to a mysterious "ty." Until this point, the poem was focused on the "ia," and there was no reason to expect a "ty." The "ty" appears to be a conflation of all the previous impressions, and the poet's turn to it an attempt to make sense of the world beyond. The questions, in which "ty" is invariably the subject, lead to a couplet in which a remarkable reversal takes place. In this final statement, the "ia" takes center stage, relegating "ty" to the accusative and prepositional cases, positions grammatically and logically subservient. The poet has taken control of the negativity and mystery that confounded him in the opening lines. This is not a formulaic poem on the subject of loss, but a struggle with the unknown

that – despite the formal exactitude that makes any poem a carefully constructed artifact – comes across as both spontaneous and deeply personal. The
concluding ellipsis can be interpreted either as an aporia (a break because
the argument can go no further) or, conceivably, as sleep, a more mundane
resolution of the poet's despair. In any case, the clear-cut conclusion of the
elegy is replaced by an attempt to comprehend and thus control external
reality.

After Pushkin's verses, sleeplessness became a common theme of Russian
poetry. In what is generally regarded as its most memorable expression,
Mandel'shtam brings together a host of new – and old – associations.

> Бессо́нница. Гоме́р. Туги́е паруса́.
> Я спи́сок корабле́й прочёл до середи́ны:
> Сей дли́нный вы́водок, сей по́езд журавли́ный,
> Что над Элла́дою когда́-то подня́лся.
>
> Как журавли́ный кли́н в чужи́е рубежи́ –
> На голова́х царе́й боже́ственная пе́на –
> Куда́ плывёте вы? Когда́ бы не Еле́на,
> Что Тро́я ва́м одна́, ахе́йские мужи́?
>
> И мо́ре, и Гоме́р – всё дви́жется любо́вью.
> Кого́ же слу́шать мне́? И во́т Гоме́р молчи́т,
> И мо́ре чёрное, вити́йствуя, шуми́т
> И с тя́жким гро́хотом подхо́дит к изголо́вью.

(Sleeplessness. Homer. Taut sails. / I read the list of ships to the middle: / This long
brood, this procession of cranes, / That once rose up above Hellas. // Like a wedge
of cranes into foreign shores – / Divine foam on the tsars' heads – / Where are you
sailing? If there were no Helen, / What is Troy alone to you, Achaean men? // The
sea and Homer – everything is moved by love. / But whom am I to listen to? Now
Homer is silent / And the black sea, orating, makes noise / And with a heavy crash
approaches the head of my bed.)

"Sleeplessness" is written in iambic hexameter with caesura after the third
foot, a form Mandel'shtam used with insistent frequency in poems about
antiquity. As in so much of his work, the primary focus is the continuity
of tradition, but it is a tradition that is constantly remade. Through a careful play of sound and sense, Mandel'shtam unites the modern and ancient
worlds.

If Pushkin began with concrete sensory impressions, Mandel'shtam draws
his first observations from a book. This is not just any book, however,
but the foundational epic of the Western literary tradition. The three terse
sentences contained within the first line produce a startling, disorienting
effect, forcing the reader to supply the missing linkages. The "fuller" version

would presumably look something like this: the poet, during a sleepless night, turns his thoughts to Homer and, more precisely, to a ship at sea. The synecdoche "Tugie parusa" ("Taut sails") conjures up the image of a ship (or ships) at full tilt, in short, rushing to battle or simply seeking adventure. This suggestion is made precise in the next lines, where we learn that the scene is the mustering of the host from the *Iliad*. Characteristically, Mandel'shtam offers less a retelling of this epic tale than a rereading of it. As we shall see, this is an epic viewed through an elegiac lens.

The motion and excitement of the opening line are illusory. In fact, the poet has been reading the catalogue of ships as a soporific. As he gradually drifts off to sleep, images of the Homeric world are refracted in his mind. Through sound, the words «Гомер» ("Homer") and «море» ("sea") become intimately linked. When the poet of antiquity falls silent, the speaker attributes the odic verb "vitiistvovat'" ("to orate") to the sea itself. Nature and culture are shown to work in tandem.

In addition to the explicit evocation of Homer, the poem enters into discussion with a number of other precursor texts. The striking formulation "vse dvizhetsia liubov'iu" ("everything is moved by love") seems to transcend the specific plot of the *Iliad*, where the love in question is really little more than lust. The phrase closely echoes the final line of Dante's *Divine Comedy* ("L'amor che move il sole e l'altre stelle" – "The love that moves the sun and the other stars"), a passage that Mandel'shtam's revered master Vyacheslav Ivanov had subjected to detailed analysis in an essay that predates Mandel'shtam's poem by a few years. Dante's conception of love is derived from the Christian tradition, which is thus indirectly invoked.

This unusually allusive love poem ends with the poet falling asleep. Where have we seen this before? Arguably, this was the conclusion of the Pushkin poem on sleeplessness, yet there is a more immediate source. Mandel'shtam's final lines feature the rhyme pair "liubov'iu/izgolov'iu" – two nouns that rhyme only if the first is in the instrumental case and the second in the dative. The rhyme is ingenious and rare; to give some idea, it occurs only once in all of Batiushkov («Мой гений») and only once in all of Mandel'shtam. When Mandel'shtam appropriates this distinctive rhyme, he calls to mind the whole poem in which it first appeared. «Мой гений», it will be recalled, praises love and the memory that allows it to triumph over distance – and it concludes with the image of the sleeping poet dreaming about his beloved. For Mandel'shtam, who always saw poetry as a means of turning spatial and temporal separation into spiritual closeness, the reference to sleep in Batiushkov supplies a crucial link in the cultural chain. In poetry, as in dreams, ordinary laws of space and time are suspended. Batiushkov's poem was written in 1815, exactly a century before Mandel'shtam's, a symmetry that the later poet surely appreciated. Mandel'shtam thus moves freely from the Western epic tradition of Homer and Dante to the lyric verse of Russia's "Golden Age." His poem revisits both ode (epic) and elegy, overcoming tradition through tradition. In developing the genres, imagery, and even specific lexical choices of his predecessors, Mandel'shtam makes himself their rightful heir.

Chapter 5

The ballad

Немо́лод о́чень ла́д балла́д,
но е́сли слова́ боля́т
и слова́ говоря́т про то́, что боля́т,
молоде́ет и ла́д балла́д.

Маяко́вский, «Про э́то»

The ballads' tune is very old
but if words hurt
and words speak about what hurts,
even the ballads' tune becomes young.

Mayakovsky, "About That"

The Russian eighteenth-century odists quarreled about virtually every aspect of versification and poetic language, but they were unanimous in their conviction that poetry was a noble endeavor that deserved the attention of a cultivated public. They attempted to codify their views in treatises so that a sufficiently educated individual, by following their clearly defined rules, could become a poet. The greatest impediment to poetry was a lack of knowledge, for nothing of worth could be produced by an unenlightened mind. Such presuppositions ensured that these poets dismissed the Russian folkloric tradition as crude and barbaric. Even the exceptional and eccentric Trediakovsky, who made the exaggerated (and largely inaccurate) claim in a treatise of 1735 that his versification system was based on native folklore, did not dispute these unschooled poets' "lack of skill." More to the point, his statement was so out of keeping with the general sentiment of the time and provoked such derision among his contemporaries that Trediakovsky himself omitted it when he republished his treatise in a "corrected" version.

Throughout the eighteenth century, then, folklore – to the extent that it attracted attention at all – existed on the periphery of serious poetry. By the beginning of the nineteenth century, however, an entirely new aesthetic had emerged. Romanticism, with its belief in divine inspiration and rejection of inherited rules, had taken Europe by storm, and it lost little time in coming to Russia. One strand of European Romanticism (strictly speaking: proto-Romanticism) led to the emergence of the elegy, which focused on individual feeling rather than the glorification of a sovereign or the edification of the public. Another strand renounced the civilized world of the city, seeking creativity among the uneducated rural populace. Romantic poets viewed the age-old unwritten poetic legacy as a precious resource, and they rejoiced in the very coarseness that had so horrified their neo-classical predecessors.

For Russia's omnivorous nineteenth-century poets, the fascination with folklore took many forms. Native traditions served as a point of departure in a number of brilliant – if free – adaptations: Pushkin's «ска́зки» ("fairy-tales"), Lermontov's «Пе́сня про царя́ Ива́на Васи́льевича» ("Song about Tsar Ivan Vasilievich"), Nekrasov's epic «Кому́ на Руси́ жи́ть хорошо́» ("Who Lives Well in Russia?"). However, the search for folk inspiration was less a question of nationalism than internationalism. Russia's great poets did not hesitate to extend their borders and domesticate Western European models.

The ballad was perhaps the most important poetic discovery of the Romantics. Innumerable ballads were written, which included transcriptions of folklore as well as adaptations, imitations, and stylizations. These "literary" ballads sometimes had a tenuous connection to actual folklore, but they delighted readers nonetheless. While there is no single feature that defines the ballad, several elements recur in these works with frequency. First of all, ballads are narratives, both in the sense that they must sound narrated (i.e., a spoken rather than written text) and in the sense that they are plot oriented. An elegy might include a rough outline of a plot, but the emphasis was always on the speaker's attitude toward it. Odes often described events (e.g., a battle), but only as a part of a larger panegyric. If the odic poet constantly interrupted his narration to express delight or emotional involvement, the balladeer tended to avoid authorial commentary and all forms of moralizing. The ballad usually assumes a distance between the teller and his subject; hence the preponderance of third-person narration. The heroes of ballads, character types rather than carefully etched portraits, act spontaneously and even irrationally, rarely considering consequences. The ballad's setting is distant from contemporary civilization both temporally and geographically. In keeping with the beliefs of the uneducated people who originally authored them, ballads often include elements of the supernatural, with folkloric or magical powers proving more powerful than human will.

The European ballad did not have any specific formal requirements, yet there were definite features that set it apart from earlier poetic tradition. Since the genre had its origins in the "artless" speech of the common people, ballad writers sought simplicity in language, relying on direct locutions rather than convoluted syntax and complicated tropes. The meter varied considerably, though ternary meters and accentual verse (dol'nik) appeared more frequently than in most other genres. Very often, lines of four stresses alternated with lines of three stresses. Rhymes were obligatory, with masculine rhymes predominant.

The problem of making the European ballad speak Russian was solved brilliantly by Vasily Zhukovsky. So successful were his verse renderings of German and English ballads that to this day his admirers often forget that they are reading translations. Sir Walter Scott's ballad "The Eve of Saint John" and Zhukovsky's translation thereof («Замок Смальго́льм, или Ива́нов ве́чер» ["The Castle of Smaylho'me or The Eve of Saint John"]) give a good idea of a typical Western European ballad and its Russian incarnation. The plot is one of infidelity and revenge. The Baron of Smaylho'me treacherously murders his wife's lover, Sir Richard of Coldinghame. Responding to the entreaties of the Baron's wife, Sir Richard returns from the grave for a final tryst three days after his death, on the Eve of Saint John. Only in the poem's laconic final stanzas are the consequences of this supernatural event revealed: the Baron becomes a monk and his wife a nun.

Scott published this dark tale (set in the sixteenth century, based on Scottish legend) in 1801. When Zhukovsky – already a famous poet – presented his version to the Russian censor in 1822, it was rejected for publication on moral grounds, since it lacked "anything useful for the mind and heart." Zhukovsky was allowed to publish the poem two years later, only after making several changes and including footnotes in which he (with questionable sincerity) emphasized the poem's religious and ethical undercurrent.

A comparison of the first two stanzas gives a clear indication of Zhukovsky's approach to poetic translation.

> The Baron of Smaylho'me rose with day,
>   He spurr'd his courser on,
> Without stop or stay, down the rocky way,
>   That leads to Brotherstone.
>
> He went not with the bold Buccleuch,
>   His banner broad to rear;
> He went not 'gainst the English yew,
>   To lift the Scottish spear.
>
> До рассве́та подня́вшись, коня́ оседла́л
>   Знамени́тый Смальго́льмский баро́н;
> И без о́тдыха гна́л, меж уте́сов и ска́л,
>   Он коня́, торопя́сь в Бротерсто́н.
>
> Не с могу́чим Боклю́ совоку́пно спеши́л
>   На вое́нное де́ло баро́н;
> Не в крова́вом бою́ переве́даться мни́л
>   За Шотла́ндию с А́нглией о́н.

(Having risen before sunrise, the famous Baron of Smaylho'me saddled his steed; And without pausing for breath, he raced his steed among crags and cliffs, rushing to Brotherstone. // The Baron hurried not together with powerful Buccleuch to martial deeds; He did not think of settling his score in Scotland's bloody battle with England.)

Zhukovsky is faithful to the spirit of the original, though certainly not to the letter. He retains the exotic names, the setting, and the plot. The changes concern minor points, some of which serve to orient the Russian reader. The hero presumably needed no introduction for Scott's readership, but Zhukovsky felt it necessary to inform his audience that the Baron was "znamenityi" ("famous"). Other changes are harder to explain and seem to have been made for metrical convenience. For example, in the original the Baron rises at daybreak, while in the Russian he gets up before dawn. In the original he travels "down the rocky way," while in the Russian he rushes "mezh utesov i skal" ("among crags and cliffs"). These are certainly inexact renderings, but it is unlikely that they would profoundly alter the poem's effect. One might quibble with the inclusion of a word like "sovokupno" ("together"), which seems too bookish and therefore stylistically wrong, but Zhukovsky otherwise retains the simple style and vocabulary of the original.

In comparison to the generally precise treatment of Scott's semantics, the choice of meter is remarkably free. The original is in accentual verse (dol'nik), with four stresses in the odd numbered lines and three in the even numbered lines. Intervals between stressed syllables vary between one and two, though most of these opening lines do not display much variation. With the exception of lines 1 and 3, they are straightforward iambs. This would seem to leave the translator two choices: either retain the "dol'nik" or use iambs. Zhukovsky does neither, opting for strict anapests. The logic behind this decision must be understood historically. At this point in the development of Russian poetry, the "dol'nik" was barely used. Whenever Zhukovsky encountered it in German and English poetry, he "regularized" it, adding syllables to create Russian ternary meters. (In the case of ballads written in strict iambs, Zhukovsky retained the meter of the original.) In the present example, preserving the exact meter was clearly less important to him than maintaining two other balladic features: the pattern of four-stress lines alternating with three-stress lines and the exclusively masculine rhyme scheme, including even the occasional internal rhyme, cf. line 3: "Without stop or *stay*, down the rocky *way*" – «И без óтдыха *гнáл*, меж утёсов и *скáл*.»

It is not necessary to dwell on "The Eve of Saint John." For present purposes, it is sufficient to recognize that this is a typical ballad in both form and content. Along with a host of other ballad translations (especially from the German), it created a firm set of expectations for the Russian ballad.

Keeping these expectations in mind, it is interesting to look at «Áнгел» ("The Angel") and «Руса́лка» ("The Rusalka"), two of the most celebrated early poems of Russia's greatest Romantic, Mikhail Lermontov. Like most poets of his generation, Lermontov wrote and translated ballads. Like all poets of his generation, he was steeped in Zhukovsky's ballad translations. (Such was his admiration, that, when attempting his own versions of Schiller's ballads, Lermontov carefully avoided those that had already been rendered by Zhukovsky.) Neither of the poems cited below was given a genre designation by Lermontov, yet both contain obvious links to the Russian ballad tradition. Equally interesting, they contain obvious links to each other, a fact that has important implications for Lermontov's sense of genre.

Áнгел

По не́бу полу́ночи а́нгел лете́л
    И ти́хую пе́сню он пе́л;
И ме́сяц, и звёзды, и ту́чи толпо́й
    Внима́ли той пе́сне свято́й.

Он пе́л о блаже́нстве безгре́шных духо́в
    Под ку́щами ра́йских садо́в;
О Бо́ге вели́ком он пе́л, и хвала́
    Его́ непритво́рна была́.

Он ду́шу младу́ю в объя́тиях нёс
    Для ми́ра печа́ли и слёз,
И зву́к его́ пе́сни в душе́ молодо́й
    Оста́лся – без сло́в, но живо́й.

И до́лго на све́те томи́лась она́,
    Жела́нием чу́дным полна́;
И зву́ков небе́с замени́ть не могли́
    Ей ску́чные пе́сни земли́.

(The Angel: An angel flew along the midnight sky / And he sang a quiet song; / And the moon, and the stars, and the clouds in a throng / Listened to this holy song. // He sang about the bliss of sinless spirits / Under the covers of heavenly gardens; / He sang about great God, and his praise / Was not feigned. // He carried in his embraces a young soul / For the world of sadness and tears; / And the sound of his song in the young soul / Remained – wordless, but alive. // And for a long time it languished in the world, / Full of a wondrous desire; / And the dull songs of earth / Could not replace for it the sounds of the heavens.)

Русáлка

Русáлка плылá по реке́ голубóй,
   Озаря́ема пóлной лунóй;
И старáлась онá доплеснýть до луны́
   Серебри́стую пе́ну волны́.

И шумя́ и крутя́сь колебáла рекá
   Отражённые в не́й облакá;
И пе́ла русáлка – и звýк её слóв
   Долетáл до крутых берегóв.

И пе́ла русáлка: «На дне́ у меня́
   Игрáет мерцáние дня́;
Там ры́бок златы́е гуля́ют стадá,
   Там хрустáльные е́сть городá;

И там на подýшке из я́рких пескóв,
   Под те́нью густы́х тростникóв,
Спит ви́тязь, добы́ча ревни́вой волны́,
   Спит ви́тязь чужóй стороны́.

Расчёсывать кóльца шелкóвых кудре́й
   Мы лю́бим во мрáке ноче́й,
И в чело́, и в устá мы, в полýденный чáс,
   Целовáли красáвца не рáз.

Но к стрáстным лобзáньям, не знáю зачéм,
   Остаётся он хлáден и не́м;
Он спи́т, – и, склони́вшись на пе́рси ко мне́,
   Он не ды́шит, не ше́пчет во сне́!..»

Так пе́ла русáлка над си́ней рекóй,
   Полнá непоня́тной тоскóй;
И, шýмно катя́сь, колебáла рекá
   Отражённые в не́й облакá.

(The Rusalka: A rusalka swam along the light-blue river, / Illuminated by a full moon, / And it tried to splash to the moon / The silvery foam of the wave. // And, sounding and circling, the river shook / The clouds reflected in it. / And the rusalka sang – and the sound of her words / Flew to the steep river banks. // And the rusalka sang: "Where I live on the bottom / The glitter of day plays, / There golden schools of fish wander, / There are crystal cities there, // And there on a pillow of bright sands, / Under the shadow of thick reeds, / A warrior sleeps, the prey of the jealous wave, / A warrior of a foreign land sleeps. // In the darkness of the nights we love / To comb the rings of his silken curls, / And at the midday hour we / Have kissed more than once the forehead and lips of this comely man. // But to our passionate kisses, I know not why / He remains cold and mute. / He sleeps – and resting his head on my breast, / He neither breaths nor whispers in his sleep!.." // Thus sang the rusalka above the dark-blue river, / Full of incomprehensible yearning; / And, noisily rushing, the river shook / The clouds reflected in it.)

In terms of form, these poems should seem familiar to anyone who has read Zhukovsky's translation of Scott. Both of Lermontov's poems employ alternating lines of four and three stresses, exclusively masculine rhymes (pair rhymes, no less common historically than the alternating rhymes of Scott's "Eve of Saint John"), and ternary meters. "The Angel" is written in strict amphibrachs, while "The Rusalka" switches (with no discernable pattern) between lines of amphibrachs and anapests. Such a combination of ternary lines is highly unusual in the Russian tradition; however, it has a precedent in German ballads, particularly if one regards ternary meters as the Russian equivalent of the German or English dol'nik. The language of both poems is remarkably simple, with virtually no tropes (though there is intricate sound play).

As far as the plot is concerned, both poems have salient supernatural elements, already reflected in the titles. Both have atemporal, nocturnal settings. However, in neither case are we dealing with a true narrative, in the sense of a plot with suspense that builds towards a climax. In fact, the human participants in these poems, clearly subservient to the mythical and folkloric figures, do almost nothing. The «душа́» ("soul") in "The Angel" incessantly yearns, but never acts (at least not by ballad standards). The actions of the hero of "The Rusalka" presumably led to his watery grave (such is the outline of the traditional "rusalka" story of Russian folklore, faithfully reflected in Pushkin's earlier poem of the same name), but this "pre-history" lies outside the purview of Lermontov's poem.

In short, "The Angel" and "The Rusalka" are not ballads in the strictest sense of the word, but they contain numerous links to that tradition. Lermontov did write some poems that he designated as ballads, so he was clearly aware that these poems were different. All of this strongly suggests that he was consciously adapting a given form for a new purpose – a common, yet highly significant step in the history of any genre. Rather than telling a story that relies on its plot development for effect, Lermontov severely restricts the plot to let an underlying idea stand out more clearly. He creates a subgenre that might be termed the "philosophical ballad."

"The Angel" and "The Rusalka" are similar not merely in form and content, but also in message. Written within a year of each other, they seem to be two complementary versions of the same poem. This is suggested even in the titles. Both poems have a one-word title that names the protagonist. The word «ангел» is masculine while «русалка» is feminine. The former is associated with the air, the latter with the water. Both are mythical creatures, one traditionally linked to goodness, to the divine world above, the other (at least in the Russian tradition) to evil and the demonic world below.

A comparison of the very first lines of these poems reveals striking parallels:

«По не́бу полу́ночи а́нгел лете́л»	(An angel flew along the midnight sky)
«Руса́лка плыла́ по реке́ голубо́й»	(A rusalka swam along the light-blue river)

In both cases, the subject (the eponymous hero, appearing in the nominative case) is conjoined with a unidirectional past tense verb of motion: "angel letel" and "rusalka plyla." Both lines include a prepositional phrase beginning with "po." Both lines are strikingly orchestrated, with alliterations and chiasmic echoes: compare "rusa*l*ka ply*la*" and "*ru*salka . . . *re*ke" with "*po* nebu *po*lunochi ang*el* let*el*." What deserves emphasis is not just that these opening lines employ suspiciously similar grammatical structure and phonological echoings, but that they serve the identical function: to draw attention immediately to a lone figure in motion at a specific – though unspecified – moment in the past.

As the poems progress, the similarities become still more apparent. The masculine "angel," accompanied by the masculine moon ("mesiats"), bears in its embraces a feminine "soul" ("dusha"): this occurs at midnight ("polunochi"). The feminine "rusalka," illuminated by the feminine moon ("luna"), describes her midday ("v poludennyi chas") embraces with the masculine "vitiaz'." An embrace generally symbolizes wholeness, the joining together of opposites, but in both cases, the embrace proves temporary and is followed by permanent separation.

Of course, the angel and the rusalka are most profoundly linked through their songs. The theme of beautiful, other-wordly singing is essential to these poems and surely the reason for their fame. Lermontov's achievement lies less in introducing the song as a theme than in recreating the sound of song itself. In "The Rusalka," one actually hears the song, while in "The Angel" one only hears about it. But in both poems, Lermontov pays special attention to the musicality of the words, using various forms of repetition to create an incantational quality.

Part of the musicality of these poems depends on anaphora. The conjunction «и» ("and") can be found at the beginning of numerous lines in both poems, particularly the odd-numbered lines. Beyond that, entire words and phrases recur: «И пе́ла руса́лка . . . И пе́ла руса́лка . . . Так пе́ла руса́лка» (in "The Rusalka") or «он пе́л» and «он пе́л» (in "The Angel"). In fact, the very words "zvuk" and "pel" (or "pela"), reiterated in both poems, create a curious echo effect whereby the repeated sounds connote sound itself.

But there is still another kind of echoing that deserves attention: from poem to poem. In "The Angel": "*И зву́к его пе́сни* в душе́ молодо́й /

Остáлся – *без слóв*, но живóй" ("*And the sound of his song* in the young soul / Remained – *wordless*, but alive). In "The Rusalka": "И пéла русáлка – *и звýк ее слóв* / Долетáл до круты́х берегóв" ("And the rusalka sang – *and the sound of her words* / Flew to the steep river banks"). Lermontov uses the identical words "zvuk" and "slov" and emphasizes the effect they have on their surroundings. The most remarkable example of such interplay occurs in the third to last line of each poem: «Желáнием чýдным полнá» ("Full of wondrous desire") and «Полнá непонятной тоскóй» ("Full of incomprehensible yearning"). In one version of "The Rusalka," the line in question reads «Непонятной печáли полнá» ("Full of incomprehensible sadness"), which brings it even closer to "The Angel," both because «полнá» ("full") then occupies the rhyming position and also because the word «печáль» ("sadness") recalls yet another passage in "The Angel": «для мúра печáли и слёз» ("for the world of sadness and tears").

The astonishing degree of formal and semantic echoes between these poems leaves little doubt that we are dealing with a case of conscious patterning, with Lermontov presenting the same idea in two incarnations. In both poems, the spirit of separation reigns supreme. The fundamental Romantic conception of a lost unity and a lengthy and unsuccessful quest for its restoration appears to have been indelibly etched in Lermontov's consciousness. Indeed, it probably gave him the impetus to transform the traditional "rusalka" from a malevolent creature into yet another victim of the inexorable law of division. By applying the unmistakable formal markers of the ballad to what are essentially philosophical poems, Lermontov extended the potential of a folkloric genre.

It would be difficult to overstate the influence that these two Lermontov poems had on subsequent Russian poets. The Symbolists in particular were drawn to them for a host of reasons: the image of two worlds that yearn for union, the conception of a memory that precedes birth ("anamnesis," an idea that can be traced to Plato), the motif of otherworldly singing. In terms of continuity of genre and meaning, Zinaida Gippius' «Баллáда» ("Ballad") provides a particularly revealing response to Lermontov's legacy:

П. С. Соловьёвой

Мосткú есть в садý, на прудý, в камышáх.
Там, пóд вечер, кáк-то, гуляя,
Я вúдел русáлку. Сидúт на мосткáх, –
Вся нéжная, рóбкая, злáя.

Я блúже подкрáлся. Но хрýстнул сучóк –
Онá обернýлась несмéло,
В комóчек вся съёжилась, сжáлась, – прыжóк –
И пéной растáяла бéлой.

Хожу́ на мостки́ я к ней ка́ждую но́чь.
Руса́лка со мно́ю смеле́е:
Молчи́т – но сиди́т, не кида́ется про́чь,
Сиди́т, на тума́не беле́я.

Привы́к я с ней, бе́лой, молча́ть напролёт
Все до́лгие, бле́дные но́чи.
Гляде́ть в тишину́ холоде́ющих во́д
И в я́ркие, ро́бкие о́чи.

И ра́дость меж не́ю и мно́й родила́сь,
Безме́рно, светла́, как бездо́нность;
Со сла́дко-горя́чею гру́стью сплела́сь,
И ста́ло ей и́мя – влюблённость.

Я – зве́рь для руса́лки, я с тле́ньем в крови́.
И мне́ она ка́жется зве́рем . . .
Тем жгу́чей влюблённость: мы си́лу любви́
Одно́й невозмо́жностью ме́рим.

О, сли́шком – увы́ – много пло́ти на мне́!
На ней, – мо́жет бы́ть – сли́шком ма́ло . . .
И во́т, мы гори́м в непоня́тном огне́
Любви́, никогда́ не быва́лой.

Поро́й, над водо́й, чуть шурша́т камыши́,
Лепе́чут о сча́стье страда́нья . . .
И пла́менно-чи́сты в полно́чной тиши́, –
Таи́нственно-чи́сты, – свида́нья.

Я ра́дость мою́ не отда́м никому́;
Мы – ве́чно друг дру́гу жела́нны,
И ве́чно люби́ть нам дано́, – потому́,
Что здесь мы, любя́, – неслия́нны!

([For P. S. Solovieva]: There are wood platforms in the garden, on the pond, in the reeds. / While taking a walk there one evening, / I saw a rusalka. She was sitting on the wood platform – / All tender, timid, evil. // I crept nearer. But a branch snapped – / The rusalka turned around cautiously, / She huddled up into a little ball, pulled herself tight, and – in a jump – / Melted into the white foam. // I go to the wood platforms to visit her every night. / The rusalka becomes bolder with me: / She is silent – but she sits, doesn't jump away, / Sits, showing white in the mist. // I have grown accustomed to remaining silent with her, the white one, / Through all the long, pale nights. / To look into the silence of waters growing ever colder / And into her bright, timid eyes. // And a joy was born between her and me, / Measureless, bright as bottomlessness; / It became entwined with sweetly-hot sadness, / And it became known as – being in love. // I am a beast for the rusalka, I have decay in my blood / And she seems to me a beast . . . / Our being in love is all the more ardent: we measure the strength of our love / By impossibility alone. // Oh, there is – alas! – too much flesh on me! / And on her, perhaps, too little . . . / And now, we burn in an incomprehensible fire / Of unprecedented love. // At times, above the water, the reeds barely rustle, / They babble about the joy of suffering . . . / And in the midnight silence our meetings are / Ardently pure and mysteriously pure. // I will not give up my joy to anyone. / We are eternally desirable to each other, / And it is given to us to love eternally, because / Though loving, we are here unmerged!)

If Lermontov's titles point directly to the protagonist, Gippius' title focuses our attention exclusively on the genre. This genre designation is firmly supported by the poem's formal features. It is written in a ternary meter (amphibrachs), with alternating lines of tetrameter and trimeter. (Gippius opts not to indent the trimeter lines, but this is a printing convention without semantic significance.) The rhyme scheme alternates (like the Scott/Zhukovsky "Eve of St. John"), but includes feminine rhymes in the even-numbered lines. Such a change is hardly unprecedented; the identical combination of meter, rhyme scheme, and stanza can be found in Zhukovsky's ballad «Покаяние» ("Repentance"), a translation of "The Gray Brother," yet another work of Walter Scott. In short, Gippius uses all of the formal means at her disposal to recall the standard Romantic ballad.

To a reader familiar with the Russian poetic tradition, the rusalka of Gippius' poem calls to mind not merely a genre, but a specific work. It invites comparison with Lermontov's «Русáлка», perhaps the most famous treatment of that theme in all of Russian literature. Like her predecessor, Gippius uses a striking degree of sound organization: her poem abounds with alliteration and internal rhymes (e.g., line 1: «в садý, на прудý,» or line 11: «Молчúт – но сидúт»). Taking her cue from Lermontov, Gippius plays on the very sounds of the word "rusalka." Lermontov had "encrypted" this key word into a line where the rusalka herself was absent: «и шумя и крутясь, колебáла рекá.» All forms of sound repetition add a mellifluous quality to verse, making it memorable and giving the impression that these sounds "belong" together. However, in a poem about a rusalka, such sound patterning has additional significance. After all, the rusalka's beautiful singing is traditionally what makes her both attractive and dangerous. The fact that the word "rusalka" appears in anagrammatic form in a line where she herself is absent suggests her dangerous proximity. Gippius not only uses the same technique, she does so twice: in line 5 («подкрáлся. Но хрýстнул») and in line 19 («слáдко-горячею грýстью»).

Despite such striking similarities in theme, form, and poetic technique, Gippius' ballad departs radically from Lermontov's poem and from virtually all other rusalka tales. The standard rusalka lures men to their death through song, yet Gippius' rusalka is silent throughout. Moreover, the protagonist's death – the unvarying element in the rusalka plot – is replaced by the image of a joyous birth: «И рáдость меж нéю и мнóй *родилáсь*» ("And a joy *was born* between her and me"). Here Gippius uses sound repetition to link the two key words of this line: rádost'/rodilás'.

The fact that the hero will not die is evident from the first stanza. The poem is written in the first person, and it would be logically difficult to imagine someone narrating his own death. This is an unusual vantage point for a ballad, but, as we shall see, it is hardly the most unusual aspect of Gippius' poem. In fact, the closer one looks, the stranger this ballad becomes. In the first two stanzas, the masculine protagonist recalls a single encounter with a rusalka who fled after he pursued her. The string of perfective past tense verbs of the second stanza is precisely what one expects in a ballad. Beginning in the third stanza, however, the narration shifts from one-time past action to a repeated present, never to return to the type of sequential narration characteristic of the genre. Rather than tracing a series of events that culminate ineluctably in death, Gippius uses present tense to emphasize repetition and describe a state of permanence.

If the traditional rusalka tale is one of temptation and fatal attraction, Gippius' ballad celebrates a paradoxical love. An oxymoron (the quintessential trope of parodox), expresses this ambiguity well: «счастье страданья» ("the joy of suffering"). More emphatic, however, is Gippius' technique of description through negation: «Мы силу любви / одной *невозможностью* мерим . . . И вот, мы горим в *непонятном* огне / Любви, *никогда не бывалой*» ("We measure the strength of our love / By *impossibility* alone . . . And now, we burn in an *incomprehensible* fire / Of *unprecedented* love"). Such expressions make clear that this love is a state of permanent desire without the possibility of fulfillment. As the final stanza has it:

> Я радость мою не отдам никому;
> Мы – вечно друг другу желанны,
> И вечно любить нам дано, – потому,
> Что здесь мы, любя, – неслиянны!

(I will not give up my joy to anyone. / We are eternally desirable to each other, / And it is given to us to love eternally, because / Though loving, we are here unmerged.)

Gippius rejects love as a unifying force, be it positive (as in traditional conceptions from Plato to Vladimir Soloviev) or negative (as in the typical "rusalka" scenario, where consummation leads to death). If the Lermontov balladic poems were characterized by a yearning for a lost unity, Gippius locates that paradise in yearning itself, in the "mysteriously pure" («таинственно-чисты») meetings that promise to continue forever.

In short, Gippius has directed the reader through meter, genre, and theme to a tradition that she then turns upside down. She presumably does so in order to let the differences stand out all the more starkly. The most radical revision concerns the gender configuration. On first glance, Gippius seems true to the tradition. As the past tense verb endings indicate, the protagonist is masculine and the rusalka is feminine. However, as soon as we realize that the author herself was a woman, complications arise. It is true that Gippius always used masculine personae in her verse, but given a theme so dependent on gender stereotypes and a poem so intent on setting up expectations in order to break them, there is surely something more profound at work here.

The Symbolist period was a time of intense speculation about sexuality, and Gippius participated both in her life as well as her work. In philosophical discussions and creative writing, she was preoccupied with issues like the transfiguration of the flesh through love, procreation without sex, androgeny. In her personal life, a source of gossip from her time to the present day, Gippius refused to conform to contemporary expectations. In a famous portrait, she appears dressed as a man. She had the reputation of a loose woman, despite the fact that none of her passionate relationships (as well as her decades-long marriage to the writer and philosopher Dimitri Merezhkovsky) ever seems to have been consummated. We are concerned here not so much with the secrets of Gippius' personal life than with the image that she herself actively projected – an image that influenced the way her poetry was understood.

An additional interpretive problem of «Балла́да» comes in the form of the dedication. Unlike epigraphs, dedications are not necessarily an organic part of the poem. Sometimes they are added at a later date, even at the request of the dedicatee, in which case they cannot be considered essential. At other times, they may have strictly biographical significance. As such, they invite the reader to consider the poem's relationship to the world of reality, just as an epigraph asks the reader to consider a poem in relationship to a prior text. Yet a poet can assume that a reader knows (or can at least reconstruct) a prior text, whereas only a few contemporaries could possibly know the subtleties of a personal dedication. At other times, particularly if the dedicatee is another poet, an interpretively meaningful link is established (if necessarily less precise than an epigraph). This seems to be the case in Gippius's «Балла́да». Poliksena Solovieva, the sister of Vladimir Soloviev (whose idiosyncratic essay «Смы́сл любви́» ["The Meaning of Love"] fascinated the Symbolists), was a poet who published verse both under her own name and under a masculine pseudonym. Moreover, she was a friend of Gippius, and, apparently, a lesbian. Nothing whatsoever suggests that Gippius and Solovieva were romantically involved, but it stands to reason that Solovieva would have been sensitive to the reversal of sex roles just beneath the surface of «Балла́да». If nothing else, the dedication of this peculiar rusalka poem by a woman to a woman seems to extend the confused gender configuration implicit in the verses themselves beyond the text.

Biographically minded readers might wish to speculate what all of this says about Gippius herself. However, the interpreter of poetry should read the poetry, not psychoanalyze the poet. Like many of her fellow Symbolists, Gippius made her personality into one of her most complex creations. It is highly unlikely that this poem faithfully reflects Gippius' own personal life, and it would be absurd to see it as a poem "à clef" (with a biographical key that would unlock its many mysteries). Gender in this poem is far too confused – and intentionally so – to allow us to create any equivalence between the protagonist and Gippius herself. What seems essential is that Gippius, as so often, sought to provoke, to test borders, and to blur boundaries.

Like much of Gippius' poetry, «Балла́да» is based on paradox and leaves us with certain unresolvable questions. What cannot be disputed, however, is that Gippius combines a highly marked – even clichéd – genre, meter, and theme in order to write a poem that radically questions all the presuppositions that she so consciously invokes. As a tradition-conscious poet, Gippius recognized that novelty stands out most effectively against a familiar backdrop. The heyday of the ballad was the Romantic period, yet Gippius finds this "outdated" genre especially conducive to a discussion of extremely contemporary issues.

Chapter 6

Love poetry

О, бы́ть поки́нутым – како́е сча́стье!
Како́й безме́рный в про́шлом ви́ден свет –
Так после ле́та – зи́мнее нена́стье:
Всё по́мнишь со́лнце, хоть его́ уж не́т.

КУЗМИН, «О, бы́ть поки́нутым»

Oh, to be jilted – what happiness!
What measureless light is visible in the past –
It's like the foul winter weather after summer:
You still remember the sun, though it's no longer there.

Kuzmin, "Oh, to be jilted"

As we have seen, the ode, elegy, and ballad have distinct formal and stylistic features; moreover, they are associated with specific literary-historical movements. The love poem, in contrast, can be found in almost every age and with great stylistic variety. What are the prime markers of this genre? The most obvious is its theme: love. But it is a peculiarity of the truly powerful, affirmative human gestures – laughter, pleasure, love – that they can be diminished by introspection and analysis. Relatively few love poems celebrate a love that actually exists. Instead, poets tend either to anticipate it or to look nostalgically (sometimes painfully) back to it. Love poems are dynamic, marked by sudden shifts in emotion and perspective. They prefer the past or future to the present tense. This is poetry that thrives on absence, on temporal and spatial displacement.

The cast of characters in love poetry rarely varies. These poems concern the poet and his/her beloved, with the former addressing the latter. Accordingly, the standard configuration of pronouns is that of "I" and "you." Since the beloved is almost without exception absent, direct address (apostrophe) might seem inappropriate, yet it is indispensable. First, the very act of apostrophizing creates an effect of immediacy, bringing the speaker closer to his beloved, in spirit if not in fact. Secondly, the reader (assuming that the reader is not the beloved) is put in the curiously pleasant position of eavesdropping on a personal, intimate appeal. In a declaration of love in a novel or film, considerable attention is given to context. The lover's speech inspires an immediate – and usually vivid – response. In contrast, the reader of a love poem has access only to the speaker's words, not to their effect. This brings us to a final aspect of love poetry – its tendency to avoid plot. The events that led to the poem are rarely recounted (since both the "I" and the "you" presumably know them) and can at best be inferred. As a result, the "action" of love poetry occurs on the psychological and linguistic planes.

In some literary traditions, one finds cycles of poems addressed to a single beloved who is named (e.g., Catullus and Lesbia in Latin verse, Petrarch and Laura in Italian Renaissance poetry). This convention, which provides a fuller narrative context, is rare in Russian poetry. Nonetheless, readers have often been tempted to study the life of the poet in order to "identify" various unnamed beloveds. Understandable as this impulse may be, it can easily lead one astray. The possible congruence between the actual poet and the "lyrical I" of a love poem is less significant than whether that "lyrical I" is psychologically plausible. The emotions of love are universal, and the reader should recognize them more easily when the "you" and "I" are *not* assigned a proper name. It is common to refer to the speaker of a lyric poem as the poet (and we shall do so here), but this is a matter of convenience rather than a claim that the speaker of a poem and his/her lyrical construct are identical.

It has been argued that love poems have a narrow range of themes. This is true, yet it by no means lessens the vitality of the genre. In general, poetry is not about creating new themes, but about finding new ways to express complex (often common) feelings and impressions. In this regard, a love poem represents the quintessence of poetry, using the highly ordered language of verse to convey a spontaneous, almost chaotic world of emotions. The poems to be examined in this chapter limit this already closely circumscribed genre in that they all concern lost love. As such, they demonstrate the extraordinary variety that great poets can bring to a single theme.

Pushkin's «Я вас любил» ("I loved you") is one of the most famous poems in the Russian literary tradition. It has been committed to memory by generations of Russian schoolchildren and – thanks to its syntactic and lexical simplicity – by many foreign students of Russian as well. Its laconicism and sparseness of traditional imagery and metaphor make it characteristic of Pushkin's mature style.

> Я вас любил: любовь ещё, быть может,
> В душе моей угасла не совсем;
> Но пусть она вас больше не тревожит;
> Я не хочу печалить вас ничем.
> Я вас любил безмолвно, безнадёжно,
> То робостью, то ревностью томим;
> Я вас любил так искренно, так нежно,
> Как дай вам Бог любимой быть другим.

(I loved you: perhaps love / Did not entirely die out in my soul; / But let it not trouble you any more; / I don't want to sadden you in any way. / I loved you silently, hopelessly, / Tormented now by timidity, now by jealousy, / I loved you so sincerely, so tenderly, / That may God grant you to be so loved by another.)

This love poem fully conforms to our (admittedly few) expectations of the genre. Its subject is obviously love – in this case unreciprocated. It has virtually no explicit narrative element, and it takes the form of the direct speech of the poet to his beloved, both of whom are designated by pronouns. The beloved is addressed as "vy" (formal "you"), which suggests a distance between the two characters, a distance that becomes clear and increasingly poignant as the poem progresses.

It might be useful to begin by emphasizing what is absent. We have no physical image of either the poet or his beloved. We have no notion of the specific events that brought them together. All that we know for certain is that we are dealing with a man and a woman (grammatical gender gives this away), that the speaker has suffered in various ways for his love, and that he recognizes the hopelessness of his situation. The few hints of plot (i.e., of their prior relationship) must be pieced together indirectly. From the alternating moods of timidity and jealousy (line 6), it would seem that the poet's love was never reciprocated. Only the phrase "no longer" in the third line allows us to surmise that the beloved was even aware of the speaker's feelings.

The "absences" also extend to poetic language. This poem has been viewed as a classic example of "poetry without images." This is not to suggest that the poem calls nothing at all to mind, but rather that it dispenses with the metaphors and similes that many readers expect from poetry (e.g., "my love is like a rose"). In fact, it demands some ingenuity to find the sole trace of metaphor in Pushkin's lines (the "flame of love," implicit in the verb "ugasnut'" ["to die out," "to become extinguished"] of line 2).

Rather than trying to dazzle the reader with poetic invention, Pushkin relies on a series of simple repetitions. In a good poem, repetition is not duplication, but variation. The identical words/sounds may recur, but they always gain in meaning based on the new context. In Pushkin's poem, the most obvious example of this phenomenon is the phrase "I loved you," which begins lines 1, 5, and 7 (an extraordinary degree of lexical repetition in so short a poem). Each time this phrase is uttered, it is further qualified. The first time it is simply a statement of fact, an introduction followed by several thematically related, yet syntactically independent statements. In the fifth line (the midway point and beginning of the second sentence), it is followed by doubled adverbs ("bezmolvno, beznadezhno" [silently, hopelessly]). In the penultimate line, it is followed by a doubled modifier ("so + adverb, so + adverb") that is syntactically completed in the final line (the Russian expression "tak . . . kak"). This basic utterance thus becomes increasingly complicated; the first time it takes up half a line, the second time a line, the third time two lines.

The poem's form displays numerous other types of repetition. The syntax (two complete sentences) indicates that we are dealing with two four-line units. The rhyme scheme (A-b-A-b-C-d-C-d) further supports this division. Alternating feminine and masculine rhymes are hardly an unusual pattern in Russian poetry, but it is noteworthy that the second set of rhymes retains a sound from the first set. In other words, "beznadezhno/nezhno" shares the "zh" phoneme with "mozhet/trevozhit," while "tomim/drugim" retains the "m" from "sovsem/nichem." In this way, the two four-line statements are linked more closely than is obligatory. The purpose of a rhyme, of course, is to bring individual words (and the concepts they embody) closer together. Pushkin himself was known to complain about the limited rhyming potential of Russian words (which is of course considerably greater than that of English words), claiming that each rhyme word immediately led the reader/listener to expect its clichéd complement. When in the poem's final rhyme pair, Pushkin uses the word "tomim," he sets up an expectation for a hackneyed rhyme. Given that this is a love poem, we might fairly expect the rhyme "liubim" ("loved"). In his final line, Pushkin fulfills that expectation, but in an unexpected way: the word "liubim(oi)" does indeed appear, but only in the middle of the line, while the true rhyme turns out to be "drugim" ("[by] another"). This substitution is of course essential to the poem's message. Instead of a successful love story ("liubim" – "[I am] loved"]), we end with the appearance of a rival ("drugim" – [by] another"), whose presence (subtly suggested in the "revnost'" of the sixth line) seals the fate, as it were, of the speaker.

But let us return to the function and effect of the "I loved you" repetitions. One might interpret them as follows: in the first words, the poet relegates his love to the past tense, yet he immediately qualifies this. It may still exist (line 2), though it is apparently not shared (line 3), and the speaker does not want it to bother his beloved. In the fifth and sixth lines, he goes beyond the simple affirmation of his love, telling how it tormented him. In the seventh and eighth lines, he emphasizes the positive aspects of this love and wishes for her to experience its equal, albeit with another. He moves from suffering to reconciliation and selfless resignation, from jealousy to generosity. In this reading, each repetition of "I loved you" accentuates still more the poet's sense of loss and sets off yet more powerfully the extraordinary generosity of his closing gesture. Such a reading takes the poet at his word, and many readers have understood the poem in precisely this fashion.

However, it is possible to interpret it quite differently. One might dispute the contention that "I loved you" has no tropes by arguing that it has one trope many times over: litotes (whereby an affirmative statement is made indirectly, through the negation of the contrary). Accordingly, when Pushkin says "Perhaps my love has not died out entirely," he means, "My love has definitely not died out." When he says "May it not trouble you any more," he means: "I certainly hope you will be troubled by it." And when he wishes that she "may be so tenderly and sincerely loved by another," he really is insisting: "There is no way you will ever find anyone who loves you as tenderly and sincerely as I do." The poet's compassion, in short, is directed toward himself.

Such an unforgiving, perhaps even punitive reading of the poem is supported by the pronouns. Not only is the word "I" exclusively in the nominative case (i.e., the subject), it occupies the initial position in four lines (with the exception of the end of the line [the rhyme], this is the point of maximum emphasis). The "you," on the other hand, while appearing with more frequency than the "I," is consistently relegated to secondary position. It always appears in the accusative case (direct object), except in the final line, where it is in the dative (indirect object). In short, this is not a poem intended to console or celebrate the beloved; she is important insofar as she is the object (and unenthusiastic recipient) of the speaker's extraordinary love.

It is fair to conclude our brief discussion by asking which of these mutually exclusive readings is "correct." Should we understand the speaker as an altruist, willing to endure suffering for the happiness of his beloved? Or should we assume that everything he says is ironic (irony often being the motive for litotes), and that resentment lurks just beneath the surface of his apparent resignation? The answer, it would seem, is that both readings are valid. This is not simply because Pushkin was a poet who generally could see multiple sides of every question. (In his work, he repeatedly revisits the same situations, viewing them now as tragic, now as comic, now as sacred, now as profane.) More to the point, Pushkin understood perfectly the effect that emotion has on logic. His portrayal of a speaker torn by contradictory impulses rings true psychologically. Anyone suffering from unrequited love (and recognizing the futility of hope) would be capable of feeling both selfish and selfless at one and the same time. Pushkin's accomplishment is to give voice to these mutually incompatible, yet inextricably linked sentiments – and to do so with an astonishing economy of means.

Anna Akhmatova, a conscious inheritor of the Pushkinian tradition, achieved early fame primarily on the strength of her love poetry. Like Pushkin's "I loved you," these poems reveal a psychological depth beneath a calm exterior. Despite the diversity of the "lyrical I" in Akhmatova's poems, contemporaries found the emotions so true to life that they (incorrectly) deemed them autobiographical. «Я не любви твоей прошу» ("I don't ask for your love") presents from a woman's perspective a variation on the theme of lost love.

Я не любви́ твое́й прошу́.
Она́ тепе́рь в надёжном ме́сте.
Пове́рь, что я твое́й неве́сте
Ревни́вых пи́сем не пишу́.
Но му́дрые прими́ сове́ты:
Дай ей чита́ть мои́ стихи́,
Дай ей храни́ть мои́ портре́ты, –
Ведь так любе́зны женихи́!
А э́тим ду́рочкам нужне́й
Созна́нье по́лное побе́ды,
Чем дру́жбы све́тлые бесе́ды
И па́мять пе́рвых не́жных дней . . .
Когда́ же сча́стия гроши́
Ты проживёшь с подру́гой ми́лой
И для пресы́щенной души́
Всё ста́нет сра́зу так посты́ло –
В мою́ торже́ственную ночь
Не приходи́. Тебя́ не зна́ю.
И чем могла́ б тебе́ помо́чь?
От сча́стья я не исцеля́ю.

(I don't ask for your love. / It's now in a safe place. / Believe me, I'm not writing your fiancée / Any jealous letters. / But take this wise advice: / Let her read my poems, / Let her keep my portraits, – / After all, bridegrooms are so kind! / Yet those little fools need more / The consciousness of full conquest / Than the bright conversations of friendship / And the memory of the first tender days . . . / But when you and your dear girlfriend / Live through the pennies of happiness / And when to your oversatiated soul / Everything suddenly becomes repulsive – / Don't come into my triumphant night. / I don't know you. / And how could I help you? / I can't cure anyone from happiness.)

Once again, the poem takes the form of direct address, this time to an informal "you" (which reflects their earlier intimacy). The "plot," while vague, is nonetheless sketched more fully than in "I loved you." The speaker is the former beloved of a man who is now engaged to another woman. Written in iambic tetrameter (Pushkin's favorite meter), the poem is organized into four-line units, which rhyme first with a "ring" scheme (a-B-B-a), then alternating (C-d-C-d). This pattern switches only in the poem's final lines, when the alternating rhymes are unexpectedly retained. This change not only emphasizes closure, but also underlines the syntactic connectedness of the final eight lines. As in Pushkin, the lexicon is simple and metaphors are few. The poem's considerable dynamism comes from the speaker's rapidly shifting thoughts, which oscillate between present and future tense and among statements, exclamations, and questions.

The first quatrain has a matter-of-fact quality, with a disarming first line that seems to question the very premise of a love poem. Love itself is treated almost as a physical object, now "in a safe place" (line 2) with the addressee's fiancée (the rhyme "nadezhnom meste" and "neveste" suggests a closeness that will soon be doubted). The speaker will send no jealous letters. However, the reader acquainted with Pushkin's "I loved you" already knows the power of negative constructions. The words "love" and "jealous" (in the Russian, both appear in genitive case as a result of negation) are the stock in trade of a love poem, even if the speaker insists that she rejects them.

The second quatrain marks a distinct change in tone. Using a series of imperatives, the speaker urges her erstwhile lover (their earlier amorous relationship is revealed indirectly in these lines) to acquaint his fiancée with her verses and portraits. This is, of course, peculiar advice. It is not immediately evident why a man should share with his fiancée souvenirs from a previous amour. Yet instead of offering an explanation, the poet presses onward with an appeal to his generosity: «Ведь так любéзны женихú!» ("After all, bridegrooms are so kind!") The use of the plural is a brilliant rhetorical strategy. Love poetry generally shuns plurals (at least as far as the participants are concerned), because the love bond itself is conceived of as unique, something that can happen only to these two people. By casting her former beloved as a type, the poet consigns him to predictability.

This technique is developed in the very next line, which begins the third quatrain. The fiancée herself is suddenly transformed into a plural, and a rather unflattering one at that ("those little fools"). While the Russian diminutive "durochka" can have a positive connotation, here it conveys a kind of innocent stupidity. Most importantly, the plural causes her to lose her individuality. In this way, the bridegroom and fiancée are no longer partners in true love, but mere caricatures playing predetermined roles. The fiancée (the type who needs victory above all else) is opposed to the sensitive individual (i.e., the speaker), who values the true sentiments of love – «свéтлые бесéды» ("bright conversations") and the power to recollect and thus reconstruct. With the line about the «пáмять пéрвых нéжных дней» ("memory of the first tender days"), the quatrain trails off into ellipsis, presumably reflecting the memories themselves. The logical question arises: why spend one line on the fiancée's triumph and two lines (plus ellipsis) on the conversations and memories that she is incapable of appreciating? While neither the "I" nor the "you" pronoun appears in this quatrain, both are clearly implicated in this reference to "memory of the first tender days." The poet mentions these things not only to remind herself, but also to admonish her former beloved, the direct addressee of the entire poem.

The final eight lines form one logical unit (we have already noted the shift in rhyme scheme that supports such a reading). This is the only instance in the poem where a four-line unit does not end with a full stop. Instead, a dash is used to separate the "when . . ." from the ". . . then" clause. In these final lines, the plurals disappear and we return to the "I" and "you" of the opening. The present tense gives way to the future, predicting a scenario diametrically opposed to the present. On the lexical level, the phrase «подру́га ми́лая» ("dear girlfriend") – a noun/adjective combination that comes up innumerable times in love poetry – clashes noticeably with the rather crass metaphor «сча́стия гроши́» ("pennies of happiness," implying "cheap happiness," mercantile imagery being invariably pejorative in Russian) and the epithet «посты́ло» ("repulsive," a word foreign to the spirit of love poetry). In the final four lines, the poet shifts to a present tense, but she still describes future events. Presumably this is done to add immediacy and minimize the uncertainty inherent in the future tense. This moment of horror, when the "you" recognizes his grave error, coincides with the poet's time of triumph. Rather than welcome her prodigal lover back, she rejects him: «Тебя́ не зна́ю» ("I don't know you"). The clipped syntax (four complete sentences in four lines) and negative constructions of the opening stanza return, suggesting that we have come full circle. But the victim is no longer the "I," but the "you." He is suffering from "happiness" (now a completely compromised concept, cf. the "pennies of happiness"), an illness that the poet cannot heal. The Russian verb "istseliat'," built on the root "tsel" ("whole"), lends a new dimension to the final line. Love is traditionally conceived of as a joining of two parts into one (cf. Plato's "Symposium"), yet the speaker implies that her former beloved will find himself in a love relationship that leaves him incomplete.

While the irony of Pushkin's "I loved you" was open to dispute, there can be no question of its presence in Akhmatova's "I don't ask for your love." Once again, the essential question concerns the poem's psychological plausibility. In this case, we encounter the inner monologue of a jilted woman. While neither "asking for his love" nor "sending jealous letters to his fiancée," she nonetheless does everything in her power to make her former beloved rue his decision to leave her. She urges him to share her verses and pictures with his new love. She mocks this new love by making it (stereo)typical ("bridegrooms" and "little fools"). Finally, she mocks the very idea of lasting happiness, describing how he will tire of the superficiality that he now enjoys. The result envisioned is the exact reverse of the present situation (hence the curious syntactic and stylistic parallels between the first and last quatrains). Now she turns to him and is rebuffed (or ignored); in the future he will come to her and receive the same treatment. This symmetry is, of course, classic – it can be found, among other places, in Pushkin's novel in verse *Eugene Onegin*, the cornerstone of the Russian literary tradition. Yet the irony does not end here, for in certain ways the speaker displays a dangerous likeness to the "little fools" she sneers at. After all, she herself is no longer interested in the sentiments of love, but in victory: «В мою́ *торже́ственную* но́чь» ("Into my *triumphant* night"). Finally, the reader – as against the listener – should appreciate that this twenty-line poem appears on the page without breaks between the quatrains. On the one hand, this could be explained by the somewhat irregular rhyme scheme. On the other hand, it gives the graphic impression of being a letter – precisely the type of "jealous letter" that the poet vowed not to send. In short, the irony turns back on the poet herself, ultimately suggesting that her plan for vengeance is – the first line notwithstanding – a thinly disguised entreaty for love.

Marina Tsvetaeva's «Попы́тка ре́вности» ("An Attempt at Jealousy") follows a similar poetic logic, but employs completely different poetic means. A line-by-line analysis of this complicated poem would take more space than we can afford. We will therefore cite and translate it in its entirety, but discuss only a few passages in order to demonstrate some of the salient differences between Russia's two greatest women poets.

> Как живётся́ ва́м с друго́ю, –
> Про́ще ведь? – Уда́р весла́! –
> Ли́нией берегово́ю
> Ско́ро ль па́мять отошла́
>
> Обо мне́, пловучем о́строве
> (По́ небу – не по вода́м!)
> Ду́ши, ду́ши! бы́ть вам сёстрами,
> Не любо́вницами – ва́м!
>
> Как живётся ва́м с *просто́ю*
> Же́нщиною? *Бе́з* боже́ств?
> Госуда́рыню с престо́ла
> Све́ргши (с о́ного сошёд),
>
> Как живётся ва́м – хлопо́чется –
> Ёжится? Встаётся – как?
> С по́шлиной бессме́ртной по́шлости
> Ка́к справля́етесь, бедня́к?
>
> «Су́дорог да перебо́ев –
> Хва́тит! До́м себе́ найму́».
> Ка́к живётся ва́м с любо́ю –
> Избра́нному моему́!
>
> Сво́йственнее и съедо́бнее –
> Сне́дь? Прие́стся – не пеня́й . . .
> Ка́к живётся ва́м с подо́бием –
> Ва́м, попра́вшему Сина́й!

Как живётся вам с чужо́ю,
Зде́шнею? Ребро́м – люба́?
Стыд Зеве́совой вожжо́ю
Не охлёствывет лба́?

Как живётся вам – здоро́вится –
Мо́жется? Поётся – ка́к?
С я́звою бессме́ртной со́вести
Как справля́етесь, бедня́к?

Как живётся вам с това́ром
Ры́ночным? Обро́к – круто́й?
После мра́моров Карра́ры
Как живётся вам с трухо́й

Ги́псовой? (Из глы́бы вы́сечен
Бо́г – и на́чисто разби́т!)
Как живётся вам с стоты́сячной –
Вам, позна́вшему Лили́т!

Ры́ночною новизно́ю
Сы́ты ли? К волшба́м осты́в,
Как живётся вам с земно́ю
Же́нщиною, без шесты́х

Чу́вств? Ну, за́ голову: сча́стливы?
Не́т? В прова́ле без глуби́н –
Как живётся, ми́лый? Тя́жче ли,
Та́к же ли как мне́ с други́м?

(How's life with another woman, – / Simpler, surely? – A stroke of the oar! – / By way of the shore's line / Did memory go away quickly // About me, the floating island / (Along the sky – not along the waters!) / Souls, souls! You were meant to be sisters, / Not lovers, you! // How's life with a *simple* / Woman? *Without* divinities? / Having deposed the empress from her throne / (After stepping down from it), // How's life – how are your worries – / How are your shivers? How's your getting up [in the morning] – how? / With the immortal tax of banality / How are you coming to terms, my poor man? // "Enough of convulsions and palpitations – / I'm going to get my own house." / How's life with just any woman – / O, my chosen one! // Are the victuals more appropriate and more edible? / If it becomes dull – don't complain . . . / How's life with a likeness – / You, who have conquered Sinai! // How's life with a foreigner, / Of this world? I'm asking you straight – is she nice? / Does shame, like Zeus' reins, / Not lash your forehead? // How's life – how's your health, / How's it going? Your singing – how? / With the immortal sore of conscience / How are you managing, poor man? // How's life with a good / From the market? Is the tax steep? / After the marbles of Carrara / How's life with the dust // From plaster? (A god is cut out of a boulder – / And broken into smithereens!) / How's life with the hundred-thousandth woman – / You, who have known Lilith! // Are you sated by / Market novelty? Having cooled toward magic spells, / How's life with an earthly / Woman, without sixth // Senses? Well, on your life now: are you happy? / No? In a hole without depths – / How's life, my dear? More difficult, / Or the same – as my life with another man?)

If the effect of the Pushkin and Akhmatova poems depended on understatement, then Tsvetaeva's verses move to the other end of the rhetorical spectrum: hyperbole. In fact, her expansiveness allows us to see just how severely Pushkin and Akhmatova restrict syntax, lexicon, and form. Characteristic is Tsvetaeva's use of the stanza. Pushkin and Akhmatova, while not introducing line breaks between quatrains, clearly use four-line units to organize their thought. In those poems, one can assume that a full stop (period, ellipsis, question mark, exclamation) will occur after every fourth line. Exceptions to this are rare, and if they occur (e.g., four lines from the end of the Akhmatova poem), they indicate a crucial shift in the poetic logic. In contrast, Tsvetaeva breaks her poem into quatrains graphically, yet she violates the boundary so frequently (and so radically) that the stanza loses its traditional shaping function. Spilling over into the first word or phrase of the new stanza, her utterance cannot be contained within the vessel that has been created for it. (The same phenomenon occurs on the level of the line, which Pushkin and Akhmatova treat as a syntactic unit, while Tsvetaeva makes enjambment the norm.) Even in her rhymes, Tsvetaeva seeks both to conjoin *and* to disorient. She uses alternating feminine and masculine rhymes in the odd-numbered stanzas and dactylic and masculine rhymes in the even-numbered stanzas. Ordinarily it is pointless to seek meaning in the conventional terms of masculine and feminine rhymes, yet Tsvetaeva realizes this dormant semantic potential: the poem's first feminine rhyme word ("drugoiu") denotes a woman, while the final masculine rhyme word ("drugim") denotes a man. This shift of attention from the "other woman" to the "other man" highlights the seismic shift of perspective that occurs in the final stanza. Tsvetaeva's rhymes themselves tend to be inexact (e.g., khlopóchetsia/póshlosti) and unpredictable (e.g., liubá/lbá). In the Pushkin and Akhmatova poems we have examined in this chapter, every rhyme is pure. In "An Attempt at Jealousy," less than half of them are. Indeed, the sudden shift in tone of the last stanza especially stands out because none of the rhymes are pure (strictly speaking, they are not rhymes at all, but merely assonance).

In terms of poetic language, Pushkin's vocabulary belongs entirely to the norms of love poetry, and Akhmatova's rarely strays beyond them. In contrast, Tsvetaeva mixes registers incessantly. Her reiterated "Kak zhivetsia vam" ("How's life") is colloquial, as are numerous other expressions, e.g., "ved'" ("surely"), "bedniak" ("my poor man"), "nu" ("well"). Yet she also includes words and forms that would never be used in spoken language and sound like they came off the pages of an eighteenth-century ode, e.g., "s onogo soshed" ("After stepping down from it" – both the pronoun [onogo] and verbal adverb [soshed] are archaic), "popravshemu" (the past active participle formed from the high-style verb "poprat'" ["to conquer"]). In short, Tsvetaeva's lexicon is, characteristically, at once more colloquial *and* more bookish than that of Pushkin and Akhmatova. And while Pushkin and Akhmatova keep metaphor (and allusion) to a minimum, Tsvetaeva relies on both, often in combination. For example, the poet equates her former beloved with Moses («Ва́м, попра́вшему Сина́й» – "you who have conquered Sinai") and with Adam («Вам, позна́вшему Лили́т» – "you who have known Lilith"). Besides these allusions to the Bible and apocrypha, one finds obvious references to classical antiquity (Zeus) and Italian Renaissance art (Carrara, the source of marble for the great sculptors). These explicit allusions are developed in extremely subtle ways. For example, once Adam has been called to mind (through the reference to Lilith), we may surmise that the expression "rebrom" (here with the unambiguous sense of "straightforwardly," but literally meaning "by the rib") is intended to recall Adam's rib, and therefore Eve (and by extension the theme of lost paradise). Likewise, the periphrastic mention of Moses is enough to recall Michelangelo's famous statue of him, which explains the phrase «мраморов Каррары» ("marbles of Carrara") a few stanzas later.

We have suggested that in poetry, any element of language can become a poetic device. Tsvetaeva makes virtuoso use of punctuation to accentuate the speaker's emotional state. Her poem contains twenty two dashes, twenty one question marks, seven exclamation points, and one ellipsis. The one and only period (stanza 5) closes the quoted speech of the former beloved and is thus associated with him. Indicative statements, it appears, are not part of the poet's own diction. Pronouns, usually crucial to the dynamism of love poetry, are surprisingly unvaried here: the "you" (formal is used) appears twelve times, but exclusively in the dative case, eight times in the identical expression, while the "I" appears only twice (neither time as the subject). Impersonal constructions dominate, creating a strange lack of agency. The "you" and "I" do not so much act as they are acted upon.

Tsvetaeva's word choice is dictated as much by aural as by semantic considerations. In the question «С по́шлиной бессме́ртной по́шлости / Как справля́етесь, бедня́к?» ("With the immortal tax of banality / How are you coming to terms, my poor man?"), the words «по́шлина» ("tax") and «по́шлость» ("banality") are brought together primarily because they sound so similar. Of course, Tsvetaeva takes advantage of their sense as well (the literal meaning of «бедня́к» ["poor man"] is activated by the reference to tax). Other aspects of Tsvetaeva's varied wordplay are apparent in the lines: «Сво́йственнее и съедо́бнее – / Сне́дь? Прие́стся – не пеня́й . . .» ("Are the victuals more appropriate and more edible? / If it becomes dull – don't complain . . ."). To begin with, «съедобнее» ("more edible") and «снедь» ("victuals") lead the reader to expect the verb «есть» (to eat). Instead of fulfilling this expectation, Tsvetaeva follows these words with the verb «приесться,» built from the root «есть» (to eat), but having a very different meaning ("to get sick of"). Moreover, she takes advantage of the repeated "s" and "n" sounds in «Свойственнее, съедобнее, Снедь» to prepare the appearance of «Синай» at the end of the stanza, an otherwise improbable lexical jump from the quotidian to the biblical.

If Pushkin's "I loved you" was based on the repetition of the initial statement (and its concomitant focus on the speaker), then Tsvetaeva's "Attempt at Jealousy" can be seen as a curious response, where a reiterated question draws attention to the addressee. Throughout the poem, the poet revisits her earlier relationship to the addressee by juxtaposing it with the addressee's present relationship with another woman. Very frequently, these oppositions are expressed in terms of earthly imagery (physical, mercantile, domestic – always pejorative in Tsvetaeva's poetic world) versus heavenly imagery (spiritual, mythological, magical – in short, the world of poetry). The addressee, who formerly participated in that extraterrestrial world, is asked how he enjoys his new, mundane existence. The implication – as in the Akhmatova poem – is that anyone who could have loved the speaker cannot possibly find true happiness with the vapid woman he now loves.

Pushkin and Akhmatova carefully crafted a "poetic argument," where each line builds on the preceding one. Tsvetaeva uses a different strategy, which could be likened to an ode. It is not so much a linear progression as a constant amplification of a single point. Her poem is structured around unrelenting contrasts, with each successive stanza emphasizing yet more the distance between the two women and (implicitly) the addressee's error in rejecting the poet in favor of the "simpler" one. In the final stanza, this pattern suddenly shifts:

> Ну, зá голову: счáстливы?
> Нéт? В провáле без глубѝн –
> Как живётся, мѝлый? Тя́жче ли,
> Тáк же ли как мнé с другѝм?

(Well, on your life now: are you happy? / No? In a hole without depths – / How's life, my dear? More difficult, / Or the same – as my life with another man?)

The interrogative intonation continues, yet the nature of the questions has changed. The first question asks about his happiness, and the poet answers it herself – negatively. She likens his existence to a «провал» (the word means a "hole," but also, figuratively, a "failure"). The one thing to be expected of a hole, of course, is depth. But playing on the figurative meaning of depth, the poet negates even this possibility. Her next question is yet more shocking in its simplicity. It is a refrain of the question asked seven times earlier «Как живётся вам» (literally: "How is *your* life?"), yet now the poet removes the formal "you" ("vam") and replaces it with the appellation "milyi" ("my dear") – one of the most time-honored epithets of love poetry. Had this word appeared in the first stanza, it would have seemed normal. After the rhetorical fireworks of the preceding stanzas, it comes as a complete surprise. Should it be understood ironically or seriously – or both at once? The final lines make it even harder to decide: the poet asks her former beloved to compare his present relationship *not* to their old relationship (as she has done throughout the poem and as we fully expect her to do once more) but rather to her *new* relationship with *another man* (about whom we learn only in the poem's final word). Thus arises the heretofore wholly unanticipated possibility that her former beloved is actually worse off than she is; that she has not only replaced his presence in her life but transcended it, transferring the pain to him. This jarring final question somewhat clarifies the poem's perplexing title. This is "An Attempt at Jealousy," but we are no longer certain whose. Is it the jealousy of the speaker (as we assumed all along) or the jealousy that she is attempting to call forth in her addressee (a possibility that arises only in the poem's final line)? In either case, Tsvetaeva – like Pushkin and Akhmatova – forces the reader to readjust perspective and reassess a seemingly clear situation. As always in Tsvetaeva, there is extraordinary control behind a highly emotional facade, a carefully articulated structure behind constantly shifting images. As always in love poetry, the actual events are overshadowed by the speaker's reaction to them. The reader, by "overhearing" this reaction, observes a complex psychological drama unfold.

Proverbs attest to the irrational quality of love: "Love is blind," we say in English – «сéрдцу не прикáжешь» ("you can't give an order to the heart") is the Russian equivalent. The challenge for the love poet is to maintain the fundamentally illogical nature of love without losing the structure that is the essence of poetry. Love is inimical to repetition, while poetry thrives on it. Love is spontaneous, while poetry demands contemplation. Not surprisingly, the three poems examined in this chapter all rest on paradox and, ultimately, interpretive indecidability. Throughout, there is a tension between passion and control, between what is directly expressed and what is implied. In all three cases, the speaker attempts to overcome a difficult situation by rejecting the present in favor of the past or future, about which he/she is extremely territorial. A seemingly emotional state does not preclude a careful weighing of guilt and meting out of punishment. In moving from Pushkin to Akhmatova to Tsvetaeva, we find unreciprocated love becoming a source of increasing heat and even punitiveness. As readers, of course, we are placed in a delicate position. On the one hand, we are detached. Having only the barest sense of the events that precipitated the poem, we observe with a certain amusement and bemusement the speaker's attempts to overcome his/her present misery. On the other hand, as human beings, we cannot but sympathize with the plight before us. In the speaker, we recognize a version of ourselves. Pushkin's verses ring as true today as they did to his contemporaries. In their mingling of self-sacrifice, self-pity, and self-praise, they epitomize the fate of the rejected lover. Akhmatova and Tsvetaeva follow a different scenario, but with no less convincing psychological portraiture. In their poems, the jilted lover comes to terms with the eternal problem of explaining how her otherwise perfect partner could make such a ghastly error as to choose a wholly inferior mate. Here jealousy and desire mix uneasily with the thirst for revenge. Such poetry moves beyond the individual, asking us to revisit ourselves, to recognize the rational and irrational composition of human emotion.

Chapter 7

Nature poetry

Ду́ма за ду́мой, волна́ за волно́й,
Два́ проявле́нья стихи́и одно́й.

Тютчев, «Волна́ и ду́ма»

Thought upon thought, wave upon wave,
Two manifestations of the same element.

Tiutchev, "Wave and Thought"

The term "nature poetry" itself connotes two distinct yet related realms: the human subject and the natural object, the observer and the observed. Like landscape painters, nature poets do not simply reproduce what they see, but filter it through their own consciousness. The prominence of the observer varies considerably from painting to painting and from poem to poem. It may be foregrounded or reduced, but never obliterated. Even the photograph, that most mimetic of art forms, cannot offer an unmediated view of nature, if only because a photographer necessarily selects one piece out of reality at the expense of others.

Of course, poets and painters rarely aspire to the degree of verisimilitude of a photographer. Nor do we expect them to render a scene "precisely as it is." It would be absurd to study the landscapes of Vincent Van Gogh or Caspar David Friedrich as a means of understanding the topology and climate of southern France or northern Germany. On the contrary: these works fascinate as much through their creators' strength of personality as through the scenes they depict. In a similar way, nature poetry tends to refract rather than reflect the landscape. These poems are often less pictorial than contemplative and associative.

Like love poetry, nature poetry cannot be defined by formal markers. The distinguishing characteristic is the theme itself. A brief poem by Afanasy Fet serves as a useful introduction to the genre:

Бу́ря на не́бе вече́рнем,
Мо́ря серди́того шу́м –
Бу́ря на мо́ре и ду́мы,
Мно́го мучи́тельных ду́м –

Бу́ря на мо́ре и ду́мы,
Хо́р возраста́ющих ду́м –
Чёрная ту́ча за ту́чей,
Мо́ря серди́того шу́м.

(A storm on the evening sky, / The noise of the angry sea – / A storm on the sea and thoughts, / Many tortuous thoughts – / A storm on the sea and thoughts, / A chorus of burgeoning thoughts – / Black stormcloud after stormcloud, / The noise of the angry sea.)

What is this poem about? On the surface, it could hardly be simpler. It is a poetic rendering of an evening storm on the waters. One could easily conceive of a landscape painting on the same subject, full of dark clouds and tempestuous waves. Such a pictorial representation could recreate the theme and even the brooding tone of Fet's poem. However, it could not even approximate the distinctiveness of his verse language.

Perhaps the easiest way to define the quality of this poem is through absence. The poem contains no verbs, no pronouns, no adverbs, no semantic figures of speech, no elaborate syntax, no complex grammatical constructions (dative and accusative cases are absent entirely; instrumental appears only once). What *is* present (mainly nouns and adjectives) stands out all the more starkly through insistent repetition. All poetry is based on various forms of repetition (rhythm, sounds, images, etc.), but few poems repeat quite this emphatically. In a work this brief, it is astounding not simply that individual words recur (as many as four times), but that entire lines are repeated verbatim.

The poem is written in dactylic trimeter, with alternating feminine and masculine line endings. With two exceptions, the lines rhyme, though in a remarkably heavy-handed way, with so-called tautological rhymes dominant ("shum" rhymes twice with "dum", "dumy" rhymes with "dumy"). Indeed, it is difficult to say what is more peculiar: that two lines do not rhyme (in Russian poems of the nineteenth century, one expects either all rhymes or no rhymes, not a mixture) or that the remaining lines rhyme so unimaginatively. These simplistic end-rhymes are complemented, however, by a series of rhymes at line *beginnings* (where rhyme is not traditionally expected). "Buria" repeats three times, while "moria" rhymes with "khor" and "chernaia." Because of the relative brevity of trimeter lines, all rhymes (and, for that matter, all repeated words and sounds) are exceptionally prominent. In other words, in most lines, two of the three stressed vowels are found in rhymed words.

Closer inspection shows the depth of Fet's attention to sound repetition. The few words that do not rhyme are all carefully embedded in the larger sound fabric. For example, neither "vechernem" (line 1) nor "tuchei" (line 7) rhyme with other words in line final position, yet "ve*chern*em" clearly echoes "*chern*aia" (the first word of the "unrhymed" line 7), and "tuchei" not only rhymes with "tucha," ("tucha za tuchei"), but also is adumbrated in the sounds of "vozras*taiushchi*kh" (line 6). In line initial positions, only "mnogo" does not rhyme, but even this word repeats the key consonant and stressed vowel of the ubiquitous "more." (In a pure rhyme, consonant and stressed vowel must be adjacent – here they are separated by the letter "n.") Of seven nouns in this poem, four share the stressed vowel "u" ("shum," "dum," "buria," "tucha") and two the stressed vowel "o" ("more" and "khor"). The sole exception, "nebo" is fixed into the sound patterning through alliteration: "*B*uria *na nebe* . . ." Moreover, all nouns conform to one of two stress patterns: either they are monosyllabic (shum, dum, khor) or bisyllabic with stress on the first syllable: (buria, nebo, more, dumy, tucha). In short, Fet's use of sound repetition goes far beyond the obvious end rhymes, extending to virtually every word in the poem.

But what was Fet seeking to achieve though such careful sound orchestration? With so many repeated nouns and no finite verbs, the poem makes an initial impression of stasis. Indeed, contemporaries ridiculed this poem for what seemed to them its plodding obviousness. Yet closer analysis reveals a complexity of meaning as well as sound texture. On the semantic level, the individual words belong to two distinct spheres: natural and human. If the first line is purely representational, the second already suggests the presence of a human observer. «Мóря сердúтого шýм» ("The noise of the angry sea") is a personification, albeit not a particularly unusual one. As in English, the "angry sea" is essentially a dead metaphor, a phrase so common that one is apt not to recognize the personification (in contrast to odd, but conceivable collocations such as "happy sea" or "angry tree"). In the course of the next six lines, however, the personification becomes more forceful. In the third line, Fet introduces "dumy," a word unambiguously associated with man (the "thinking reed," in Pascal's famous formulation). This passage from "angry sea" to "tortuous thoughts" may seem arbitrary to an English speaker, but the whole point is that this occurs in Russian, where sound repetitions support the semantic development. The very phonemes of the word "dumy" have been adumbrated in the previous lines: «*M*óря сердúтого шýм – / *B*ýря на *m*óре и *d*ýмы». The fluidity of the border between the human and the natural is reflected in the word choice – not simply in terms of meaning but, equally important, in terms of the specific sounds that compose these words.

If, in line 2, «Мóря сердúтого шýм» was primarily a nature description with only a hint of personification, the final line (identical except for the punctuation) is a statement completely imbued with human presence. How can the same words have a such a different meaning? In between the second and final lines, the process of personification becomes increasingly pronounced. Already in line 4, the human element is dominant. In «Мно́го му́чи́тельных ду́м» ("Many tortuous thoughts"), nature has disappeared entirely. Still, one might suggest that this line should be understood figuratively, as an internalization of the impending storm. The ambiguity here cannot be resolved. Indeed, it is essential to the poem's ultimate meaning, which is based on constant intersections – through sound, syntax, and meaning – of the spheres of the human and the natural. By the end, it is unclear whether the troubled thoughts are a reflection of the stormy seascape or whether the entire seascape is merely a metaphor for the poet's troubled thoughts. In other words, tenor and vehicle have become inseparable to the point where we can no longer say for certain which is which.

Fet's poem, then, contains considerably more development than is initially evident. More overtly than visual art – and more *dynamically*, because it unfolds in time – his "verbal painting" accentuates the degree to which a depiction of the natural world is ultimately a landscape of the mind. Observation inspires meditation, making the observer a part of the observed. Fet's "simple" poem about nature turns out to be a statement about human consciousness and its relationship to the external world.

Fet's poem contains not a single pronoun, yet it invokes the authorial self through personification. A more radical version of this same technique can be found in Mikhail Lermontov's «Па́рус» ("The Sail"). The poem focuses not on nature *per se*, but on an inanimate, man-made object within a natural scene.

> Бе́леет па́рус одино́кий
> В тума́не мо́ря голубо́м!. .
> Что и́щет он в стране́ далёкой?
> Что ки́нул он в краю́ родно́м?. .
>
> Игра́ют во́лны – ве́тер сви́щет,
> И ма́чта гнётся и скрипи́т . . .
> Увы́! он сча́стия не и́щет
> И не от сча́стия бежи́т.
>
> Под ни́м струя́ светле́й лазу́ри,
> Над ни́м луч со́лнца золото́й . . .
> А о́н, мяте́жный, и́щет бу́ри,
> Как бу́дто в бу́рях есть поко́й!

(A sail shows white / In the sea's light-blue mist! / What does it seek in a distant country? / What has it abandoned in its native land? // The waves play – the wind whistles, / And the mast bends and creaks . . . / Alas! it does not seek happiness / And does not flee happiness. // Beneath it is a stream brighter than azure, / Above it is a golden ray of sun . . . / But it, the rebellious one, seeks a storm, / As if in storms there were peace!)

«Па́рус» consists of three quatrains of iambic tetrameter with alternating feminine and masculine rhymes. This is the most common stanzaic form in the history of Russian poetry, and Lermontov makes no striking departures from tradition in his realization of it. The poem has no enjambment, no explicit metaphors, and both vocabulary and syntax are strikingly simple (so simple, in fact, that this poem is often assigned to first-year students of the Russian language). However, beneath this uncomplicated surface lies a subtle degree of patterning.

Each stanza is structured in precisely the same fashion. The first two lines are descriptive and conclude with an ellipsis, while the second two lines might be called "interpretive," in that they comment on the first two. The first stanza ends with a question, the second with a statement (perhaps an answer to that prior question), and the final stanza with an exclamation. This structure reflects a gradual increase of emotional involvement on the part of the observer.

In each stanza, the descriptive half leads somewhat unexpectedly to the interpretive half. The first stanza initially establishes the existence of a lone sail shrouded in the fog of the sea. Yet the questions that immediately follow suggest much more: that it is "seeking" something far away and "abandoning" something in its homeland. One can surmise that the sail is moving away from the observer, but the oppositions used in these grammatically parallel lines (iskat'/kinut' [to search/to abandon], dalekaia strana/krai rodnoi [distant country/native land]) suggest a level of animacy that one ordinarily does not grant to a sail.

The second stanza is still more puzzling. Because the first focused on a sail (rather than on the entire ship), it gave the impression that the ship was being viewed from a considerable distance. However, the observer in the second stanza is close enough to hear the mast as it creaks in the wind. And where did this violent wind come from? The first stanza had given the setting as «в тума́не мо́ря голубо́м» ("in the sea's light-blue mist"), not a particularly threatening image. In short, not only has the observer's position shifted; the weather itself appears to have changed. The second half of the stanza again departs radically from the descriptive tone of the first. Now questions are replaced by answers. The sail, we learn, neither seeks nor flees happiness. What might have been surmised based on lines three and four now becomes obvious beyond a doubt. The sail is a symbol. It is not simply a synecdoche, where the sail stands for the entire ship, but a metaphor, i.e., it represents something else entirely. The ubiquity of the masculine singular pronoun «он» ("it," but literally: "he"), which replaces the noun «па́рус» ("sail") after line one, suggests that we are not really discussing a sail or even a boat, but a man. And the exclamation «Увы́!» ("Alas!") implies that this is not just any man, but a projection of the observer himself.

If one could reconcile the settings of the first two stanzas by arguing for a shift in perspective, the third stanza challenges even this approach. It defies ordinary logic that a «луч со́лнца золото́й» ("golden ray of sunlight") and a «струя́ светле́й лазу́ри» ("stream brighter than azure") can coexist with the misty, even stormy weather of the first two stanzas. Yet the beautiful weather appears not to influence the interpretive half of the stanza. The sail, now modified by the striking epithet «мяте́жний» ("rebellious"), *seeks* storms. The poem's numerous hidden paradoxes culminate in the explicit paradox of the alliterative final lines: «и́щет *бу́ри*, / Как *бу́дто* в *бу́рях* есть поко́й!» ("seeks a storm, / As if in storms there were peace!").

Looking back on the poem as a whole, certain essential features emerge that were scarcely noticeable on first reading. The only pronoun in this poem is the third-person singular, yet every moment is controlled by the observations and commentary of an implicit "I." This invisible but highly emotional speaker completely manipulates our view (both literal and figurative) of the sail, to the extent that each stanza appears to depict an entirely different scene. To paint Fet's seascape would be a relatively simple task. If one wished to reproduce Lermontov's poem in pictorial form, it would probably be necessary to produce three different works. A quintessentially Romantic poet, Lermontov dominates his surroundings. Fet's poem, in constrast, showed a certain balance between observer and observed; indeed, the boundary could not be fixed precisely. In «Па́рус», there is no attempt to picture nature "as it is" – rather, nature reflects the poet's consciousness. What superficially resembles a seascape (the portrait of a single sail on the water) is actually a psychological projection of the poet's inner struggle.

Russian Romanticism was a diverse movement. While Lermontov's poetic persona reflected the Byronic ideal, Fedor Tiutchev was much closer to the German Romantics. Tiutchev spent years in Munich and was fully aware of the developments of *Naturphilosophie*, a highly abstract area of philosophy that used man's relationship to nature as a way to investigate the subject/object problem. Tiutchev raises similar questions in his verse, though without the formal rigor of a philosophical system. Indeed, the search for such systematization (and the consistency it implies) may be the most fundamental difference between the philosopher and the poet. Tiutchev's «Есть в о́сени первонача́льной» ("There is in earliest autumn") serves as a good example of his approach:

Есть в о́сени первонача́льной
Коро́ткая, но ди́вная пора́ –
Весь де́нь стои́т как бы хруста́льный,
И лучеза́рны вечера́ . . .

Где бо́дрый се́рп гуля́л и па́дал ко́лос,
Тепе́рь уж пу́сто всё – просто́р везде́, –
Лишь паути́ны то́нкий во́лос
Блести́т на пра́здной борозде́.

Пусте́ет во́здух, пти́ц не слы́шно бо́ле,
Но далеко́ ещё до пе́рвых зи́мних бу́рь –
И льётся чи́стая и тёплая лазу́рь
На отдыха́ющее по́ле . . .

(There is in earliest autumn / A short, but wondrous time, – / The entire day is as if crystalline / And the evenings are radiant . . . // Where the cheerful scythe wandered and the grain fell, / Now everything is empty – everywhere there is space, – / Only the slender strand of a spider web / Glistens on the empty furrow. // The air becomes empty, birds are heard no more, / But the first winter storms are still distant – / And the pure and warm azure air streams / Onto the resting field . . .)

This poem is written in free iambs, that is to say, in iambic lines of varying and unpredictable lengths. Such a meter is not unusual in lyric meditations of this period, and it would be unwise to seek a precise "meaning" in each line length. That is to say, it is unlikely that the pentameter lines are semantically consistent or, for that matter, opposed to the tetrameters. Like other poets of the time, Tiutchev probably chose this relatively free metrical scheme as a formal equivalent to his wandering train of thought.

Tiutchev's nature poems are philosophical in spirit rather than in careful argument or syllogism. The tone is set by the first word. Experienced readers of Russian poetry expect that a poem beginning with the word «Есть» ("there is") will be meditative. Whenever this word begins a line of verse – and the malleability of Russian syntax easily allows such constructions – it draws attention to itself (though it does not receive metrical stress in iambic lines such as these).

Tiutchev focuses on a brief period in early autumn. The harvest is already over (line 5), the birds have migrated (line 9), but the first winter snowstorms are still distant (line 10). Throughout, this «ди́вная пора́» ("wondrous time") is characterized by fragility, silence, motionlessness, and absence (note how the adjective "pusto" in line 6 anticipates the verb "pusteet" in line 9). A person is mentioned only in the fifth line, and even here indirectly. The synecdoche ("serp" ["scythe"]) and personification ("bodryi" ["cheerful"]) call to mind the presence of the harvester, while the two past tense verbs (all other verbs are in the present tense) relegate his activities to a prior time, suggesting his irrelevance to the autumnal scene. It is worth noting how Tiutchev emphasizes these verbs still more through syntax, using a chiasmic construction to place them next to each other («се́рп *гуля́л* и *па́дал* ко́лос»).

This contrasts sharply with the remainder of the poem, where verbs are less frequent, always in present tense, and depict stasis rather than action (the final verb "l'etsia" ["streams"] being a significant exception in this regard).

The poem concludes with the image of a "resting" field. The Russian word "otdykhaiushchee," etymologically linked to the word for breath, suggests life, but in this poem life is equated with nature, not man. In the final lines, the "lazur'" ("azure air") streams downward, creating a mysterious communion between above and below, the heavens and the earth. It is as if the earth itself is experiencing what in religious thought is called *kenosis*, the emptying out of the human so that it can become a receptacle for the divine. The poem does not so much conclude as trail off, with ellipses lending a sense of perpetuity to this fleeting moment.

Insofar as the poet is a representative of mankind, he celebrates in this poem his own absence. As in the examples by Fet and Lermontov, there is no authorial "I." However, whereas in those other poems the "I" was implicit through frequent personification, here Tiutchev reduces the human presence in every way possible. One inevitably senses the poet's presence in the exquisite imagery, but the urgency and turmoil that so marks the observer in the earlier poems is absent. Indeed, this harmonious picture comes into being only because mankind has been removed from it. More precisely, man becomes maximally an observer and minimally a participant. This seemingly unmediated vision of nature is, of course, a very particular view, a Romantic's dream of an "organic," peaceful, and self-contained world independent of the observing subject. Such a state cannot exist for long – hence the fragility of so much of the imagery and the emphasis on the brevity of this privileged moment.

Tiutchev was a poet of paradox. While contemporary philosophers aspired to a precise and systematic understanding of nature, he allowed for a multitude of mutually contradictory perspectives. The omniscient yet maximally distanced observer of «Есть в óсени первоначáльной» is countered by a participatory, even anguished poet in another of his poems, «О чём ты вóешь»:

О чём ты вóешь, вéтр ночнóй?
О чём так сéтуешь безýмно? . .
Что знáчит стрáнный гóлос твóй,
То глýхо жáлобный, то шýмно?
Понятным сéрдцу языкóм
Твердúшь о непонятной мýке –
И рóешь и взрывáешь в нём
Порóй нейстовые звýки! . .

О, стра́шных пе́сен сих не по́й
Про дре́вний ха́ос, про роди́мый!
Как жа́дно ми́р души́ ночно́й
Внима́ет по́вести люби́мой!
Из сме́ртной рвётся он груди́,
Он с беспреде́льным жа́ждет сли́ться! . .
О, бу́рь засну́вших не буди́ –
Под ни́ми ха́ос шевели́тся! . .

(What do you howl about, night wind? / What do you lament so wildly? . . / What does your strange voice mean, / Now mutely, now noisily complaining? / In a language comprehensible to the heart / You reiterate incomprehensible torment – / And you burrow and arouse in the heart / Sounds that are at times furious! . . // O, do not sing these terrible songs / About ancient, native chaos! / How greedily the world of the night soul / Drinks in its favorite tale! / It tears itself from the mortal breast, / It strives to fuse with the infinite! . . / O, do not rouse storms that have fallen asleep – / Beneath them chaos stirs! . .)

In this poem, the punctuation alone indicates the high degree of emotional engagement. In «Есть в о́сени первонача́льной» each stanza was composed of a single sentence, culminating once in a period and twice in ellipses. Such punctuation aptly reflected the meditative quality of that poem. In contrast, «О чём ты во́ешь» relies on question marks and exclamation points that come at much briefer intervals. The tone is urgent and the poetic voice deeply implicated.

The flurry of opening interrogatives creates an immediate sense of uncertainty. However, within that uncertainty, important assumptions are revealed. For example, in the first line, the poet addresses the wind, thereby suggesting that it is an entity with a consciousness and even positing the possibility of genuine communication with it. In «Есть в о́сени первонача́льной» a detached effect was created through avoidance of all pronouns. This poem begins with an explicit "you" addressed by an implicit "I," thus setting the stage for a confrontation between these two forces.

The second question qualifies and develops the first. The wind is not simply howling, but lamenting, i.e., it expresses sorrow, a human emotion. The word "bezumno," meaning "madly" or "wildly," may have an additional sense in this context. Literally, of course, it means "without a mind," and Tiutchev perhaps wishes to underscore the fact that he is concerned here with a different type of consciousness – "mindless" nature versus the rationality of man. In any case, the third question goes so far as to lend a "strannyi golos" ("strange voice") to the wind, thus completing the personification of the first line. Now, however, there is an assumption that the wind indeed *has* a meaning. The final four lines of the stanza already begin to answer the questions posed. Through close proximity of the opposed adjectives "poniatnym" and "neponiatnoi," Tiutchev emphasizes a fundamental paradox. In these lines, nature speaks directly to the heart (i.e., not to the mind), which can comprehend it but not the torment it describes. The final two lines of the stanza mark a sudden and important shift. The object (wind) leaves its mark on the subject (poet), tearing from his heart "neistovye zvuki" ("furious sounds"). Now the emotional qualities of the opening lines become clear: the poet does not simply address the wind as a distanced "other," but as something intimately linked to himself.

In the second stanza, this link is explored and explained, not in a discursive manner but in a series of exclamations. The earlier sound imagery – through which a howl became in turn a lament, a voice, and a language – reaches its final point as a song with a specific narrative component [*povest'*]. This narrative is nothing less than a cosmology, according to which man yearns to return to his origins in primordial chaos. The human element, represented by the "mir dushi nochnoi" ("world of the night soul"), recognizes its kinship with this "bespredel'noe" ("endlessness" or, literally, "boundlessness") and seeks to merge with it by breaking forth from its mortal confines.

However, the pathos of this second stanza lies in the two negated imperatives ("ne poi"/"ne budi"), both emphatically placed in rhyming position. The poet in no way denies the powerful bond between man and nature, finite and infinite, microcosm and macrocosm. Yet he urgently warns against this attraction, presumably because any unification would entail the death of the individual consciousness. The poem posits the annulment of the subject/object relationship, but at the cost of the subject's very existence. The peaceful, if momentary, resolution of «Есть в осени первоначáльной» is replaced by a vision of triumphant chaos, alluring, yet terrifying in its permanence. In retrospect, the almost frantic opening questions posed to the wind can be understood as masking the poet's true concerns: human impermanence, the imminence of chaos, and the longing for death. The distance between nature poetry and landscape painting could hardly be more pronounced than in this poem. There is virtually nothing visual here at all; the development comes about through a series of images, drawing on (and eventually leaving behind) the howling of the night wind.

The previous four poems concerned man's relationship to nature, but each used a different setting to come to its own distinct conclusions. The following two poems – one from the nineteenth century and one from the twentieth – treat a common theme. The first is by Tiutchev, the second by Boris Pasternak, arguably Russia's greatest nature poet of the twentieth century. Pasternak's verse is highly individualistic and idiosyncratic, yet he consciously draws on the work of his predecessors, often borrowing specific words and images. (Curious readers may wish to compare his «Стéпь» ["The Steppe"] with two Fet poems written half a century earlier:

«Стéпь вéчером» ["The Steppe in the Evening"] and «На стóге сéна нóчью ю́жной» ["On a hayrick on a southern night"].) However, in the poems below, there are no obvious links between the texts beyond the theme of a thunderstorm. Just as one can learn a great deal about the specific interests of landscape painters by comparing how differently they portray the same object, so poetic distinctiveness stands out most clearly in apposition.

Весéнняя грозá

Люблю́ грозу́ в начáле мáя,
Когдá весéнний, пéрвый грóм,
Как бы резвя́ся и игрáя,
Грохóчет в нéбе голубóм.

Гремя́т раскáты молоды́е,
Вот дóждик бры́знул, пы́ль летúт,
Повúсли пéрлы дождевы́е,
И сóлнце нúти золотúт.

С горы́ бежúт потóк провóрный,
В лесу́ не мóлкнет птúчий гáм,
И гáм леснóй и шýм нагóрный –
Всё втóрит вéсело громáм.

Ты скáжешь: вéтреная Гéба,
Кормя́ Зевéсова орлá,
Громокипя́щий кýбок с нéба,
Смея́сь, на зéмлю пролилá.

(Spring Thunderstorm: I love a storm in the beginning of May, / When the first thunder of spring, / As if frisking about and playing, / Crashes in the blue sky. // The young peals of thunder resound, / Now a shower has gushed forth, the dust flies, / Pearls of rain hang [in the air], / And the sun turns their threads golden. // From the mountain rushes a swift flood, / In the woods the birds' din does not fall silent, / And the din of the woods and the noise from the mountain / All the while merrily echo the thunderclaps. // You'll say: Frivolous Hebe, / Feeding the eagle of Zeus, / Laughing, poured a thunder-seething goblet / From heaven onto the earth.)

In Tiutchev's poem, the poet's presence and attitude toward his subject matter are established immediately, in the very first word: "liubliu" ("I love"). This is not a love poem, of course, but a loving depiction of nature. In certain contexts, storms are associated with the sublime, a feeling of fear and awe in the presence of natural phenomena. Tiutchev's speaker, however, reveals a much more light-hearted relationship to nature. His word choice suggests that this is a scene of playful exuberance: "rezviasia i igraia" ("frisking about and playing") are verbs ordinarily used to describe children, an association supported by the personification *"molodye* raskaty" ("*young* peals of thunder"). The first three stanzas are essentially descriptive and attend especially to the sounds of the storm. Tiutchev does this both by using numerous words that connote sound (e.g., "raskaty" ["peals"], "gam" ["din"], "shum" ["noise"]) and, more subtly, through emphatic alliteration: *g*rom, i*g*raia, *g*rokhochet, *g*remiat. (In this context, even "i*g*raia" obtains a "noisy" quality – a classic case of phonetic "guilt through association.") One is struck throughout by the sense of movement, achieved partially by an overwhelming number of active verbs (five in the second stanza alone), partially through the constant shift in attention from one object to the next.

The poem is written in quatrains of iambic tetrameter with alternating rhymes, the most common form in Russian poetry. Each stanza corresponds to a single thought, and is marked as such by the punctuation. In terms of overall structure, the final stanza stands out for several reasons. To begin with, it suddenly includes another human observer. "Ty skazhesh'" ("You will say") represents a wholly unexpected direction, introducing, as it were, a new interpretation of the same scene. This unidentified second eyewitness has no less playful a perception, but expresses it through recourse to myth. Hebe, cupbearer to the gods according to the ancient Greeks, is pictured impishly emptying her wares onto the earth. To set off the final stanza from the first three, Tiutchev draws on a more archaic lexicon. Not only does he introduce two mythological figures, but the goddess bears a "kubok" ("goblet") which is itself described with the neologism "gromokipiashchii" ("thunder-seething"), a compound epithet that imitates Greek word formation.

Experienced readers of Russian nature poetry may know that the phrase "Ty skazhesh'" is used elsewhere to introduce a supernatural reading of nature that develops the more realistic perspective of the speaker (e.g., Tiutchev's own «Проблеск» ["The Flash"] or Khodasevich's «Гляжу на грубые ремёсла» ["I look at coarse trades"]). But even without this context, one can recognize that this allusion to antiquity lends a new dimension to the scene depicted in the first stanzas. Looking back, one might even say that it draws on the consciously unrealistic (personified) elements of those predominantly pictorial verses. As a whole, the poem presents two different yet complementary visions of a thunderstorm, both celebratory: one describes the storm as it unfolds, the other anchors these impressions in the world of ancient myth. Myth itself arose when primitive man attempted to explain the world around him, and many of Tiutchev's poems show him to be a conscious inheritor of this pre-literary impulse.

These "mythopoetic" qualities are worth bearing in mind as we turn our attention to Pasternak's poem:

Гроза́ момента́льная наве́к

А зате́м проща́лось ле́то
С полуста́нком. Сня́вши ша́пку,
Сто́ слепя́щих фотогра́фий
Но́чью снял на па́мять гро́м.

Ме́ркла ки́сть сире́ни. В э́то
Вре́мя о́н, нарва́в оха́пку
Мо́лний, с по́ля и́ми тра́фил
Озари́ть упра́вский до́м.

И когда́ по кро́вле зда́нья
Разлила́сь волна́ злора́дства
И, как у́голь по рису́нку,
Гря́нул ли́вень всем плетнём,

Ста́л мига́ть обва́л созна́нья:
Вот, каза́лось, озаря́тся
Да́же те углы́ рассу́дка,
Где тепе́рь светло́, как днём!

(A Storm Forever Momentary: And then summer said farewell / To the small railway station. Taking off its cap / Thunder took as a souvenir / One hundred blinding photographs at night. // A branch of lilac gradually darkened. At this / Time it [the thunder] having plucked an armful / Of lightning bolts, aimed to please, using them from the field / To illuminate the manager's house. // And when along the roof of the building / A wave of *Schadenfreude* poured out / And, like charcoal along a drawing, / The shower crashed along the whole wattle fence, // The avalanche of consciousness began to blink: / There, it seemed, will become illuminated / Even those corners of reason, / Where it is now light as day!)

Had Pasternak simply called this poem «Гроза́» ("A Thunderstorm"), he could have created a pictorial impression worthy of a painting. Instead, he chose to modify the visual element with the oxymoron «момента́льная наве́к». This disorients the reader by prompting the question: how can a storm simultaneously be "momentary" and "forever"? His title is the first of many surprises, for the poem as a whole challenges our fundamental assumptions about reality.

In formal terms, Pasternak's poem has a number of unusual elements. While there is nothing particularly startling about trochaic tetrameter, Pasternak's distinctive treatment of the quatrain as such forces us to reassess its function. Ordinarily, stanzas are self-contained units, but Pasternak undermines this convention through his rhyme scheme: A–B–C–d–A–B–C–d. This renders the individual stanza incomplete, since each rhyme straddles the stanzaic boundary (four lines removed). Pasternak emphasizes this still more by using a comma instead of the expected period at the end of the third quatrain, which postpones the logical conclusion from its usual place at the stanza's conclusion to the end of the first line of the subsequent stanza. Had the poem been written as two eight-line stanzas (and some of the drafts suggest that it was originally conceived as such), this effect would have been greatly minimized. But the fact that Pasternak opted for the quatrain configuration indicates that he actively sought to create a jarring effect, in this case a disjunction between visual presentation (four well-defined quatrains) and the actual poetic development. These verses, as it were, break out of their formal constraints. Even within the stanzas, Pasternak runs roughshod over another traditional boundary, using enjambment to erase the unit of the line (e.g., lines 5–6: «В э́то / Вре́мя», an outrageous pause from the point of view of syntax and logic).

Pasternak's poem begins with the words "A zatem" ("And then"). Such an opening belongs more to the sphere of narrative than to lyric poetry. In any case, it is odd, since readers find themselves entering into a story midway through it, with the expectation that they will somehow know what has happened before. This is, of course, not the case (even for those who know the entire book of poetry where this poem appears); such narrative sleight-of-hand is simply one of Pasternak's myriad devices for throwing the reader off guard.

In much of the nature poetry we have examined, there is a strong tendency toward personification. Since nature is akin to man and unimaginable without man, it stands to reason that poets endow it with human qualities. Pasternak, however, brings personification to a new level altogether, making it ubiquitous and always surprising. The first stanza alone contains three examples. The end of summer is portrayed in terms of summer parting with a rural train station, with the thunder doffing its hat and taking photographs. The image «стó слепя́щих фотогра́фий» ("a hundred blinding photographs") makes clear that the actual scene being described is a sudden burst of lightning, which is likened to the flash of a camera. Pasternak even includes a pun, relying within the same sentence on two different meanings of a single verb: "sniat'" as "to take off (a hat)" as well as "to take (a picture)." Such playfulness is characteristic of the entire poem, which – as we shall see – offers an almost childish perception of nature.

Pasternak's subject matter, in a word, could hardly be more traditional, but his verbal representation is peculiar. The second stanza continues the personification of thunder, portrayed no longer as a photographer, but as a gardener of sorts. The phrase «нарва́в оха́пку / Мо́лний» requires some commentary. «Нарва́ть цветы́» is the standard Russian expression for "to pick flowers," but Pasternak changes it in two important ways. First, he introduces the word "okhapka," which would be more appropriate for bundles of hay than for flowers. Still, the combination "narvat' okhapku" makes sense as a hyperbole: "to pick by the armful." The line – but not the syntactic construction! – concludes at this point, thus augmenting the surprise when the noun "lightning bolts" appears (in lieu of the long anticipated "flowers"). If the lightning in the first stanza was meant to produce a souvenir photograph, in the second stanza it serves as a surrogate for electricity, illuminating the administrative building next to the train station. This is also a bit of a joke; "trafit'" is a rather colloquial verb, which makes the accompanying (higher style) verb "ozarit'" ironic. After all, it is hard to imagine that anyone in that administrative building would appreciate the abundance of lightning bolts directed at it.

This idea of human discomfort is developed in the third stanza, where lightning yields to rain. Pasternak eschews direct naming, preferring to use the metaphor «волнá злорáдства» ("a wave of *Schadenfreude*" [English has no word that renders the key concept here: pleasure in someone else's misfortune]). In other words, nature (the rain) crashes down on man (present as a synecdoche in the roof of the building where he resides) and takes pleasure in the suffering it causes. Curiously, a similar phenomenon (the downpour against the wattle fence) is then compared to «ýголь по рисýнку» ("charcoal along a drawing"). A few explanations of this simile are possible. To begin with the most literal, the image of darkness (the blackness of charcoal) may be meant to describe the type of heavy rain that renders everything black. (Throughout the poem Pasternak has contrasted darkness with moments of sudden illumination.) Yet it also calls to mind an aesthetic issue. The storm is depicted as a visual artist, just as it was earlier likened to a photographer. Sketching in charcoal is characterized by swift strokes; Pasternak seems to want us to perceive the rapid downpour as a linear phenomenon (much as Tiutchev did in his image of the raindrops as *strings of pearls*).

As the words "soznan'e" (consciousness) and "rassudok" (reason) indicate, the final stanza moves the external storm to an internal location. The thunderstorm leads to destruction ("obval" ordinarily means "avalanche" or more generally a physical collapse), yet here it is the destruction of everyday consciousness ("obval soznan'ia"). If the poem began with emphatic personification of the observed, it concludes with the observer, presumably the speaker himself, but perhaps humanity in general. Many of the words in this stanza are chosen to recall and develop the lexicon of the earlier stanzas. "Ozarit'" in stanza two meant "to illuminate" in the literal sense, but here the figurative sense is invoked. The essential play of darkness and light continues, but now within the mind. (The final word, "day" in the instrumental case, recalls "night" in the instrumental case in line 4.) In another pun, the word "ugol'" ("charcoal") of the third stanza recurs as its unpalatalized counterpart "ugol" ("corner"). The most striking change, however, is in verb tense. After a sequence of past tense verbs, Pasternak shifts to future tense in the final lines, in which he anticipates a complete spiritual cleansing that will "enlighten" not only the dark areas of consciousness, but «Даже те углы́ рассу́дка, / Где тепе́рь светло́, как днём» ("Even those corners of reason, / Where it is now light as day"). In other words, the storm will bring about a complete reevaluation of the world as we know it.

With this in mind, we return to the title. Pasternak's poem focuses on a single moment (or, perhaps, a few moments) which lead to permanent liberation, to a completely new way of experiencing reality. His poem has taken a momentary phenomenon and rendered it permanent. This is, of course, a function commonly attributed to art, and it is no coincidence that Pasternak refers in his imagery to photography and drawing. In this epiphanic moment, man leaves his everyday consciousness behind and experiences nature as a spontaneous, fully animated force. This is not to say, of course, that Pasternak truly believed that thunder doffs its hat and takes pictures. But just as Tiutchev ultimately animated his thunderstorm to the point that it became part of ancient myth, so Pasternak creates a new myth, granting a face and personality to the natural world. His poem owes its extraordinary vitality to the verbal presentation, which defies expectations on virtually every level – phonetic, syntactic, and semantic. Such constant play with conventions makes Pasternak a difficult poet, but the difficulty is very much part of the message. The sudden shifts in focus reflect the imagination itself, as it leaves the realm of the everyday and is rejuvenated through a sense of wonder. Pasternak's poem concludes on the verge of a spiritual breakthrough. It is as if we wait – permanently, but with full confidence – for that imminent illumination.

Pasternak's poetic voice is highly individual, yet his poem fits squarely within the genre of nature poetry as established by the nineteenth-century poets we have examined. Like his predecessors, Pasternak moves back and forth between an object in nature and the observing subject. Perhaps even more transparently, Pasternak recognizes that any depiction of nature involves an act of interpretation, be it aesthetic or overtly philosophical. His poem is essentially a celebration of this act, as the spontaneity and power of a thunderstorm call forth mental fireworks within the consciousness of the observer.

If love poetry is predicated on psychological plausibility, on creating a bond between speaker and reader, nature poetry functions differently. Even after reading their poems, few of us would experience a thunderstorm as playfully as Tiutchev or Pasternak. Nor would we view a solitary boat with the urgency and uneasiness of Lermontov. However, the general tendency to see the world beyond us as mysteriously related to ourselves is universal. It is precisely this element that so fascinates in nature poetry and, it would seem, in landscape painting as well. Van Gogh's "Starry Night" tells us a lot less about the evening sky than it does about Van Gogh. Yet we are attracted to his depiction notwithstanding its strangeness. We delight in the contact with an imagination that forces us to see something that we ordinarily do not. Likewise, the aesthetic pleasure in nature poetry lies less in the specific subject matter than in its presentation. In the subtle interplay of the observer with the observed we sense a familiar but infinitely variable phenomenon. In this sense, the poem about nature tells us a great deal about the nature of poetry.

Chapter 8

Patriotic verse

Ру́сь моя́! Жена́ моя́! До бо́ли
Нам я́сен до́лгий пу́ть!

Блок, «На по́ле Кулико́вом»

My Russia! My wife!
The long path is painfully clear to us!

Blok, "On the Kulikovo Field"

Virtually all national literatures have poems on patriotic themes, but the Russian tradition is particularly extensive. To some extent this can be attributed to the influence of patronage systems that have so frequently put the Russian poet in the position of supplicant. However, despotic autocrats and their illegitimate communist progeny by no means account for the full range of this phenomenon. For reasons both cultural and philosophical, Russian poets have often proudly viewed their language as inextricably linked to their country, using artistic achievement to compensate for – or even overcome – the backwardness of the society as a whole. Patriotic verse, then, does not always entail flattery of a monarch and the ruling interests; it can also present with unfeigned praise natural beauty, the common man, the national spirit. Many great Russian poets have contributed to this genre, making it significant politically, sociologically, and artistically.

Vasily Trediakovsky, one of the creators of Russian secular poetry, spent the years 1727–1730 studying in Paris. All evidence suggests that he enjoyed himself immensely, but, as his «Стихи́ похва́льные Росси́и» ("Verses in Praise of Russia") indicate, the pleasures of the French capital did not diminish his patriotic zeal.

Начну́ на фле́йте стихи́ печа́льны,
Зря на Росси́ю чрез стра́ны да́льны:
Ибо все днесь мне её добро́ты
Мы́слить умо́м есть мно́го охо́ты.

Росси́я ма́ти! свет мой безме́рный!
Позво́ль то, ча́до прошу́ твой ве́рный,
Ах, как сиди́шь ты на тро́не кра́сно!
Небо росси́йску ты со́лнце я́сно!

Чем ты́, Росси́я, не изоби́льна?
Где ты́, Росси́я, не была́ си́льна?
Сокро́вище всех до́бр ты еди́на,
Всегда́ бога́та, сла́ве причи́на.

Коль в тебе́ звёзды все здра́вьем бле́щут!
И россия́не коль гро́мко пле́щут:
Вива́т Росси́я! вива́т драга́я!
Вива́т наде́жда! вива́т блага́я.

Скончу́ на фле́йте стихи́ печа́льны,
Зря на Росси́ю чрез стра́ны да́льны:
Сто́ мне язы́ков на́добно б бы́ло
Просла́вить всё то, что в тебе́ ми́ло!

(I will begin my sad verses on my flute / Looking at Russia across distant countries: / For there is much desire to think with my mind / Today about all its virtues. // Oh, mother Russia! my infinite light! / Allow this, I ask, your loyal child, / Oh, how you sit beautifully on the throne! / For to a Russian you are the bright sun! [. . .] // In what, O Russia, are you not bountiful? / Where, O Russia, were you not powerful? / You alone are the source of all virtues, / Always rich, the cause of glory. // How in you all stars shine with well-being! / And how the Russians loudly applaud: / Long live Russia! Long live the dear one! / Long live hope! Long live the good one. // I will finish my sad verses on my flute / Looking at Russia across distant countries: / I would need one hundred tongues / To glorify everything that is dear in you!)

These stanzas – the first two and final three of a nine-stanza work – suffice to give a sense of the whole. Written in syllabic lines of 10 syllables (with caesura after the fifth, exclusively feminine rhymes and almost exclusively feminine cadences before the caesura), the poet uses exclamations, rhetorical questions, apostrophe, personification, metaphor, and emphatic parallelisms to heap praise on his distant homeland. The verses are "sad," presumably because they were composed at so great a distance (cf. the thematically significant repeated rhyme "pechal'ny/dal'ny"). But everything else about the poem is positively jubilant. "Mother Russia" (this appellation, cemented by grammatical gender, was already hackneyed in Trediakovsky's day) is associated with beauty, abundance, power, kindness, glory, vigor, etc. Her virtues cannot be fully enumerated; hence the poet signs off with a version of the modesty topos: he would need one hundred tongues to praise his subject sufficiently.

Upon reflection, what is most striking in this panegyric is the conventionality of description. Nothing in it is distinctly Russian; with the possible exception of "Mother Russia," every epithet could be attributed to any other country. It is noteworthy that at approximately this time, Trediakovsky also composed «Стихи́ похва́льные Пари́жу» ("Verses in Praise of Paris"), a work no less enthusiastic and without a hint of the homesickness of its "partner" poem. Today we would probably attribute this inconsistency to hypocrisy, but such criticism misses the point. Most likely, Trediakovsky conceived of these works primarily as genre exercises. That is to say: he was not necessarily voicing his own convictions, but only the sentiments appropriate for a *laus patriae* (the Latin term, meaning "praise of the fatherland," makes clear that the genre predates the modern period).

Certainly this was the case in Trediakovsky's «Торже́ственная о́да о сда́че го́рода Гда́нска» ("Solemn Ode on the Surrender of the City of Danzig") of 1734. This poem, which – together with Lomonosov's "Khotin Ode" of 1739 (see Chapter Four) – established conventions of the Russian ode, begins not with an account of the battle (which only enters in the fourth stanza), but with the praise of the monarch.

> Кое тре́звое мне́ пиа́нство
> Сло́во даёт к сла́вной причи́не?
> Чи́стое Парна́са убра́нство,
> Му́зы! не ва́с ли ви́жу ны́не?
> И зво́н ваших стру́н сладкогла́сных,
> И си́лу ли́ков слы́шу кра́сных;
> Всё чи́нит во мне ре́чь избра́нну.
> Наро́ды! ра́достно внемли́те;
> Бурли́вые ве́тры! молчи́те:
> Хра́бру прославля́ть хощу́ А́нну.

(What sober inebriation / Gives me word for a glorious cause? / Pure adornment of Parnassus, / Muses! Is it not you whom I see now? / I hear both the sound of your sweet-voiced strings, / And the power of your beautiful choruses; / Everything causes me to make a special speech. / O peoples! Listen joyously; / O wild winds, be silent! / I wish to praise courageous Anna.)

Before turning to the Russians' military feat, Trediakovsky addresses the muses (the classical source of inspiration) and his sovereign Anna, who embodies the heroism of all Russia. Any temptation to read these lines as a reflection of Trediakovsky's imperialistic beliefs is undone by literary history. The poem's politics – as well as its structure and imagery – are borrowed wholesale from Boileau's "Ode on the Taking of Namur," written approximately four decades earlier. Indeed, entire stanzas (such as this one) are essentially translated from the French, with the name Louis crossed out and Anna put in its place. Interestingly, the most original feature of this stanza is the epithet "trezvoe pianstvo" ("sober inebriation"), an oxymoron that presumably connotes inspiration and thus adds considerable power to Boileau's "docte et sainte yvresse" ("learned and holy inebriation"). The Russian poet felt free to alter precise details of poetic language, but the larger rhetorical strategies, structure, and themes formed an inviolable template.

Trediakovsky's ode is written in syllabic verse, with nine syllables per line and exclusively feminine rhymes. (Even the rhyme scheme is that of Boileau, though without the alternation of masculine and feminine rhymes of the French model.) About two decades later, Trediakovsky rewrote the poem in the new syllabo-tonic system (trochaic tetrameter), yet he preserved the content with remarkable fidelity – even though Anna was no longer alive. It is safe to say, then, that Trediakovsky was far more interested in the formal execution of the ode (and the patriotic genre in general) than in the political opinions it expressed. In keeping with his epoch, he viewed these sentiments as a given. The task of the individual poet was not to vary the ideas, but to find the appropriate formal means to express them.

Of course, patriotic verse was particularly well-suited to the realities of Russian eighteenth-century society. When Trediakovsky returned to Russia from France, he became a court poet and the first Russian ever to be named a professor at the Academy of Sciences (his colleagues were mainly Germans). These positions forced him to hone his skills in the panegyric genres. In subsequent years, his poetic authority was challenged by Lomonosov and others, but none of these rivals ever questioned the basic themes of ode writing. Rather, they found fault with Trediakovsky's system of versification, with his specific imagery and lexicon.

Only at the very end of the eighteenth century did the content of patriotic verse change. Radishchev genuinely admired Trediakovsky and Lomonosov for their genius and technical prowess, but he was dissatisfied with the elements of the ode that his predecessors had considered inviolable. In «Вольность» ("Liberty"), Radishchev replaced the image of the faultless sovereign with that of the tyrant. The following stanza is the twelfth of fifty four:

> Чело́ надме́нное вознёсши,
> Схвати́в желе́зный ски́петр, ца́рь,
> На гро́мном тро́не вла́стно сёвши,
> В наро́де зри́т лишь по́длу тва́рь.
> Живо́т и сме́рть в руке́ име́я:
> «По во́ле, – рёк – щажу́ злоде́я,
> Я вла́стию могу́ дари́ть;
> Где я смею́сь, там всё смеётся;
> Нахму́рюсь гро́зно, всё смятётся.
> Живёшь тогда́, велю́ коль жи́ть».

(Having raised his haughty brow, / Having grabbed his iron scepter, the tsar, / Having seated himself powerfully on his threatening throne, / Sees in his people only a lowly creature. / Holding life and death in his hands / He spake: "If I so wish I pardon the villain, / I can make gifts through power; / Where I laugh, everything laughs, / If I frown threateningly, everything becomes agitated. / You live if I order you to live.")

The traditional ten-line odic stanza, the archaic lexicon (e.g., "chelo" [forehead] "gromnyi" [threatening], "zrit" [sees], "zhivot" [in the meaning of "life"]), syntax ("veliu kol' zhit'"), grammatical forms (e.g., the truncated adjective "podlu"), and cacophonous sound fabric (e.g., the consonantal cluster of "ski*petr, ts*ar'"') give these verses a distinctly eighteenth-century flavor, but the image of despotism – one is tempted to say "proto-totalitarianism" – leaves the Russian eighteenth century far behind. The patriotic ode is here informed by an enlightenment sensibility (though baroque in expression!), which divorces the concept of freedom from the sovereign who would misuse it.

This idea of separating patriotism from the blanket praise of the ruler was perhaps Radishchev's most influential innovation, at least as far as nineteenth-century poets were concerned. With a radically different poetic style, the young Pushkin wrote a number of political works that were patriotic in precisely this sense. His own ode «Вольность» ("Liberty"), though it has no precise lexical borrowings from Radishchev beyond the title (even the eight-line stanzaic form is borrowed from Derzhavin), recalls the critical spirit of Radishchev's example. The much shorter «К Чаадаеву» ("To Chaadaev") is still more representative of the way Pushkin assimilated Radishchev's politics to a new poetic style:

> Любви, надежды, тихой славы
> Недолго нежил нас обман,
> Исчезли юные забавы,
> Как сон, как утренний туман;
> Но в нас горит ещё желанье,
> Под гнётом власти роковой
> Нетерпеливою душой
> Отчизны внемлем призыванье.
> Мы ждём с томленьем упованья
> Минуты вольности святой,
> Как ждёт любовник молодой
> Минуты верного свиданья.
> Пока свободою горим,
> Пока сердца для чести живы,
> Мой друг, отчизне посвятим
> Души прекрасные порывы!
> Товарищ, верь: взойдёт она,
> Звезда пленительного счастья,
> Россия вспрянет ото сна,
> И на обломках самовластья
> Напишут наши имена!

(The deceit of love, hope, and quiet glory / Did not coddle us for long. / Youthful amusements disappeared, / Like a dream, like the morning mist; / But a desire still burns in us, / Beneath the weight of a fateful power / With an impatient soul / We perceive the call of the homeland. / We await with the languor of hope / The moment of holy liberty, / As a young lover awaits / The moment of certain *rendez-vous*. / While we burn with freedom, / While our hearts are alive for honor, / My friend, let us dedicate to the homeland / The beautiful impulses of our soul! / Comrade, believe: it will ascend, / The star of captivating happiness, / Russia will rise up from sleep, / And on the shards of despotism / Our names will be written!)

Addressing a free-thinking friend and mentor, Pushkin here clearly distinguishes between love of the fatherland and hatred for its tyrannical rulers. In terms of genre and style, little is left of the traditions of the eighteenth century. Though retaining the iambic tetrameter, Pushkin replaces the odic stanza, reserved by earlier poets for solemn subjects, with a nonstanzaic form with unpredictable rhyme scheme. (Four-line sequences are rhymed in different ways, then impressively amplified by a triple rhyme and alliteration to draw emphasis to the exclamatory conclusion: "o*na*/*sna*/*Na*pishut *na*shi ime*na*!") In general, this form is associated more with personal poetry (cf. Pushkin's «К Каве́рину» ["To Kaverin"], written a year earlier) than with civic themes. Yet in this poem, lyric and epic mix; political sentiments coexist with personal impressions and vows of friendship. The oppositions come out most strikingly in the simile found at the exact center of the poem, in which the poet's yearning for "holy liberty" (note the marked word "vol'nost'", which directly invokes Radishchev) is compared to the impetuousness of a young lover awaiting a *rendez-vous*. Indeed, Pushkin's lexicon is as indebted to love poetry and elegy (e.g., "liubov'" [love], "nezhit" [coddle], "obman" [deceit], "zabava" [amusement], "gorit eshche zhelan'e" [desire still burns], "serdtsa" [hearts], "prekrasnye poryvy" [beautiful impulses], "plenitel'noe schast'e" [captivating happiness]) as to the odic tradition ("slava" [glory], "vlast'" [power], "gnet" [weight], "chest'" [honor], "otchizna" [homeland], "samovlast'e" [despotism]). The poet's devotion to his country, if not precisely that of a lover, recalls chivalric traditions. The feminine noun "otchizna" (rather than the neuter "otechestvo") is used twice, both times in passionate declarations of duty and service. While the first person plural pronoun makes clear that this is a civic passion, it is only in the prophetic final passage, with the first appearance of the word "Russia" (personified and accompanied by a high-style verb in an archaic form ["*vs*prianet" rather than the pleophonic variant "*vos*prianet"]), that the political truly dominates. The awakening of Russia marks the doom of despotism and the concomitant glorification of the poet and his friend. Of course, the reader looks in vain for an explicit political program in these verses. Pushkin avoids specifics, concentrating on giving voice to the relatively new notion of patriotic dissent.

In «Ро́дина» ("Motherland"), one of his last and most famous poems, Lermontov continues this tradition with an important change.

> Люблю́ отчи́зну я́, но стра́нною любо́вью!
>   Не победи́т её рассу́док мо́й.
>   Ни сла́ва, ку́пленная кро́вью,
>   Ни по́лный го́рдого дове́рия поко́й,
>   Ни тёмной старины́ заве́тные преда́нья
>   Не шевеля́т во мне отра́дного мечта́нья.
>
>   Но я́ люблю́ – за что́, не зна́ю са́м –
>   Её степе́й холо́дное молча́нье,
>   Её лесо́в безбре́жных колыха́нье,
>   Разли́вы ре́к её, подо́бные моря́м;
>   Просёлочным путём люблю́ скака́ть в теле́ге
>   И, взо́ром ме́дленным пронза́я но́чи те́нь,
>   Встреча́ть по сторона́м, вздыха́я о ночле́ге,
>   Дрожа́щие огни́ печа́льных дереве́нь.
>   Люблю́ дымо́к спалённой жни́вы,
>   В степи́ ночу́ющий обо́з
>   И на холме́ средь жёлтой ни́вы
>   Чету́ беле́ющих берёз.
>   С отра́дой мно́гим незнако́мой
>   Я ви́жу по́лное гумно́,
>   Избу́, покры́тую соло́мой,
>   С резны́ми ста́внями окно́;
>   И в пра́здник, ве́чером роси́стым,
>   Смотре́ть до по́лночи гото́в
>   На пля́ску с то́паньем и сви́стом
>   Под го́вор пья́ных мужичко́в.

(I love my homeland, but with a strange love! / My reason cannot vanquish it. / Not glory, bought with blood, / Not peace full of proud faith, / Not the cherished legends of dark antiquity / Stir in me a joyous dream. // But I love – I know not why – / The cold silence of its steppes, / The swaying of its boundless forests, / The flooding of its rivers, which are like seas; / I love to gallop in a cart down a country road / And, penetrating the shadow of night with my slow gaze, / Sighing for night lodgings, to encounter off to the side / The quivering lights of sad villages; / I love the smoke of the burning field after harvest, / The caravan of carts spending the night in the steppe / And on the hill among the yellow meadows / A pair of birch trees showing white. / With a joy unfamiliar to many / I see a full barn, / A hut, covered with thatch, / A window with carved shutters; / And on a holiday, of a dewy evening, / I am ready to look until midnight / At the dance with stamping of feet and whistling / Accompanied by the speech of drunken peasants.)

Lermontov's poem begins in free iambs (rhymed unpredictably), which eventually become stricter, culminating in twelve lines of iambic tetrameter with alternating rhymes. The poem is divided into two sections, the first considerably shorter than the second. The logical structure of the whole is suggested by the word «Но» ("But"), which begins the second stanza and makes clear that it will oppose the first.

The poem opens with a declaration of patriotism that is immediately qualified in a series of striking repetitions. The two forms of the word "love" in the first line (strategically situated in first and final positions) yield to a litany of negatives in lines 2–6. These negated lines contain a virtual catalogue of the standard topoi of patriotic verse: military prowess, peace, history, legend. In short, Lermontov expresses his love through negation – he emphasizes what it *is not*. The second line, with its play on martial vocabulary ("pobedit" ["vanquish"]), emphasizes the irrational aspect of such a love of country. Patriotism, it follows, cannot be logically defined or explained.

This idea is confirmed in line 7 – («за чтó, не знáю сáм» ["I know not why"]), which also repeats the key concept of love. At this apparent recapitulation, the tone shifts radically. Turning from negatives to positives, Lermontov expresses his delight in specific scenery, people, and objects. In the final twelve lines, the change in versification signals another thematic change. If the opening was abstract, almost philosophical, the conclusion presents, as it were, a set-piece with an ever-narrowing focus. The beginning of the second section offers a panoramic picture of Russia in its vastness (steppes, forests, rivers, villages), but the final lines focus on a single place and, ultimately, a single moment (a holiday evening with attendant celebrations).

If Pushkin's patriotism rested on a politics yet to be achieved, Lermontov divorces patriotism from politics, glorifying Russian nature and the age-old elements of peasant life. In the context of this idealization of the Russian countryside and "simple folk" (note the untranslatable diminutive in the final word, which imparts a quality of tenderness), the odd status of the poet himself stands out. This poet is in no way an organic part of the scene he describes: he is an enthusiastic observer, but never a participant (cf. the repeated emphasis on looking: «взóром мéдленным пронзáя нóчи тéнь», «вѝжу», «смотрéть до пóлночи готóв» ["penetrating the shadow of night with my slow gaze," "I see," "I am ready to look until midnight"]). Lermontov leaves us with the image of the poet as a wanderer who encounters and loves the vast expanses and folk customs of Russia, but cannot become one with them.

In patriotic verse as in much else, Tiutchev and Lermontov represent the extremes of Russian Romanticism. While Lermontov's poem reflects the admiration of the mysterious outsider for the common folk, Tiutchev, in «Эти бéдные селéнья» ("These poor settlements") erases the boundary between the poet and the people, steeping his views in myth and building on the religious concept of a chosen people.

Э́ти бе́дные селе́нья
Э́та ску́дная приро́да –
Кра́й родно́й долготерпе́нья,
Кра́й ты ру́сского наро́да!

Не поймёт и не заме́тит
Го́рдый взор иноплеме́нный
Что сквози́т и та́йно све́тит
В наготе́ твое́й смире́нной.

Удручённый но́шей крёстной,
Всю тебя́, земля́ родна́я,
В ра́бском ви́де ца́рь небе́сный
Исходи́л, благословля́я.

(These poor settlements, / This sparse nature – / Native realm of long suffering, / You realm of the Russian people! // The proud foreign gaze / Cannot understand and cannot notice / What shows through and mysteriously shines / In your humble nakedness. // Weighed down by the burden of the cross, / In the guise of a slave, the heavenly king / Walked through all of you, my native land, / Giving blessing.)

Tiutchev's three trochaic tetrameter stanzas vary radically in terms of syntactic structure. The first is characterized by unusually simple sentences (no verbs, only nouns and adjectives in nominative and genitive cases). The second contains a single sentence organized around parallel pairs of verbs. Word order is more complicated than before, though still rather straightforward. The final stanza is marked by genuine syntactic complexity, with the placement of the two essential verbal forms delayed until the concluding line. This stanza is certainly the most important, and the convoluted grammatical constructions slow the reader down, lending profundity to the subject.

The syntactic distinctiveness of each stanza corresponds to the themes treated therein. The opening quatrain begins with simple statements: the first line is devoted to the people, the second (parallel not only in grammatical structure, but even in syllable breaks between words) to the land itself. This pared down sentiment seems appropriate for the subject at hand (poverty). Yet the purely descriptive opening then turns into an exclamation and, in line four, an apostrophe ("ty"). In this way, the speaker's attitude to his subject matter (by no means obvious in the first two lines) becomes highly emotional. The second stanza also sets the first two lines against the second two, albeit to different effect. Pride ("gordyi") is contrasted with humility ("smirennyi") as the foreigner surveys the barren landscape. In the final stanza, all such oppositions disappear. The four lines form a single unit, focused entirely on a mythical explanation of Russia's spiritual strength. While accounts of Apostle Andrew's visit to Russia can be found in apocryphal writings, the image of Christ himself wandering through Russia is entirely Tiutchev's invention. According to this conception, Russia itself performs an *imitatio Christi*. The poverty and suffering, viewed with scorn by the outsider, signals heightened spirituality. Though the stanza is governed by a past tense verb ("iskhodil" [walked through]), the final word "blagoslavliaia" (blessing) – foregrounded by virtue of its being the only nongrammatical rhyme in the poem – suggests that the act of blessing continues, as it were, permanently. In short, the poem moves from a present tense (first stanza) to a modal future (second stanza) to a past tense that – thanks to the verbal adverb – continues mysteriously into the present and beyond.

If Lermontov's poem showed a certain alienation of the poet from the country he so admired, Tiutchev emphasizes throughout the notion of belonging. In many ways, the poem's entire development can be traced in the usage of the Russian root «род», which designates birth and kinship. In the first stanza, the rhyme "pri*rod*a" (nature) and "na*rod*a" ([of the] people) establishes the crucial link between the land and the people who inhabit it. The fact that the country is labeled «Кра́й *род*но́й долготерпе́нья» ("Native realm of long suffering") introduces the notion of suffering as not a temporary condition, but a permanent feature. In the second stanza this crucial morpheme disappears as such, but it is varied in the phrase "go*rd*yi vzor" ("proud gaze"). This distorted echo represents the force inimical to Russia. Note that Tiutchev chooses the word "inoplemennyi" rather than the synonymous "inorodnyi," thus restricting the crucial root to passages connected to Russia. When, in the final stanza, Tiutchev addresses his country as "zemlia *rod*naia" ("native land") he is not simply repeating a patriotic cliché, but emphatically claiming kinship with the land itself.

No mere apology for material backwardness, Tiutchev's poem is a messianic vision of Russia as the Christ of nations. It purports to show Russia in its spiritual purity, elevating poverty to the highest virtue and tagging any dissenters with the sin of pride. Tiutchev's physical image of Russia is almost intangible – the only lines that even purport to describe it are the first two. But in the absence of the physical the spiritual stands out yet more starkly.

Tiutchev's conception of Russia proved highly influential to both contemporaries and successors. Dostoevsky cited it frequently and fervently, as did the mystically-inclined Symbolists. Vyacheslav Ivanov repeatedly named Tiutchev the forefather of Russian Symbolism, and his own poem «Óзимь» ("Winter Crop") amply demonstrates why:

Как о́сенью нена́стной тле́ет
Свята́я о́зимь – та́йно ду́х
Над чёрною моги́лой ре́ет,
И то́лько ду́ш легча́йших слу́х

Незадрожа́вший тре́пет ло́вит
Меж ко́сных глы́б, – так Ру́сь моя́
Немо́тной сме́рти прекосло́вит
Глухи́м зача́тьем бытия́ . . .

(Just as in the foul weather of autumn / The holy winter crop moulders – the spirit secretly / Hovers above the black grave, / And only the hearing of the most ethereal souls // Detects the trembling not yet begun / Among the stasis of the clods of earth, – so my Russia / Defies mute death / Through the imperceptible inception of life . . .)

Formally, Ivanov brings extraordinary inventiveness to an extremely common meter (two stanzas of iambic tetrameter with alternating rhyme). Most immediately striking is the fact that, stanza division notwithstanding, the entire poem consists of a single complex sentence. The frequent enjambments (and the interstanzaic run-on) propel the poem forward, yet the syntax is so intricate that the poem's underlying grammatical structure (Kak . . . tak [Just as . . . so]) only becomes evident at the end of the sixth line. Until then, the opening "Kak" is apt to be misunderstood as part of a simple simile comparing the crop with the spirit.

But what is the purpose of such complex syntax? Ordinarily, two-stanza poems are structured as oppositions, whereby the first stanza is played off against the second. Yet here Ivanov makes considerable effort to create seamless continuity. His poem is essentially an extended comparison, and the structure serves to intertwine tenor and vehicle in manifold ways. The title suggests that the tenor is the winter crop, a crop planted in cold climates in the fall, which then ripens invisibly beneath the earth in the harsh winter months. Yet "ozim'" turns out to be a vehicle or, in Ivanov's special sense of the term, a symbol: a physical object that contains within itself the germ of a higher reality. As such, the winter crop does not simply point to the tenor of the poem ("Rus'"), but becomes another instance of it. Importantly, both "Rus'" and "ozim'" are feminine in gender. Already in line 2, this allows for the unexpected transfer of the epithet "sviataia" (formulaically associated with "Rus'") to the unlikely noun "ozim'". It is the first of several instances where Ivanov invests the winter crop with a religious quality. Ultimately, Ivanov's poem is about birth. Just as the winter crop emerges after a long period of *apparent* stagnancy (cf. Tiutchev's "gordyi vzor" ["proud gaze"], unable to distinguish the hidden richness), so Russia itself is pictured as an organism that experiences a symbolic death in order to be reborn. The word "zachat'e" ("the inception of life") indicates that the feminine gender of the two key terms (ozim', Rus') really does signify a feminine entity. The poem ends with the word "bytiia" ("[of] life"), additionally marked as the only instance of nongrammatical rhyme; Tiutchev used the same technique in «Эти бе́дные селе́нья». It trails off without explaining the significance or consequences of this new birth, but the imagery strongly recalls John 12:24, the famous passage that served Dostoevsky as the epigraph to *The Brothers Karamazov*. Though less explicit than Tiutchev, Ivanov also creates a myth according to which Russia is superficially barren, but endowed with a divine Christian essence accessible only to the most sensitive and congenial observer.

None of the Symbolists developed the genre of patriotic poetry so extensively as Aleksandr Blok. In Blok, Russia's feminine quality transcends the traditional epithet of "Mother Russia." She is a bride, a beloved, a lost love, even a fallen beauty who awaits – and grants – imminent resurrection. There is no single poem that encapsulates Blok's vision of Russia. Indeed, Blok carefully organized his poetry into cycles so that each individual poem shared its power and meaning with those adjacent to it. The more than twenty poems of the cycle «Ро́дина» ("The Motherland") reveal a variety of attitudes toward Russia, some grounded historically or mythically, some looking prophetically forward. (The final poem ends with two questions, suggesting that the poet himself had not come to any ultimate resolution.) Within the parameters of this chapter, the poem «Росси́я» ("Russia") seems particularly appropriate, as it reveals both Blok's significant debt to tradition as well as some of his distinctive innovations.

> Опя́ть, как в го́ды золоты́е,
> Три стёртых тре́плются шлеи,
> И вя́знут спи́цы росписны́е
> В расхля́банные колеи . . .
>
> Росси́я, ни́щая Росси́я,
> Мне и́збы се́рые твои,
> Твои́ мне пе́сни ветровы́е, –
> Как слёзы пе́рвыя любви́!
>
> Тебя́ жале́ть я не уме́ю,
> И кре́ст свой бе́режно несу́ . . .
> Како́му хо́чешь чароде́ю
> Отда́й разбо́йную красу́!
>
> Пуска́й зама́нит и обма́нет, –
> Не пропадёшь, не сги́нешь ты,
> И лишь забо́та затума́нит
> Твои́ прекра́сные черты́ . . .
>
> Ну, что́ ж? Одно́й забо́той бо́ле –
> Одно́й слезо́й река́ шумне́й,
> А ты́ всё та́ же – ле́с, да по́ле,
> Да пла́т узо́рный до брове́й . . .
>
> И невозмо́жное возмо́жно,
> Доро́га до́лгая легка́,

Когда́ блеснёт в дали́ доро́жной
Мгнове́нный взо́р из-под платка́,
Когда́ звени́т тоско́й остро́жной
Глуха́я пе́сня ямщика́! . .

(Again, as in the golden years / Three worn-out harnesses are fraying / And the painted spokes get stuck / In the loose ruts . . . // Russia, destitute Russia, / For me your gray huts, / For me your windy songs / Are like the tears of first love! // I cannot pity you, / And I carefully bear the cross . . . / Give your predatory beauty / To whatever sorcerer you wish! // Let him tempt and deceive, – / You will not disappear or perish, / And only care will darken / Your beautiful features . . . // And what of it? By one more care – / The river will be noisier by one tear / But you are always the same – forest and field, / And a patterned kerchief down to the eyebrows . . . // And the impossible is possible, / The long path is easy, / When in the distant road / A sudden glance flashes from behind the kerchief, / When the muted song of the coachman / Rings out with a prisoner's yearning! . .)

Blok's poem is written in quatrains of iambic tetrameter with alternating rhyme, augmented by a six-line concluding stanza. This strophic change is less radical than it might initially seem, since the final lines parallel the preceding two grammatically, logically, and in terms of rhyme. As a whole, the poem shows clearly how Russian Symbolism was in many ways a summation and synthesis of earlier artistic achievement. Blok conflates – but also develops – virtually all the models of patriotic verse that his nineteenth-century predecessors had bequeathed to him: the love poem (Pushkin), the outsider poet who admires the beauty of nature and the elemental common folk (Lermontov), poverty as kenotic ideal (Tiutchev). In writing about this poem, Blok's comrade-in-arms Andrei Bely explicitly pointed to the influence of both Lermontov and Tiutchev: "Blok loved our motherland with a strange love [strannoiu liubov'iu], a love that blessed [blagoslavliaiushchei] and cursed [proklinaiushchei]." Bely's reference to "cursing" points to one of the elements that Blok freely added. Many of his trademark motifs (the path, the wind, the song) appear in this poem next to virtual citations from his predecessors.

The poem begins with the precise image of a troika stuck in the mud. At the famous conclusion to the first part of *Dead Souls*, Nikolai Gogol' had sung the praises of a troika that symbolized Russia. In that optimistic passage, the troika is characterized by its great speed. Blok's virtually motionless troika introduces a different mood altogether, but it leads to a similarly patriotic vision. While the first stanza creates a fixed and rather desperate setting, the second initiates a meditation, beginning with a highly emotional address to Russia and eventually leading to an image of an eternally renewable and miraculously rejuvenated Russia. As in Tiutchev, a forlorn physical setting conceals unfathomable spiritual riches. The true tone of the poem, then, is found not in the opening description, but in the second stanza, where the poet apostrophizes Russia in its destitution and simultaneously expresses his love for it. Not simply a Christian love of suffering (though it is also that, cf. "Krest nesu" ["I bear the cross"] of stanza 3), this is an erotic love for a country personified as a beautiful woman (e.g., "Tvoi prekrasnye cherty" ["Your beautiful features"], a line borrowed directly from the tradition of love poetry). Into the stylistic and generic mix come the folkloric images of the "charodei" ("sorcerer") and the peasant woman, identified through synecdoche as "plat uzornyi" ("patterned kerchief" – "plat" is a synonym for "platok," but with folk connotations).

Stanzas three to five introduce a paradox frequent in Blok's patriotic verse. Russia appears as a violated or even predatory beauty, yet this cannot ultimately corrupt her essence. Russia inevitably rises up and rejuvenates the pilgrim: «И невозмо́жное возмо́жно, / Доро́га до́лгая легка́ ("And the impossible is possible, / The long path is easy"). The four consecutive stressed "o" vowels, combined with numerous alliterations, give these crucial lines an acoustic emphasis that underscores their semantic significance. The oxymoron "nevozmozhnoe vozmozhno" ("the impossible is possible") signals the culmination of a series of paradoxes. This miraculous salvation is contingent on one of two things: a woman's sudden glance or the song of the coachman. Both of these people are clearly conceived of as "types" rather than individuals. The woman who looks out from beneath a kerchief (this "platok" is presumably another reference to the "plat" four lines earlier) is yet another hypostasis of the mysterious feminine figure who haunts Blok's poetry from the very beginning, and who comes to be associated with Russia. The coachman, metonymically linked to the "doroga" ("road"), is the embodiment of wandering (a crucial element of Blok's world-view and especially of his discovery of Russia). His indistinct song calls forth a desire for freedom. Already in the second stanza of this poem, song was the nostalgic expression of longing and loss. These final images of vision and song mirror the poet's own yearning, giving him the power to move forward into the salvation of Russia's immensity. The poet thus leaves the "rut" of the first stanza, moving hopefully and longingly onward. As so often in Blok's poetry, the entire poem is set in mythic time. Events repeat (note the first word of the poem: "opiat'" ["again"]) time and again, suffering is always present, yet ultimately transfigured. The folkloric, the mythical, and the literary combine in Blok's profoundly mystical conception of Russia.

After the Soviet Union was established, such overt mysticism was no longer in step with the times, but the need for patriotic poetry was in no way diminished. It was up to the self-proclaimed revolutionary poet

Vladimir Mayakovsky to provide the new models. In 1925, on a world tour as poster-boy for the new regime, Mayakovsky wrote his uncharacteristically brief poem «Прощанье» ("Parting"), a superlative example of the relevance of an old genre in a new society:

> В авто́,
>   после́дний фра́нк разменя́в.
> – В кото́ром часу́ на Марсе́ль? –
> Пари́ж
>   бежи́т,
>   провожа́я меня́,
> во всей
>   невозмо́жной красе́.
> Подступа́й
>   к глаза́м,
>   разлу́ки жи́жа,
> се́рдце
>   мне́
>   сантимента́льностью расква́сь!
> Я хоте́л бы
>   жи́ть
>   и умере́ть в Пари́же,
> если б не́ было
>   тако́й земли́ –
>   *Москва́.*

(Into the car, having changed my last franc. / "What time is the train to Marseilles?" / Paris runs, seeing me off, / in all its impossible beauty. / Step up to my eyes, swill of parting, / bloody my heart with sentimentality! / I would want to live and die in Paris, / If there wasn't such a land as *Moscow*.)

Culturally speaking, the Soviet period was in many ways a return to the eighteenth century. The state once again became the primary sponsor of poetry, controlling its creation and dissemination. Consequently, genres that extolled the state quickly claimed a central position. Mayakovsky's "Parting" recalls in several ways the Trediakovsky poems discussed at the beginning of this chapter. This is probably not an instance of direct influence, but rather of shared assumptions and a common personal predicament. (Mayakovsky would have been forced to encounter Trediakovsky's work as part of the mandatory school program in the early twentieth century, but it is hard to imagine that this reading made much of an impression on him.) Like Trediakovsky, however, Mayakovsky found himself in Paris, a city he loved. Like Trediakovsky, he needed to write poetry that would extol his homeland. In 1925, of course, political circumstances gave the situation an added piquancy. Paris, which had long exercised a strong attraction on the Russian imagination, had become the capital of the Russian emigration. Mayakovsky had to direct his patriotic message toward two unsympathetic audiences – the hostile émigré community who had little desire to return to Soviet Russia as well as his compatriots at home, who would never have the chance to travel abroad.

"Parting" is constructed with extraordinary attention to form. Looking past the superficial "stepladder" layout of the verses to their deeper structure, one can see that the poem consists of eight lines, each beginning flush left and ending with a rhyme. The rhyme scheme, a-b-a-b-C-d-C-d, may not be immediately obvious, since Mayakovsky characteristically appends unrhymed letters to the rhyming syllables. Metrically, he uses an intriguing and unusual mix of accentual and syllabo-tonic verse. The first four lines are written in alternating dol'nik of three and four stresses, while the final four lines are trochaic (one line of pentameter followed by three of hexameter). Such a formal structure sets the two halves of the poem against each other, an opposition that corresponds to the semantics.

The first four lines present the physical setting in a few brief strokes. The poet is leaving Paris for the port city of Marseilles, presumably to sail away from France (hence the reference to changing his last franc). As he rushes toward the train station, Paris itself appears to be moving, even seeing him off. (This "false" perception of motion is typical of Futurism, an avant-garde artistic movement at the root of Mayakovsky's pre-revolutionary poetics.) In these lines, the mundane (changing money) mixes with the elevated image of Paris «во всéй невозмóжной красé» ("in all its impossible beauty," cf. Pushkin's praise of Petersburg in "The Bronze Horseman" as «Полнóщных стрáн *красá* и дúво» ["The *beauty* and marvel of the northern countries"]).

In the final four lines, the observation moves from without to within, as the poet records his emotional response to the situation. Initially this takes the form of two imperatives addressed to his tears, which are named metaphorically through the unusual image of "razluki zhizha" ("swill of parting"). "Zhizha" is a particularly crude word, yet Mayakovsky uses rhyme to pair it with Paris: zhizha/Parizhe. The same sort of lexical tension is found in the expression "santimental'nost'iu raskvas'" ("bloody with sentimentality"). "Raskvasit'" is a highly physical word (it usually refers to a battered nose or face rather than a heart), more appropriate for a police blotter than for a lyric poem. Hence it clashes with the gentle associations of sentimentality, even in Mayakovsky's spelling. (The standard form would be "sentimental'nost'iu" rather than "santimental'nost'iu" – Mayakovsky's variant imitates [and perhaps mocks] French nasal pronunciation.) In this way, the traditional image of tears of parting is simultaneously called forth and undercut. Once again, these lines reflect Mayakovsky's avant-garde origins: the transformation (through synecdoche) of the poet into eyes and a heart recalls Cubism.

In the closing two lines the poet changes tone once again. The physical poet disappears entirely, replaced by his "metaphysical" musings. Shifting from histrionic imperatives to a contrary-to-fact (subjunctive) statement, Mayakovsky expresses his closeness to Paris only to reject it in favor of Moscow. Moscow was indeed Mayakovsky's home, but in this poem it has added significance as Russia's new capital city. (Petersburg/Petrograd had been the imperial capital, and one of the earliest decisions of the Soviets was to change the seat of power.) Mayakovsky uses grammatical gender to underscore the contrast. The fact that Moscow (feminine in gender) is described as a "zemlia" (also feminine, but a word usually applied to a country or at the very least a region) suggests that he is drawing on the feminine aspects of Russia so prominent in the patriotic verse of his predecessors. This stands out even more when it is opposed to Paris (masculine in gender). «Москва» closes the poem, italicized, as a rhyme word, and on its own step of the graphic stepladder. It is as if the mere naming of the poet's beloved city obviates the need for further commentary.

In short, if the first part of Mayakovsky's poem is factual and descriptive (statements and questions), the second is evaluative and emotional (imperatives and subjunctives). The actual departure scene (first half of the poem), conveyed through time and motion, yields to an atemporal meditation on the act of parting and an uncharacteristically laconic yearning for Russia (second half).

Three stanzas of a recent poem (published in 2000 and probably written not much earlier) by Timur Kibirov give a good indication of where Russian patriotic verse stands today.

> Только вы́молвишь сло́во «Росси́я»,
> а тем бо́лее «Ру́сь» – и в башку́
> тотчас по́шлости ле́зут таки́е,
> вра́ки, глу́пости сто́ль прописны́е,
> и таку́ю наво́дят тоску́

> гра́фа Ну́лина вздо́рное чва́нство,
> Хомяко́ва небри́тая спесь,
> ба́рство ди́кое и мессиа́нство –
> тут как ту́т. Завсегда́ они́ е́сть. [. . .]

> Ру́сь-Росси́я! От сих коннота́ций
> нам с тобо́ю уже́ не сбежа́ть.
> Не РФ же тебе́ называ́ться!
> Как же зва́ть? И куда́ ж тебя́ зва́ть?

(Just utter the word "Russia," / Or better yet "Rus'" – and into your noggin / In an instant such banalities will crawl, / Such lies, such hackneyed stupidities, / And they'll cause such boredom // Count Null's stupid arrogance, / Khomiakov's unshaven conceit, / Wild gentry and messianism – / There they all are. They're always there. [. . .] / Rus'-Russia! From these connotations / The two of us cannot escape. / You can't just be called RF [Russian Federation]! / But what should we call you? And where should we summon you to?)

Kibirov begins by invoking the two historical designations of Russia, leading the reader to anticipate yet another poem in the patriotic mode. "Rus'" is usually distinguished from "Rossiia" as a spiritual community rather than a political entity. However, both words can connote patriotic pride, as the poems of Ivanov and Blok indicate. By the end of the second line of Kibirov's poem, all such elevated expectations are made problematic by the word "bashka" ("noggin") – a decidedly low lexical item. And when we reach the rhyme "Rossiia/propisnye" ("Russia/hackneyed"), there can be little doubt that the first two lines were essentially a provocation, as the poem is devoted to demolishing the hallowed image of holy Russia. A similarly striking stylistic clash occurs in a rhyme of the second stanza: "chvanstvo/messianstvo" ("conceit/messianism"). In this stanza, Kibirov cites specific figures both literary (Count Null is from Pushkin's eponymous poem, a snobbish Francophile who despises Russia) and historical (the poet and philosopher Aleksei Khomiakov, one of the guiding lights of the Slavophile movement). In the final stanza, he again sets various lexical registers – and their concomitant associations – against each other. For example, in the phrase "ot sikh konnotatsii" ("from these connotations"), the archaic "sikh" is followed by a pretentious and distinctly modern-sounding loan word. An experienced reader will recognize in these concluding lines some of Blok's trademark intonations: emotional apostrophes («нам с тобо́ю уже не сбежа́ть» ["The two of us cannot escape"]) and urgent short questions («Как же зва́ть?» ["But what should we call you?"]). However, the phrase "RF," an obvious anachronism, undercuts these pathos-inducing allusions. The (post)modern poet plays on rhetoric and themes still immediately recognizable to the Russian reader, but uses the familiar intonations to subvert the underlying assumptions. Less a dismissal of prior Russian poetry than of present reality, it is an homage to the powerful poetic models of Lermontov, Tiutchev, and especially Blok.

Kibirov's poem reflects a skepticism toward Russian nationalism, a phenomenon that has become disturbingly prominent in political and popular discourse since the demise of the Soviet Union. The rhetoric of the past, he suggests, fits incongruously with present aspirations. However, his poem also allows us to reach a broader conclusion: namely, that great poetry has a way of overcoming even its own subject matter. Most of the poems discussed in this chapter express sentiments that are uncomfortable for today's readers – both Russian and foreign. Yet there is no denying their power. By building on the work of their predecessors, Russian poets have created a unique tradition of civic verse that rises above the historical and social circumstances that gave rise to it.

Conclusion: poetry and pattern

С бесчеловечною судьбой
Какой же спор? Какой же бой?

Г. Иванов, «С бесчеловечною судьбой»

With an inhuman fate
What argument can there be? What battle?

G. Ivanov, "With an inhuman fate"

The specific poetic genres discussed in Part Two were hardly exhaustive. Several equally important genres could be adduced (e.g., religious poetry, the metapoetic poem [poetry about poetry], poetry of the city). And even our chosen genres could be divided into a host of subgenres. The three exemplary love poems (Chapter Six) could all be categorized as poems of jealousy, but there are many other types of love poem: anticipatory (e.g., Fet's «Я пришёл к тебе с приветом» ["I came to you with a greeting"]), disappointed (e.g., Pasternak's «Марбург» ["Marburg"]), ecstatic (e.g., Pushkin's «Нет, я не дорожу мятежным наслажденьем» ["No, I do not value wild pleasure"]. The chapter on patriotic poetry omitted the substantial tradition of civic verse directed *against* Russia, e.g., Viazemsky's «Русский бог» ("Russian God"), Lermontov's «Прощай, немытая Россия» ("Farewell, unwashed Russia"), and most of Nekrasov's verse. A no less vexing problem is that a single poem can combine genres. Blok's «Предчувствую тебя» ("I anticipate you"), discussed in Chapter Three, wavers between love poetry and religious poetry. Pasternak's «Гроза моментальная навек» ("A Storm Forever Momentary") is at once a nature poem and a metapoetic poem (see Chapter Seven). Even the genres that are defined by strict formal characteristics are not necessarily pure (recall Derzhavin's «Фелица» ["Felitsa"] in Chapter Four).

Such fluidity notwithstanding, genre remains an invaluable tool for understanding both individual poems and poetic tradition. A poet seeking to express his or her thoughts invariably retains or revises the paradigms of earlier poets. Likewise, readers encountering a new work will try to make sense of it by comparing it to things they already know. At times, poets foreground genre, designating a given work as an "elegy" or an "ode." In other cases, poets write without a conscious model, yet their particular situation (and response to it) recalls that of prior poets, perhaps wholly unknown to them. For this reason, even poems that were created independently can prove mutually illuminating when read together.

Poetry has been defined as "violence done to language," but it might be more accurate to define it as patterning imposed on language, patterning that extends far beyond the rules that govern everyday grammar and style. As we have seen, virtually any constituent part of language (sound, syntax, rhythm, grammatical categories) can be used *poetically*, to establish a symmetry that directly influences the way a poem is perceived and understood. Were these effects to appear in everyday usage (e.g., the iambic trimeter supermarket observation: "The léttuce cósts a dóllar, / the sóup a dóllar tén"), no one would impute significance to them. In a poem, however, one justly assumes that their use is both deliberate and meaningful. A translator can retain only a small fraction of a poem's numerous symmetries. A scholar can draw attention to many, but can never replicate the effect of their simultaneous combination.

The poet's fascination with pattern answers a fundamental human need for order. A common topos of world literature portrays the poet as a second God, whose creation reflects (albeit on a small scale) the perfection of divine provenance. And while the notion of an omniscient being who regulates the tiniest details of human existence may seem more in keeping with the mind-set of the Middle Ages than of our own epoch, the desire for a structured environment remains an indelible part of human consciousness. Even people who believe that the world is random and fundamentally meaningless inevitably create their own order, establishing a routine in daily life and developing a personal philosophy that makes spiritual existence possible. For the poet, this order resides in language itself, which remains even in the absence of reason, justice, happiness, and basic human freedoms.

The relationship of poetry – with its careful patterning – to the chaotic and often distinctly "unpoetic" world beyond the poem is the subject of this concluding chapter. Our two exemplary poems were written by émigrés, which gives them a special pathos. Emigration always uproots and disrupts, but for poets it also entails severe linguistic dislocation, a permanent separation from the only audience capable of appreciating their work. Anna Akhmatova, who stayed in Russia through thick and thin, probably had this in mind when she wrote in her «Поэма без героя» ("Poem Without a Hero") of the «изгнания воздух горький» ("bitter air of exile"). The daunting task facing the émigré poet – which did not confront émigré musicians or painters to the same degree – was to create meaningful art in an alien and inhospitable climate.

In the course of four decades of emigration, Georgy Ivanov had ample opportunity to reflect on the fate of the émigré poet. The poem «Отвлечённой сло́жностью перси́дского ковра́» ("Like the abstract complexity of a Persian carpet"), a profound meditation on this subject, concludes the final section of his final book of poetry (first published in 1958, a few months after his death).

> Отвлечённой сло́жностью перси́дского ковра́,
> Суетли́вой ро́скошью павли́ньего хвоста́
> В не́бе расцвета́ют и темне́ют вечера́,
> О, совсе́м бессмы́сленно и всё же неспроста́.
>
> Голуба́я я́блоня над кру́жевом моста́
> Под прозра́чно-при́зрачной верле́новской луно́й —
> Миллионноле́тняя земна́я красота́,
> Ве́чная бессмы́слица – она́ опя́ть со мно́й.
>
> В о́бщем, э́то пра́вильно, и я́ ещё дышу́.
> Подверну́лась му́зыка: её я запишу́.
> Си́ней паути́ною (хвоста́ или моста́),
> Ли́нией павли́ньей. И всё же неспроста́.

(Like the abstract complexity of a Persian carpet, / Like the frivolous luxury of a peacock's tail / In the sky the evenings bloom and darken, / Oh, completely meaningless but nonetheless not without purpose. // The light blue apple tree above the lace of a bridge / Below the transparently phantom-like Verlainian moon – / The million-year-old earthly beauty, / Eternal meaninglessness – it is with me again. // In general this is right, and I am still breathing. / Music has turned up: I will write it down. / Like a dark blue spider web (of a tail or a bridge), / Like a peacock line. But nonetheless not without purpose.)

With the significant exception of the final line, the poem is written in the highly unusual meter of trochaic heptameter. As in most poems with long lines, there is a caesura, here after the fourth foot and almost always corresponding to a logical pause. This fourth foot is always unstressed, creating a rhythmic regularity that allows one to reconceptualize each individual line as being composed of two trochaic trimeters, the first with unrhymed dactylic endings, the second with masculine rhymes. The essential point here is not that this poem is in heptameter and hexameter at the same time, but that – already within the sphere of meter – a hidden pattern emerges that forces us to revise our initial impression.

The richness of the poem's sound organization is immediately evident. The rhyme scheme itself shows a more extensive patterning than one expects to find in quatrains. The "b" rhyme of the first stanza recurs throughout the poem, uniting a series of essential words: «хвоста́» ("of a tail"), «неспроста́» ("not without purpose"), «моста́» ("[of a] bridge"), «красота́» ("beauty"). In the final stanza, all of these words recur except for «красота́» (which is unique aurally as well, with its –со́та ending instead of the –ста endings in the words it rhymes with). In addition to rhyme, Ivanov relies on emphatic alliteration (*прозра́чно-при́зрачной, верле́новской луно́й*), sometimes combined with assonance (*Ли́нией павли́ньей*).

But what is the poem "about"? The fact that it begins in the most abstract and ambiguous grammatical case (instrumental) is telling – this is not a poem that makes its point directly. The two first lines are strikingly similar in structure – a feminine adjective and noun in the instrumental case are followed by a masculine adjective and noun in the genitive case. Moreover, the word boundaries of these lines coincide exactly (falling after syllables 4, 7, and 11). Such careful symmetry is particularly appropriate since both the Persian carpet and the peacock's tail are images of intricate patterning. Only in the third line, however, does the basic meaning of the first two lines become apparent. It is here that we discover that the opening instrumental case is functioning as a simile. The evening sky that repeatedly "blooms" and "darkens" is likened to the complex patterns of the peacock and carpet. (Since the verb "расцвета́ть" ["bloom"] ordinarily describes a flower, it suggests another image of complex patterning.) The final line shifts directions, moving from description to interpretation. At the basis of this line is an undisguised paradox. The clash of «совсе́м бессмы́сленно» ("completely meaningless") and «неспроста́» ("not without purpose") brings to the fore the fundamental tension between pattern and meaning (or lack thereof).

The second stanza seamlessly develops the first. «Кру́жево моста́» ("the lace of a bridge") presumably depicts the intricate ironwork on a bridge railing and thus supplies an additional instance of complex patterning, recalling in particular the Persian carpet, another creation of man. In a similar way, the «я́блоня» ("apple tree") parallels the peacock's tail, both images belonging to the natural world. The «верле́новская луна́» ("Verlainian moon") combines the natural and human spheres. The great French Symbolist Paul Verlaine wrote two famous moon poems ("Clair de lune" ["Moonlight"] and "La lune blanche" ["The White Moon"]), both of which rely on rich sound orchestration to depict a scene of melancholic beauty. The "Verlainian moon" appears to place the poem in Paris, where Verlaine spent his formative and final years and where Ivanov lived throughout his emigration. It also calls to mind the struggling and destitute poet (the "poète maudit" ["cursed poet"], as Verlaine called himself), whose miserable physical existence provides a marked contrast to his hauntingly euphonic verse. As in the first stanza, there is an emphasis on time, which passes without affecting change. For all its parallels to the first stanza, however, the second adds a new and crucial element: beauty. Curiously, beauty is associated with the earth and equated not with pattern, but with "eternal meaninglessness."

The second stanza closes by introducing the poet himself, but – in a by now familiar strategy – only in the instrumental case.

In formal terms, the third stanza departs from the previous two. The rhyme scheme changes from a "ring" pattern to couplets, and the final line contains a metrical irregularity (a missing syllable). Such exceptions from the carefully constructed norm suggest that the theme of the poem will also undergo a significant change. The first lines certainly support such an expectation, since they position the poet in the foreground for the first time. The rhyme words bring together his basic physical existence (дышу́ [I breathe]) and his artistic creation (запишу́ [I will write down]). The reference to music, that most abstract of the arts, invokes Verlaine's dictum of "De la musique avant toute chose" ("Music before all else"), a rallying cry for poets in both France and pre-revolutionary Russia.

The final two lines recall the opening stanzas, recapitulating the images of peacock's tail and bridge and supplementing them with a spider web. In this new context, however, these images are related not only through their complex patterning, but through their proximity to art and, by extension, to beauty. In the closing lines of the previous stanzas, the first half of the line was explicitly devoted to the subject of meaninglessness: «О, совсе́м бессмы́сленно» ("Oh, completely meaningless") and «Ве́чная бессмы́слица» ("Eternal meaninglessness"). In the third stanza this by now anticipated exclamation is replaced by yet another image of pattern: «Ли́нией павли́ньей» ("a peacock line"). This phrase is striking in its very obscurity. Presumably the contour of a peacock is meant, the sweep of its entire body. «Ли́ния» ("line") is thus being used to describe something that is, strictly speaking, curved. Yet even this odd phrase connotes pattern, not only because it recalls the peacock's tail, but also because it expresses pattern through sound. Though etymologically unrelated, the second word echoes the first so closely that their similarity seems preordained. Language itself, in short, creates the pattern. After this comes the poem's rhythmic "error." A syllable is omitted, creating an eerie pause – a hesitation – which nevertheless leads to the familiar and now conclusive assertion: «И всё же неспроста́» ("But nonetheless not without purpose").

In the first two stanzas, the poet presented images of the most detailed patterning, describing them as at once meaningless and meaningful. These images included natural objects and human artifacts. They were not delimited temporally, as was indicated by the fact that the poet spoke of many evenings (rather than a single evening) in the first stanza and about the "million-year-old" beauty in the second. In short, the poet's purview extended beyond his own brief lifetime. He was searching not simply for personal, but for universal meaning. In the final stanza, he begins by focusing within, examining his own activity as a living being and poet. His creative activity seems as involuntary as breathing: «Подвернýлась мýзыка: её я запишý» ("Music has turned up: I will write it down"). The source of the music is mysterious (the verb подвернýться connotes an accidental quality), but whatever its origin, music – which one may safely equate with poetry – represents yet one more instance of careful patterning. This artistic activity is in turn associated with the symmetries discussed earlier, an implicit linkage created by imagery (the spider web recalling the carpet, lace, etc.) and grammatical parallelism (the instrumental case of «сúней паутúною» ["like a dark blue spider web"] reminiscent of the opening lines).

The poet looks out into the "meaningless" world and confronts a series of patterns: visual, aural, syntactic, even biographical (the Russian poet and his French counterpart). Though he is unable to discern the precise logic that would explain them, their very existence appears to convince him of an overriding plan to the universe itself. His initial response (lines one and two) to pattern is hardly positive: «отвлечённой слóжностью» ("abstract complexity") and «суетлúвой рóскошью» ("frivolous luxury"). However, as the poem progresses, these constantly recurring patterns create a sense of ubiquitous order, which ultimately becomes the mark of beauty and art. That these myriad repetitions cannot be understood is less significant than the undeniable fact of their presence. In spite of himself, the poet continues to write, mimicking in his verse the intricate patterns of the "meaningless logic" that surrounds him.

Georgy Ivanov was one of the great poets of the "first wave" of Russian emigration. Within fifteen years of his death, the "third wave" of émigrés began to appear in the West. One of the outstanding figures of this new group of dispossessed intellectuals was Joseph Brodsky, whose poetry reflects – in a very different idiom than Ivanov's – surprisingly similar concerns. Shortly after emigration, Brodsky wrote a cycle of enigmatic and uncharacteristically brief poems entitled «Часть речи» ("A Part of Speech"), from which the following poem is cited in its entirety (including the opening ellipsis).

> . . . и при слóве «грядýщее» из рýсского языкá
> выбегáют мы́ши и всéй орáвой
> отгрызáют от лáкомого кускá
> пáмяти, что твой сы́р дыря́вой.
> После стóльких зи́м уже безразлúчно, чтó
> или ктó стоúт в углý у окнá за штóрой,
> и в мозгý раздаётся не неземнóе «дó»,
> но её шуршáние. Жи́знь, котóрой,
> как дарёной вéщи, не смóтрят в пáсть,
> обнажáет зýбы при кáждой встрéче.
> От всегó человéка вам остаётся чáсть
> рéчи. Чáсть рéчи вообщé. Чáсть рéчи.

(. . . and at the word "the future" out of the Russian language / rush mice and in a whole horde / gnaw away at the dainty morsel / of memory like that hole-ridden cheese of yours. / After so many winters it doesn't matter any more, what / or who is standing in the corner at the window behind the drapes, / and in one's mind resounds not the unearthly "do," / but its rustling. Life, which, / like a gift thing, you don't look in the maw, / bares its teeth at every meeting. / From the whole man you are left with a part / of his speech. An actual part of speech. A part of speech.)

Like most of the cycle, this poem is written in accentual verse, with stresses per line varying from three to six and unstressed intervals varying from one to four. The rhymes are alternating masculine and feminine, which creates a completely predictable rhythmic patterning at the end of each line. Curiously, rhythmic regularity is also built into the beginning of the lines, since twelve of fourteen start with an anapest. In the two exceptional cases (lines four and twelve), stress falls on the opening syllable and coincides with a striking enjambment. In these instances, the expected rhythmic flow is altered to mark two crucial words: «па́мяти», «ре́чи» ("[of] memory," "[of] speech").

Brodsky constantly disorients the reader with surprising images and clashing stylistic registers. Even the opening ellipsis suggests that we have already missed some of the essential presuppositions. The word «гряду́щее» ("the future") with its archaic and distinctly literary quality, leads one to expect a meditation in the high style. (In everyday speech, the synonym «бу́дущее» is used). Yet any such expectations are dashed in the second line, with the appearance of a horde of mice. The combination of the mice and the future recalls Pushkin's «Стихи́, сочинённые но́чью во вре́мя бессо́нницы» ("Verses Composed at Night at a Time of Sleeplessness"), discussed in Chapter Four, but Brodsky's treatment of the subject is unique. While Pushkin's poem traced the path from uncertainty to control, Brodsky's leads only to increasing fragmentation and disintegration. Already in this opening passage, Brodsky creates confusion by reversing the tenor and vehicle of his metaphor. Ordinary logic would dictate the following sequence: the mice eat Swiss cheese, which is like a brain (because of its porous physical appearance), which in turn represents memory (an abstract concept associated with the brain). In this passage, however, these very physical mice take a bite directly out of the abstraction that is memory. Memory is then compared to Swiss cheese, with the potentially mediating term «мозг» ("brain") appearing only four lines later and in another context.

This resulting image, while intentionally imprecise, concludes the unambiguously grim view of the future presented in the opening four lines. In the next few lines, the poet's attention turns from the future to the past and present. The passage of time – «после сто́льких зим» ("after so many winters") – has apparently led to a state of utter indifference. Inanimate and animate («что или кто» ["what or who"]) are no longer categories that matter. Moreover, spatial positions (indicated by the rapid succession of prepositions в, у, за) seem interchangeable. The only sound that occurs is not the otherworldly «до», but a distinctly mundane rustling – of drapes or possibly mice, since the feminine possessive pronoun could refer to «штóра» ("drapes") or – less probable but nonetheless conceivable – «орáва» ("horde [of mice]"). The Russian word «до» itself contains rich ambiguities. It may refer to the first note of the musical scale (in which case the «неземнóе «дó»» ["unearthly 'do'"] would call to mind the ancient belief in the music of the spheres) or to the preposition "before," which has spatial *and* temporal meanings, both of which are relevant to the present context. Whatever that transcendent «до» may represent, however, it remains inaudible and therefore inaccessible.

Confusing imagery notwithstanding, the first four lines of the poem make a formally irreproachable quatrain, containing a single sentence and ending with a full stop. Against this backdrop, the second four lines display a discontinuity. The full stop that "should" occur at the end of line eight is pushed forward, so that it falls in the middle of the next line. The new beginning is thus, strictly speaking, out of kilter. As usual in Brodsky, this break comes on a particularly significant word: «жизнь» ("life"). From this point on, the sense of dislocation already established becomes yet more insistent. The Russian proverb «Дарёному коню в зýбы не смóтрят» (literally: "One doesn't look a gift horse in the teeth"), appears in fractured form in lines eight to ten. By its very nature, a proverb is fixed in language and therefore not subject to even the slightest change. When Brodsky alters it, he shakes the very foundations of communication. In accordance with the equivalence of animate and inanimate averred earlier, Brodsky compares the proverbial horse (in Russian, a «кто») to a thing («вещь», that is, а «что»). Most interesting, he omits the word «зýбы» ("teeth") from the proverb, but includes it in another fixed expression («обнажáет зýбы» ["bares its teeth"]), thereby making the gift horse (life itself) menacing, even predatory. Like the mice of the opening, it becomes a direct threat to human existence.

From this highly metaphorical passage (mixed metaphors, one might add) emerge the two final lines, bereft of figurative language, but containing one of the most powerful enjambments in all of Russian poetry. «От всегó человéка вам остаётся чáсть / рéчи.» If this sentence is pronounced correctly (with the requisite pause at the line ending), it initially reads: "From the whole person you are left with a part." Only after this pause does one realize what it *really* says: "From the whole person you are left with a part . . . of his speech." The poem closes by breaking down this sentence into sentence fragments. (To appreciate the brevity of the closing lines, one must recall the sprawling run-on sentences that preceded them. Likewise, the finality of the closing line's three periods should be contrasted with the ellipsis that opened the poem.) The final line focuses our attention ever more closely on this disembodied "part of speech" as the sole survivor and the ultimate reality.

Brodsky's poem posits a future where language is more a relic than a means of communication. As the rhyme «языкá/кускá» ("[of] language/[of] a piece") suggests, language is itself repeatedly broken into parts. Individual words such as «грядýщее» and «до», set off by quotation marks, appear as if suspended in space. Quotation marks ordinarily designate speech and, implicitly, a speaker. Perhaps the most disturbing aspect of Brodsky's poem is the absence of that speaker. Indeed, the most traditional component of lyric poetry, the "I," never appears. Pronominal usage is limited to «твой» (possessive pronoun, second personal singular, informal) and «вам» (dative case, formal singular or plural). Both of these words invoke an interlocutor, yet Brodsky uses them in constructions that erase the sense of a real person. The first instance («как твой сыр») simply means "like that old cheese" (i.e., that cheese that everybody knows about). The second («вам остаётся») could be rendered most idiomatically as "all that's left is . . ." Tellingly, when Brodsky himself translated the poem into English, he removed both cases of pronominal usage. Yet these depersonalized uses of "you" in the Russian poem make the absence of humanity more palpable than their complete omission. They raise the possibility of human contact only to annul it. The result is a world in which shards of language continue to exist, but divorced from speakers and listeners. Even the graphic layout contributes to this effect. In all editions of "A Part of Speech" that Brodsky supervised, each brief poem is allotted its own page, even though two poems could easily have fit on the same page. Brodsky clearly wished to create a visual impression of sparseness by presenting each laconic poem against a void.

Brodsky's poem represents a "poem of the end," and therefore provides a convenient place to close our study. However, it would be wrong to read it as an epitaph for Russian poetry. After writing "A Part of Speech," Brodsky himself had another two prolific decades ahead of him, and Russian poetry remains robust to this day. More to the point is that Brodsky's poem shows the extraordinary degree of poetic control necessary to write about fragmentation and communicative breakdown. The haunting effect of this poem results from a virtuoso manipulation of syntax, lexicon, and figurative language. In this work, poetry is powerful enough to discuss its own undoing, and to do so in a way that – paradoxically – continues to engage us.

The émigré poetry of Georgy Ivanov and Joseph Brodsky has now returned home and found a new generation of readers. This burgeoning interest in their work can be explained less by a fascination with the émigré experience than by the world-view that it gave rise to: searching, disoriented, at times despairing, but never cynical. One might say that emi-gration represents a distinctly modern – some might say "post-modern" – sense of alienation and spiritual homelessness. Yet if the poetry of emigration teaches us anything, it is that language creates a home. In the patterning of poetry, in the concision of a lyric poem, we find perhaps the best substitute for the wholeness that continually eludes us in life.

Bibliography

Note: Since the "Biblioteka poeta" editions are generally reliable and often the most accessible, I have used them whenever possible, even if it meant altering an inaccuracy (in the case of Viacheslav Ivanov) or changing the orthography to conform with modern norms (in the case of Lomonosov). At times (e.g., Akhmatova), this was not possible, because the Soviet "Biblioteka poeta" editions omitted important poems for ideological reasons.

Akhmatova, Anna, *Sochineniia*, Washington: Inter-Language Literary Associates, 1965–83.
Al'fonsov, V. N., and S. R. Krasitskii (eds.), *Poeziia russkogo futurizma*, Saint Petersburg: Akademicheskii proekt, 1999.
Baratynskii, E. A., *Polnoe sobranie stikhotvorenii*, Leningrad: Sovetskii pisatel', 1989.
Batiushkov, Konstantin, *Polnoe sobranie stikhotvorenii*, Moscow: Sovetskii pisatel', 1964.
Blok, Aleksandr, *Stikhotvoreniia*, Moscow: Sovetskii pisatel', 1955.
Briusov, Valerii, *Sochineniia*, Moscow: Sovetskii pisatel', 1987.
Brodskii, Iosif, *Sochineniia Iosifa Brodskogo*, Saint Petersburg: Pushkinskii fond, 1998.
Derzhavin, Gavrila, *Stikhotvoreniia*, Leningrad: Sovetskii pisatel', 1957.
Fet, Afanasii, *Stikhotvoreniia i poemy*, Leningrad: Sovetskii pisatel', 1986.
Gippius, Zinaida, *Stikhotvoreniia*, Saint Petersburg: Akademicheskii proekt, 1999.
Iazykov, Nikolai, *Stikhotvoreniia i poemy*, Leningrad: Sovetskii pisatel', 1988.
Iskrenko, Nina, *Ili: Stikhi i teksty*, Moscow: Sovetskii pisatel', 1991.
Ivanov, Georgii, *Sobranie sochinenii v trekh tomakh*, Moscow: Soglasie, 1994.
Ivanov, Viacheslav, *Stikhotvoreniia, poemy, tragediia*, Saint Petersburg: Akademicheskii proekt, 1995.
Kantemir, Antiokh, *Sobranie stikhotvorenii*, Leningrad: Sovetskii pisatel', 1956.
Khodasevich, Vladislav, *Stikhotvoreniia*, Leningrad: Sovetskii pisatel', 1989.
Kibirov, Timur, *Kto kuda – a ia v Rossiiu*, Moscow: Vremia, 2001.
Kuzmin, Mikhail, *Stikhotvoreniia*, Saint Petersburg: Akademicheskii proekt, 1996.
Lermontov, Mikhail, *Polnoe sobranie stikhotvorenii v dvukh tomakh*, Leningrad: Sovetskii pisatel', 1989.
Lomonosov, Mikhailo, *Izbrannye proizvedeniia*, Leningrad: Sovetskii pisatel', 1986.
Maiakovskii, Vladimir, *Polnoe sobranie sochinenii*, Moscow: Khudozhestvennaia literatura, 1955–61.

Mandel'shtam, Osip, *Polnoe sobranie stikhotvorenii*, Saint Petersburg: Akademicheskii proekt, 1997.

Nekrasov, N. A., *Polnoe sobranie sochinenii v trekh tomakh*, Leningrad: Sovetskii pisatel', 1967.

Pasternak, Boris, *Stikhotvoreniia i poemy v dvukh tomakh*, Leningrad: Sovetskii pisatel', 1990.

Prigov, Dmitrii, *Napisannoe s 1975 po 1989*, Moscow: Novoe literaturnoe obozrenie, 1997.

Pushkin, Aleksandr, *Polnoe sobranie sochinenii v desiati tomakh*, Leningrad: Nauka, 1977–79.

Radishchev, Aleksandr, *Izbrannoe*, Leningrad: Molodaia gvardiia, 1949.

Scott, Sir Walter, *Poetical Works*, London: Macmillan, 1935.

Soloviev, Vladimir, *Stikhotvoreniia i shutochnye p'esy*, Leningrad: Sovetskii pisatel', 1974.

Sosnora, Viktor, *Verkhovnyi chas: stikhi*, Saint Petersburg: Peterburgskii pisatel', 1998.

Tiutchev, Fedor, *Polnoe sobranie stikhotvorenii*, Leningrad: Sovetskii pisatel', 1987.

Trediakovskii, Vasilii, *Izbrannye proizvedeniia*, Moscow: Sovetskii pisatel', 1963.

Tsvetaeva, Marina, *Stikhotvoreniia i poemy*, Leningrad: Sovetskii pisatel', 1990.

Viazemskii, Petr, *Stikhotvoreniia*, Leningrad: Sovetskii pisatel', 1958.

Zhukovskii, Vasilii, *Sobranie sochinenii v chetyrekh tomakh*, Moscow: Khudozhestvennaia literatura, 1959–60.

Suggested further reading

I. Bilingual anthologies of poetry

Kelly, Catriona (ed.), *An Anthology of Russian Women's Writing, 1777–1992*, Oxford: Oxford University Press, 1994. Contains mainly prose, but also almost one hundred pages of Russian poetry in English translation, with the originals printed in an appendix.

Obolensky, Dimitri (ed.), *The Heritage of Russian Verse*, Bloomington: Indiana University Press, 1976. Originally published as *The Penguin Book of Russian Verse*, London: Penguin Books, 1962. Offers an excellent selection of major poets with reliable English prose translations.

Smith, Gerald S. (ed.), *Contemporary Russian Poetry*, Bloomington: Indiana University Press, 1993. Conceived of as a sequel to the Obolensky; includes the work of many significant poets of the last twenty-five years.

II. General studies of poetry

Hofstadter, Douglas, *Le Ton Beau de Marot: In Praise of the Music of Language*, New York: Basic Books, 1997. Uses theory and practice of translation as a means to discuss the uniqueness of poetry. One chapter is devoted to Russian poetry, but the entire book raises important questions in a quirky yet highly readable way.

Steele, Timothy, *All the Fun's in How You Say a Thing: An Explanation of Meter and Versification*, Athens: Ohio University Press, 1999. While limited to English-language poetry, this book is an accessible and intelligent introduction to many questions that are equally relevant to the Russian tradition.

III. Russian textbooks on poetry

The following works, written for Russian high school and college students, assume a knowledge of the Russian school program in literature. They are not appropriate for beginners, but more advanced students will find them enormously helpful.

Bogomolov, N. A. *Stikhotvornaia rech': Posobie dlia uchashchikhsia starshikh klassov*, Moscow: Interpraks, 1995.

Gasparov, M. L. *Russkie stikhi 1890-kh–1925-go godov v kommentariiakh*, Moscow: Vysshaia shkola, 1993. Republished under the title *Russkii stikh nachala XX veka v kommentariiakh*, Moscow: Fortuna Limited, 2001.

Lotman, Iu. M. *Analiz poeticheskogo teksta*, Leningrad: Prosveshchenie, 1972. Republished in Iu. M. Lotman, *O poetakh i poezii*, Saint Petersburg: Iskusstvo–SPB, 1996. This work also exists in an English version, though long out of print: Yuri Lotman, *Analysis of the Poetic Text*, edited and translated by D. Barton Johnson, Ann Arbor: Ardis, 1976.

IV. Classic studies of Russian poetry:

Gasparov, M. L. *Ocherk istorii russkogo stikha*, Moscow: Nauka, 1984. Republished under the same title – Moscow: Fortuna Limited, 2000. Divides Russian poetry into six periods and highlights for each one the distinguishing features of rhythm, meter, rhyme, and stanzaic forms. Encyclopedic and brilliant, but not an easy read.

Ginzburg, Lidiia, *O lirike*, Leningrad: Sovetskii pisatel', 1974, republished under the same title – Moscow: Intrada, 1997. An insightful study of Russian poetry from the elegiac school to the early twentieth century with emphasis on genre and style.

Jakobson, Roman, *Language in Literature*, Cambridge: Harvard University Press, 1987. Contains numerous seminal essays of poetic analysis as well as influential statements about the nature of poetry.

V. Recent Western studies of Russian poetry

Sandler, Stephanie (ed.), *Rereading Russian Poetry*, New Haven: Yale University Press, 1999. Analyses from a variety of theoretical positions of specific poems of both canonic and lesser-known poets.

Scherr, Barry, *Russian Poetry: Meter, Rhythm, and Rhyme*, Berkeley: University of California Press, 1986. A detailed yet clear discussion of all aspects of Russian versification.

Wachtel, Michael, *The Development of Russian Verse: Meter and Its Meanings*, Cambridge University Press, 1998. Focuses on the connection between form and meaning, considering many issues not treated in the present study.

Index of poetic terms

(Note: in certain cases [e.g., "rhythm"] this index gives only the page where the term is defined rather than every single reference to it.)

Index of names and works